Crimes of Passion Since Shakespeare

Bringing key Shakespeare texts into dialogue with feminist socio-legal research, this book investigates the notion of a 'crime of passion' – indicatively, wife-killing.

Its key concern is to bring attention to a cultural and legal revolution widely overlooked even in the law field where it occurred. In 2009, the English Parliament passed a controversial law abolishing the defence of provocation. Explaining the new law, reformers said that this so-called 'heat of passion' defence had allowed men to get away with murder by blaming the victim. Abolishing it in cases of alleged 'infidelity' would 'end the culture of excuses'. Unpacking what was at stake in the reformers' revolutionary challenge to the English law of murder's age-old concession to 'human frailty' in 'red mist' rage cases, this book charts passion's progress in wife-killing cases over the centuries. It commences in the early modern era when jurists were busy distinguishing murder from manslaughter and, contemporaneously, Shakespeare set about querying culturally inscribed excuses for femicide in his plays, *Titus Andronicus* and *Othello*.

This book will appeal to feminist and socio-legal scholars, criminologists and those working in the fields of law and literature, legal theory and Shakespeare studies. More widely, it will appeal to anyone interested in so-called 'crimes of passion'.

Adrian Howe is an Honorary Principal Fellow in the School of Historical and Philosophical Studies, University of Melbourne, Australia.

Crimes of Passion Since Shakespeare

Red Mist Rage Unmasked

Adrian Howe

Routledge
Taylor & Francis Group
a GlassHouse Book

First published 2023
by Routledge
4 Park Square, Milton Park, Abingdon, Oxon OX14 4RN

and by Routledge
605 Third Avenue, New York, NY 10158

Routledge is an imprint of the Taylor & Francis Group, an informa business

A GlassHouse book

British Library Cataloguing-in-Publication Data
A catalogue record for this book is available from the British Library

ISBN: 978-1-032-29518-3 (hbk)
ISBN: 978-1-032-29520-6 (pbk)
ISBN: 978-1-003-30197-4 (ebk)

DOI: 10.4324/9781003301974

Typeset in Bembo
by Deanta Global Publishing Services, Chennai, India

To the memory of London charwoman Hannah Abbott (1797–unknown) who lived to tell her story

Contents

Acknowledgments

My first thanks go to Peter Johnston who read the entire manuscript and offered invaluable suggestions for improving it. I am deeply indebted to him. Thanks also to Santo de Pasquale, David Truex and Robyn Wood for their most helpful comments on individual chapters and to the Routledge reviewers who were so enthusiastic about the book proposal.

Special thanks to Eric Heinze, professor of law and humanities at Queen Mary University of London, for introducing me to 'his' Shakespeare. Eric's brilliant lectures and publications in the law and literature genre was what it took to move me on at last from Foucault. I also acknowledge the post-humanist Shakespeare scholars whose superb readings of *Titus Andronicus* and *Othello* helped keep me relatively sane as I conducted what turned out to be deeply traumatising research for this book. Unprepared for and frequently overwhelmed by the sheer volume of cases of impassioned femicide lying dormant in the archives, I found solace in the scintillating Shakespeare scholarship and, of course, in Shakespeare himself. The support of my friends through this process was also invaluable. Thank you.

The book focuses on one jurisdiction, that of England and Wales. But the story it tells of slaughtered women, legally sanctioned excuses for killing them and feminist demands for law reform is the same story that could be told in any Anglophone jurisdiction. I have referenced as many as possible of the key feminist legal and criminological studies produced in the UK, Canada, United States and Australia over the last three decades. I would especially like to acknowledge all those feminist scholars, activists and law reformers who have long advocated for the curtailment or abolition of legal defences that allow men to get away with murdering women.

Karen Ingala Smith, co-founder of the UK Femicide Census, deserves my lasting gratitude for tirelessly compiling her 'Counting Dead Women' lists. Karen's contribution to the fight against femicide has been immense. I wish to thank her for identifying all the women killed by men since 2012, thereby saving me hours of research time needed to unearth hundreds of cases of intimate partner femicides committed prior to 2012.

Finally, a judge in an 1828 trial discussed in the book made what was described as a 'very feeling address' as he delivered the death penalty to a wife-killer. After all, these were, and still are, very feeling cases and this is a very feeling book, one whose sympathies lie unapologetically with the victims, overwhelmingly women, of impassioned homicide. It has been written as a contribution to the global movement that is naming intimate partner femicide as a first-order political problem and demanding justice for its victims.

Introduction

In his landmark history of emotions, *The Navigation of Feeling: A Framework for the History of Emotions*, William Reddy identified three late twentieth-century revolutions in this newly emergent field of inquiry. One was in psychology, another in ethnography, while in the third, historians and literary critics were discovering that emotions have 'a kind of history', though what kind was 'not entirely clear'.[1] *Crimes of Passion Since Shakespeare* brings attention to a fourth contemporaneous revolution, one that has flown under the radar and has been widely overlooked even in the law field where it occurred. In 2009, the English Parliament passed a highly controversial law abolishing the defence of provocation, a partial defence that, when successful, reduce murder to manslaughter. It was replaced by a new loss of control defence for England and Wales which expressly excludes sexual infidelity as a trigger for loss of control. The reformers defended this monumental change to the English law of murder thus: the provocation defence, or more specifically, provocation by sexual infidelity – the so-called 'heat of passion' defence – had 'allowed men to escape a murder charge in domestic homicide cases by blaming the victim'. It was 'a terrible thing', they said, 'to lose a sister or a daughter, but to then have her killer blame her and say he is the victim of her infidelity is totally unacceptable. The relatives say "he got away with murder" and they're right'. It followed that abolishing the defence in cases of alleged 'infidelity' was an important law change that would 'end the culture of excuses'.[2]

At stake in this law reform was not only the question of what should constitute sufficient provocation to warrant a conviction for the lesser offence of manslaughter, now that infidelity was off the table. In naming the 'provocation by infidelity' defence as a cultural defence for Englishmen and, even more astonishingly, specifying it as '*our own* version of honour killings', the reformers shook to the core the self-contradictory received view of so-called 'crimes of passion' as at once an un-English, foreign indulgence *and* as an emotionally laden partially excusable killing that anyone, man or woman, might commit.[3]

DOI: 10.4324/9781003301974-1

The reformers' insistent specifying of infidelity-inspired 'honour' killers as *ours* is the latest expression of a critical approach to domestic homicide that can be traced back to Shakespeare's querying of culturally inscribed excuses for femicide in his plays, *Titus Andronicus* and *Othello*. Unpacking what the reformers meant by calling provocation by infidelity 'our own version of honour killing', this book charts passion's progress in wife-killing cases in the courts, commencing in the early modern era when England's leading cultural authority penned an astonishing critique of the notion of a warrant for femicide.

In defence of 'French-style' crime passionnel

Unsurprisingly, the proposal to abolish provocation as a defence was adamantly opposed by a wide cross-section of the legal fraternity and upper echelons of the judiciary. After all, the passions distinguishing hot-blooded manslaughter from cold-blooded murder had a venerated, only occasionally contested, place in English law. Their resistance to change warrants a close analysis, serving as it does to highlight the tenacity of the received view of impassioned killing as a lesser form of homicide. Shrillest objections were raised in the House of Lords where emotions ran very high over the idea of depriving men of the ancient right to plead provocation after killing an unfaithful wife. Lord Neill's objections to the reform proposal, raised in the House of Lords in 2009, are a case in point and an apt testament to the incoherent fictions informing the conservative jurist's understanding of heat of passion homicide. The 'most common thing', he said, that one 'reads in the press in murder cases' is that

> the wife *or* husband finds the other spouse in the sexual act, loses control, picks up a bread knife or whatever comes to hand and stabs and sometimes kills the other spouse. That is French-style *crime passionnel*. Are we now turning this into something that the English, with their stiff upper lip, will take as an ordinary incident of marital life? That is ridiculous and out of line with the way in which people think about human passions.[4]

Lord Neill would later admit that 'it is mainly men killing women' – Antigone, he recalled, was an exception proving the rule that 'on the whole, it is the men'. Nevertheless, he persevered in opposing the proposed reform on the ostensibly gender-neutral ground that banning infidelity as a trigger for an 'individual' to lose self-control was absurd:

> We would make ourselves look extraordinarily foolish if we say a jury cannot take account of what most people recognise as being the most dominant cause of violence by one individual against another. Every opera you go to, every novel you read has sexual infidelity at some point or another. Otherwise it is not worth reading or listening to.[5]

So here we have a retired judge relying on newspaper reports to disavow the sexed asymmetry of offenders and victims. Evidently, he had not noticed in his long career that it is almost exclusively husbands, not wives, who appear in English courts on murder charges after losing control ostensibly over infidelity, as over three decades of feminist investigative research has documented. Moreover, they rarely if ever do so after catching their partners 'in the sexual act' as Lord Neill puts it. Far more commonly, men kill women who have left them or plan to. Lord Neill is also confused about his classical precedent. In Sophocles' play, Antigone commits suicide. She does not kill anyone else. There is still more confusion as he descends into avowing the supposed foreignness of infidelity-inspired homicidal rage. On the one hand, he is alarmed that 'French-style' impassioned crime is something that stiff upper-lipped Englishmen are now to forgo – take as an ordinary incidence of marital life – thus inadvertently giving it away that they certainly did not forgo it in the past. On the other hand, everyone thinks about 'human passions' in the same way. We all, evidently, believe sexual infidelity to be the primary and readily understandable cause of interpersonal violence. Every opera you go to, every book you read endorses it.

What an extraordinary lapse of memory this was on the part of the law lord. Not only did he somehow forget that stiff upper-lipped Englishmen have been killing unfaithful and allegedly unfaithful wives for centuries. He also overlooked the tried and true defence they have offered for doing so. For all his efforts to differentiate the English from their supposedly more impassioned others – the French, Italians, colonial subjects – the merest glance at the case law proves beyond reasonable doubt that provocation by 'infidelity' has always been the English wife-killer's defence *par excellence*. Lord Neill's protest encapsulates the stubborn drive to disavow the endlessly rediscovered empirical fact that it is overwhelmingly men who commit 'red mist' impassioned homicide and, on the other hand, avow its foreign otherness. Challenging this wilful blindness, breaking through the wall of disavowals about impassioned homicide's sexed asymmetry is no easy task. Nor is contesting the derisory, othering practice of insisting it is foreigners and ethnic minorities who commit impassioned femicides. But that's what this book sets itself to do, fortified by the overwhelming evidence that the provocation defence has operated over the centuries as a profoundly sexed excuse for any man to commit femicide.

What kind of history of crimes of passion?

Bringing histories of emotion in the early modern period into dialogue with criminological research, legal history and Shakespearean scholarship, this book fills a gap in the history of impassioned homicide. Our conversationalists will include judges, legal and social historians, legal commentators, Shakespeare scholars and, most importantly, Shakespeare himself. We begin by flagging the central analytical importance of registering the sexed asymmetry of explosions of homicidal 'passion'. For it is not only the likes of Lord Neill and his fellow opponents of the proposed reforms to defences to murder who have overlooked the fact that it is almost always men, not women, who succumb to homicidal fury against their intimate partners. This has also frequently passed scholars by, even those working in the field of the history of emotions, or at least, not been deemed worthy of close attention. Consider, for example, Brigid Escolme's reflections on the early modern shift from passion to emotion in common usage. The *OED*'s 1602 citation, she notes, places 'passion' and 'emotion' in 'interesting proximity'. It reads as follows: 'The king entered into a strange passion … and in this emotion or rage of jealousie … hardly contained he himselfe from killing his wife'. For Escolme this entry signals a shift from the use of emotion to mean 'political agitation or unrest' or 'movement, disturbance or perturbation' to its current definition as 'any strong mental or instinctive feeling, such as pleasure, grief, hope, fear'.[6] Left unmarked is the sexed specificity of the passion in question – surely a telling omission. Is it not notable that it is specifically a king's, and not a queen's, barely containable jealous rage tempting him to kill his wife that is described in the *OED* entry? To take another example, consider the *Othello* chapter in a recent edited collection which maps emotions in Othello's era, including the emotions leading to his downfall.[7] Astonishingly, there is no mention of the fact that those emotions centred on an impassioned belief in his wife's infidelity that propelled him into killing her.

The kind of history this book offers is one that begins by specifying who, historically, have entered into that 'strange passion' – 'seeing red' or 'red mist' rage, in today's parlance – a specification that is also frequently missing in legal histories of heat of passion defences to murder. Non-feminist law scholars tend to dig no deeper than noting how the defence of provocation has operated as a historically mandated concession to a generic 'human frailty'. They leave unnoticed the overwhelming empirical evidence of a pronounced sexed asymmetry in the matter of whose so-called 'human frailty' is raised in intimate partner homicide cases. An exception is Jeremy Horder's magisterial *Provocation and Responsibility*.[8] Published three decades ago and informed by contemporaneous feminist critiques, it remains the definitive historical account of the development of the English defence of provocation. I will be engaging with its key findings throughout this book, but I will do so from a victim-orientated rather than the usual offender-focused approach that has proved to be such an obstacle to feminist challenges to the received view that over-emotional wife-killers deserve sympathy. Taking this approach is no mean feat, the victims being, specifically, dead. But some women survived homicidal attacks to tell their stories and, where they didn't, a victim advocate can step in to tell a counter-narrative to that provided by defendants in passion murder cases. Accordingly, this book is firmly on the side of those who argue we can and must 'over-read', that is, read to excess the possibility of women's subjectivity, agency and resistance.[9] This methodology has a long pedigree, from the 'new' social histories of the 1970s bent on writing history from the bottom up through to postcolonial queries as to whether the subaltern can speak. Is it possible to attribute agency to the subaltern in the face of what Shakespeare scholar Ania Loomba calls 'indifferent archives and hostile historiography' that bears no trace of her?[10] To take a pertinent example, she notes that the deaths of young Indian women killed for lack of adequate dowry are recorded as suicides. The victims' voices are either not recorded or are manipulated by their killers. Despite the fact that these victims sometimes concur in this construction to protect their family or their killers' honour, Loomba insists that 'we have to recognise that they are murders'.[11]

Insisting that the intimate partner femicide cases I discuss in this book were also murders, I have strived to recover something of their lives and subjectivities from a hostile offender-focused archive and a historiography indifferent to her fate. Recording subjugated voices, deploying them as a counterpoint or counter-hegemonic challenge to dominant common sense knowledges, has long been my methodology of choice.[12] Recognising women killed in England and Wales by male partners claiming they provoked them into a homicidal rage as a marginalised group demanding to be brought back into history fulfils an ethical obligation to the dead. It also enlists them to this book's cause, adding their voices to those of late twentieth-century critics who challenged the received view, one reinforced by offender-biased legal histories, that men who kill women while emotionally distraught deserve law's compassion. More, it is to insist that defence tales of provocative blameworthy women not only posthumously slander the victims; they perpetrate a social injury against all women dead and alive.[13] Not that this in any way suggests that the lives and lived experience of these femicide victims had any parallel with those of subaltern women in colonial societies. Its premise is rather that in their deaths at the hands of their male partners, women everywhere achieve a kind of ghastly equality of condemnatory erasure.[14]

It is from this history written from below perspective that I shall explore the nature of the passion that Othello and his non-fictional counterparts could not shake, the passion driving them to kill women. Keeping in mind Thomas Dixon's caution against too simply conflating the early modern understanding of passion with the later psychological category of emotion, I pay close attention to the variety of feelings inflamed in and by 'crimes of passion'.[15] Is it really, as is usually assumed, simply jealousy that whips men up into a homicidal rage? Certainly, Iago asserted as much, famously warning Othello to beware 'the green-eyed monster'. But Iago was a notoriously unreliable source. Alternatively, some Shakespeare scholars insist Othello was overwhelmed by shame rather than jealousy when he became convinced of his wife's adultery.[16] Complicating the analysis, jealousy has been associated with different behaviours in men and women, legitimating them in men, condemning them in women, as Niamh Cullen points out in her study of love, honour and jealousy in post-war Italy.[17] Similarly, Masha Belenky argues that jealousy was seen as a 'legitimate emotion' for men in nineteenth-century France inasmuch as it was linked to the legal and social status of the wife as property.[18] Was that the case in England? Was it anxieties about losing proprietary rights in women rather than jealousy that drove nineteenth-century Englishmen to kill wives they suspected of adultery? Carolyn Conley found that men tried for wife-killing in late nineteenth-century England cited jealousy or suspicion of infidelity as their motive 'in only 15 percent of cases'.[19] What about twentieth-century wife-killers? What, precisely, was at stake for all these men? More crucially, what can account for the continuing purchase of the view that men's feelings, whether classified as passions or as emotions, should have mitigating force when it comes to killing their women partners and former partners?

If twenty years ago William Reddy felt that emotions had 'a kind of history' though he was not clear what kind exactly, this book is more assured of the sort of history it wants to write.[20] It follows the chequered career of extreme emotion – 'being wrought, perplexed in the extreme' as Shakespeare's Othello put it, 'seeing red' as modern-day wife-killers put it – in English intimate partner femicide cases since the early modern period. My focal concerns are first, to unpack the extraordinary tenacity of the view that the feelings aroused in men who kill their wives in so-called 'crimes of passion' should have excusatory force, reducing their crimes from murder to manslaughter. Second, I show why the law reform banning the age-old 'heat of passion' defence and with it, effectively, the whole notion of a 'crime of passion', was so revolutionary and why, nevertheless, the revolution is far from over.

Shakespearean glosses on method

The enduring sympathy expressed in the courts, criminal law scholarship and more generally for impassioned men who kill their current or former women partners while in a 'red mist' rage, has preoccupied me for some time.[21] Challenging the ancient right to passion embodied in provocation by infidelity defences to murder; addressing the normative questions raised by the conceit that a woman's infidelity is sufficiently grave provocation to reduce murder to manslaughter; demonstrating how the residual compassion still shown today by some juries for over-emotional wife-killers can be linked to the traditional belief that men have possessory rights over women – these remain my all-consuming passions.[22] To address them, I deploy the Foucauldian methodology I have developed over the last 25 years, one that follows Carol Smart's influential feminist reading of law as a discursive field in which law, broadly understood, is a 'most important site of engagement and counter-discourse'.[23] More specifically, I will continue to read criminal law cases as crucially important sites for exploring and contesting the notion that provoked killing, including intimate partner femicides, is manslaughter, not murder. In short, I read these cases as highly revealing sites of cultural contestation over the notion of excusatory passion. This same problematising methodology, one legible not only to scholars in the fields of law and humanities, critical criminology and socio-legal studies but also to those in English literature, Shakespeare studies and especially to new historicist, feminist and critical race Shakespeare scholars, is applied to the cases and also to key Shakespeare texts.

But why Shakespeare? Which Shakespeare? The Shakespeare recruited here is the one who emerged over the last four decades in transgressive interpretations of his work. Challenging the humanist view that Shakespeare offers universal 'mirrors of truth', these 'resistant' studies have rewritten the canonical Shakespeare text in ways that 'contest traditional or canonical readings'. This post-humanist Shakespeare queries established authority, parodies cultural conventions and breaks down the distinction between civilisation and barbarism. In short, his work denaturalises the dominant order of things.[24] Informed by this 'alternative' but by now established interpretative tradition, the two Shakespeare texts I examine, *Titus Andronicus* and *Othello*, will be read as problematising the cultural inscription of men's self-justifying passions leading them to commit femicide. That is to say, I will analyse the Shakespeare texts in the same way as Shakespeare scholars like Jean Howard have: that is, as dramatisations of 'a world in which truth is discursively produced and authorised' by a 'set of practices, including theatre practices, which secure one understanding of the world at the expense of another'.[25] Such a methodology is alert to various appropriations of Shakespeare's authority either to naturalise or to contest the notion of excusatory passion. Shakespeare's plays, I will argue, are most illuminatingly read as counter-hegemonic contestations of inherited truths about justifications for murdering women. Interpreted this way, the two Shakespeare plays I discuss stand out as early challenges to the conventional practice of naturalising men's violent emotions. As I will show, such challenges occasionally surfaced in legal judgments over the centuries before being embraced and fully articulated by late twentieth-century feminist-led law reform movements taking place in anglophone and other jurisdictions.[26]

What's to come

Chapter 1 dives into the murky field of what has been called 'the perplexing borders of justification and excuse' in English criminal law, borders which, defying systematic categorisation, have been thrashed out by legal scholars primarily in discussions of the provocation defence.[27] My starting point is the late sixteenth century when a convergence of cultural and legal developments helped forge the English defence to what the French call *crime passionnel*. It was then that English jurists set about devising the legal rule that cold-blooded murder could be distinguished from the lesser crime of hot-blooded manslaughter. In a parallel development, honour theorists were busy revising the Aristotelian notion that angry retaliation in men of honour was virtuous, a notion that would inform the legal fiction that killing an adulterous wife befitted a man of honour. Here begins my conversation with Jeremy Horder's *Provocation and Responsibility*, focusing on his analysis of the early modern foundational conceptualisation of the provocation defence. I then explore these legal developments through the lens of Shakespeare's contemporaneous revenge drama, *Titus Andronicus*, a play that troubles the notion that murder can itself be justice. Read as a scathing indictment of justification-via-precedent for retaliatory violence, the play provides an illuminating window into the culturally inscribed, and therefore contestable, constitution of excuses and justifications for femicide. The gift that keeps on giving, *Titus Andronicus* makes whiteness racially visible, thereby disrupting its cultural force and anticipating late modern feminist critical race scholarship's insistence that excuses for femicide are always racialised, even when the killers are members of dominant groups. Finally, Chapter 1 highlights the move in Shakespeare criticism to transform Lavinia, the play's central femicide victim, from an object into a subject, giving her a voice and agency, a move that I will replicate for other victims in subsequent chapters.

Chapter 2 focuses on early modern understandings of the rage driving men to kill wives, giving centre stage to *Othello*, Shakespeare's brilliant dissection of the feelings driving an impassioned man to kill his wife. *Othello*'s significance for a history of crimes of passion cannot be overestimated, dramatising as it does the cultural inscription of the passions attending these homicides. Shakespeare scholarship, especially Marxist and critical race scholarship, makes an important contribution here. They offer insights into the origins of the fictions of possession that are still being retailed today in cases of 'infidelity'-inflected homicidal rage, fictions that have proved to be immensely difficult to dislodge embedded as they are into centuries of 'our' understanding of men's entitlements. Crucially too, Shakespeare's attribution of extreme possessive jealousy to a racialised character instantiates the insidious othering practice that continues to bedevil dominant cultural beliefs about the likely perpetrators of intimate partner femicide. Finally, as Shakespeare scholars have noted, *Othello*, like *Titus Andronicus*, is permeated with the language of law. It is especially intrigued by what constitutes evidence and what murder. Drawing on and occasionally taking issue with Shakespeare and law scholarship, the chapter highlights Shakespeare's uncanny anticipation of the passion-based legal defences of provocation by sexual infidelity and mental incapacity, later diminished responsibility, deployed by English wife-killers over the next 400 years.

Switching from Shakespeare's theatre back to the theatre of law, the next four chapters unpack passion's fortunes in English criminal courts. Starting in the eighteenth century, I chart how the expanding and sometimes contracting excusatory passions invoked in provocation by infidelity wife-killing cases have fared in the courts over time. While cuckoldry, real or imagined, was too potent a transgression to be confined to provocation cases, spilling over into insanity, attempted murder and wounding cases, we will see that it is provocation cases that have provided the precedents enshrining the legal idea that a man is justified, or at least can be excused, for killing an adulterous wife. We shall also see how legal opinion about the role of passion in murder trials was to wax and wane. Over the centuries, judges, lawyers and academics would occasionally enlist *Othello*, some to support an exculpatory view of possessive jealousy, others to contest it.

Chapter 3 examines whether legal precedents authorising men to kill adulterous wives discovered *in flagrante* proved as 'lively' in nineteenth-century English criminal courts as the one Titus Andronicus seized upon to justify killing his daughter. Reading the English law of murder through the prism of the evolving exculpatory sexual infidelity script, I trace excusatory passion in the courts, commencing with some important late eighteenth-century cases before concentrating on nineteenth-century and especially Victorian-era intimate femicide cases. My dialogue here is with Martin Wiener's *Men of Blood: Manliness and Criminal Justice in Victorian England*, his analysis of hundreds of criminal trials of 'men of blood', most of them defendants in intimate partner femicide cases.[28] Though his account is written from a relentlessly pro-offender perspective, the rich archive he amassed from a wide array of sources can be raided from a victim-focused perspective. Such an approach reveals that the received idea of an impassioned man's right to a conviction for the lesser offence of manslaughter for killing his wife was contested not only by 'punitive' nineteenth-century judges but also by some all-male juries and, far more frequently, by witnesses, many of them women neighbours. Very occasionally survivors of men's murderous attacks also got the chance to voice their views. Viewing the cases from their perspectives reveals how far removed the typical wife-killing case was from the classic scenario of an impassioned man finding his wife *in flagrante*.

Chapter 4 continues the story of passion's progress during its low point as an effective defence to murder in the first half of the twentieth century. This is the story of passion contained, of marked judicial intolerance of wife-killers, judges keeping a close check on what constituted mitigating provocation, refusing to extend it beyond the classic case of finding a wife *in flagrante*. But they could not hold out forever. Chapter 5 examines the mid-century reforms to the law of murder that would unleash passion's excusatory force for femicidal men. Juries would now be able to consider 'everything done and said' by the victim to upset her killer, thereby opening the floodgates to impassioned provocation pleas. It was now open to 'passion' – the passion of men aroused by taunting, departing women in scenarios far removed from discovering her *in flagrante delicto* – to follow an unabashedly subjectivising path, becoming embedded in what is colloquially referred to in Britain as 'the nagging and shagging defence'. Or he might raise a defence of diminished responsibility, perhaps even claiming he suffered from 'Othello Syndrome', Shakespeare shadowing this history of men's homicidal rage against women from beginning to end.

'Infidelity'-provoked rage continued to exonerate wife-killers of murder until the early twenty-first century. By then three decades of victim-focused feminist investigative research highlighting ethical problems with the operation of the defence in 'domestic' cases finally came into its own. Chapter 6 tells the story of the early twenty-first-century English law reform movement, how it overcame trenchant opposition to abolish provocation as a defence and ban sexual infidelity, real or imagined, as a trigger for loss of control in a new loss of control defence. Constituting a stunning counter-hegemonic challenge to the concept of a 'crime of passion', these reforms, it will be argued, ushered in nothing less than a legal and cultural revolution in the English understanding of excusatory homicidal passion. Finally, I examine the post-reform cases to assess how successful the reforms have been in preventing men getting away with murdering women. What remains of men's time-honoured right to passion? Has 'seeing red' – killing a woman while in a 'red mist' or under other clouding circumstances – finally lost its excusatory force?

A final introductory point: my book's inquiry into the continuing purchase of the notion that femicidal men deserve compassion and their victims blame for inciting men's homicidal fury is informed by a wide array of feminist scholarship, none more influential than Italian philosopher Adriana Cavarero's Arendtian account of ethical narration. It is crucial, she argues, if one is to narrate ethically, to tell the story of the 'who' rather than the 'what' of human existence. Moreover, despite Arendt's 'reticence' on this point, 'one must affirm that, being born, there always appears to the world a sexed *who*'. All actors leave behind a story, but 'nothing guarantees that this story will later get told', a telling observation when transferred to the killing scenarios I discuss in this book. The standard tale told in court by the wife-killer is that of a man aggravated by a 'what', a nagging, unfaithful or departing wife who is never elevated into a 'who', a 'you', a subject in her own right. In the courtroom it is only the killer's story that is told, allowing him, a deeply sexed 'who', to become a 'narratable self' while the victim is reduced to an annihilated 'what', an exemplary case if ever there was one of ethical bankruptcy.[29]

Following Cavarero, I have set myself the challenge of reversing this order of things. It is intent on elevating the victim of intimate partner femicide into a subject, bringing her back into history as a 'who' with her own story to tell, while reducing her killer to a nameless 'what'. The trick however, is to do so without losing sight of law's complicity with the impassioned killer's standard reductionist defence strategy. Retaining a focus on the discursive constitution of the she-asked-for-it woman annihilated in his victim-blaming narrative is essential for exposing it as an exemplary instance of post-mortem slander. For the victims' families and for survivors of attempted femicide, this injurious slanderous speech, incessantly repeated in English courtrooms over the centuries, compounds the physical wounds suffered by women at the hand of 'their' men. Shakespeare put this best. Speaking in a different context, he sums up the problematic addressed in this book in one stunning sentence: 'oftentimes the excusing of a fault/Doth make the fault the worser by th'excuse'.[30] That it takes an entire book to make Shakespeare's point in the context of femicidal men's murder trials is powerful testimony to the blinding power of the legal fiction that killing while in a 'red mist' rage should mitigate murder.

Chapter 1

Honourable anger, moral warrants for murder – Glossing *Titus Andronicus*

TITUS
My lord the emperor, resolve me this:
Was it well done of rash Virginius
To slay his daughter with his own right hand,
Because she was enforced, stained and deflowered?

SATURNINUS
It was, Andronicus.

TITUS
Your reason, mighty lord?

SATURNINUS
Because the girl should not survive her shame,
And by her presence still renew his sorrows.

TITUS
A reason mighty, strong and effectual;
A pattern, precedent and lively warrant
For me, most wretched, to perform the like.
Die, die, Lavinia and thy shame with thee,
And with thy shame thy father's sorrow die.

Titus Andronicus 5.3.35–46[1]

Introduction

The origins of the idea that a wife's adultery could provide a warrant, a moral warrant no less, for a husband to kill her can be traced back to *Leviticus*. Chapter 20:10 is translated thus today: 'If a man commits adultery with another man's wife – with the wife of his neighbour – both the adulterer and the adulteress are to be put to death'. Over the centuries, Englishmen have killed their adulterous and allegedly adulterous wives far more frequently than their wives' lovers, but the commandment laid down in *Leviticus* seems

DOI: 10.4324/9781003301974-2

clear. A wife's adultery warrants death. And yet compare the 1611 King James Bible translation: 'And the man that committeth adultery with another man's wife, even he that committeth adultery with his neighbour's wife, the adulterer and the adulteress shall *surely* be put to death'.[2] Surely? Might that 'surely' possibly register a miniscule doubt about the harshness of the biblical injunction against adulterers? Probably not, but just such a doubt would periodically arise in judgments in English wife-killing cases over the centuries.

This chapter takes as its starting point the late sixteenth century when a convergence of significant cultural and legal developments lay the foundations of the English version of *crime passionnel*. It was then that English jurists set about devising the legal rule that cold-blooded murder could be distinguished from the lesser crime of hot-blooded manslaughter. In a parallel development, honour theorists were busy reviving the Aristotelian notion that angry retaliation in men of honour is virtuous, a notion that would underline the legal fiction that killing an adulterous wife befits a man of honour. Contemporaneously, Shakespeare was writing *Titus Andronicus*, a play traditionally seen as a simplistic revenge drama, famously dismissed by TS Eliot as 'one of the silliest and most uninspired plays ever written'.[3] From that lowly place in humanist scholarship, the play has been reclaimed over the last four decades by various strains of post-humanist Shakespeare studies that have opened up new ways of interpreting it. Most compellingly, it is now read as a damning parodic indictment of established authority. It is these studies that will inform my reading of the play as querying and problematising contemporaneous developments in the English law of murder.

Titus Andronicus may seem an unlikely choice for my first Shakespearean glosses on the tenacity of the view that the murderous feelings women arouse in men are entirely understandable. After all, those feelings are not addressed in the play. So why not commence with Shakespeare's jealousy plays, *The Merry Wives of Windsor*, *Much Ado about Nothing*, *Cymbeline* or *The Winter's Tale* where men's obsessions with and fantasies of cuckoldry take centre stage? Better still, why not start with *Othello*, that brilliant dissection, unsurpassed in English literature, of the explosive emotions leading men to kill wives? And inasmuch as Shakespeare's jealous men are all Italians or soldiers surrounded by Italians, it is surely these plays that illuminate one of my key themes: the propensity of early and late modern English writers alike to conceive of impassioned wife-killing as a foreign phenomenon. To English eyes, it was an indulgence of hot-headed strangers slavishly acting out an exaggerated sense of honour. Indeed, when they are interpreted as problematising contemporary truths about men's fears about wayward wives, the jealousy plays stand out as foundational literary challenges to the conventional practice of naturalising men's violent emotions.[4]

And yet, there are good reasons for prioritising *Titus Andronicus*, and not only because it precedes *Othello* by about ten years. Most revealingly, in picking a literary precedent to justify slaying his daughter, the play's protagonist not only deploys the language of law. More particularly and most intriguingly, Shakespeare has him searching for a precedent or 'lively warrant' to legitimate committing femicide at the very time early modern English jurists were developing the idea of a warranted excuse for reducing murder to manslaughter.

Why Shakespeare, which Shakespeare?

It is well to be clear about the Shakespeare that informs this book and the approach to the Shakespeare text that it takes. 'My' Shakespeare is hardly mine. He emerged from the waves of 'new' or 'alternative' Shakespeare studies that emerged in the late twentieth century. Parading under the names of new historicist, cultural materialist, feminist, critical race and postcolonial Shakespeare scholarship, they have been producing transgressive, 'post-humanist' interpretations that contest canonical readings of his work over the last four decades. Their Shakespeare is no longer the universalising everyman credited in traditional humanist scholarship with enshrining a universal human nature. For all their differences in approach and emphasis, the 'new' critical scholarship converges on presenting the Shakespeare text as denaturalising the dominant order of things. This Shakespeare is a questioner of inherited truths about all manner of things – war, sovereignty, nationhood, social and political order, including the gender order in which he lived.[5] He is more 'unexpectantly relevant' to our times, more 'fluent to our contemporary concerns' than those wedded to a view of him as presenting 'timeless values of tolerance and humanity' could imagine. Far from glorifying early modern England as the apex of civilisation, he was one of the first writers to register that 'there is no document of civilisation that is not also a record of barbarism'.[6]

For these scholars, no other writer goes beyond Shakespeare's ability 'to challenge, to interrogate, to illuminate and to insist we rethink ourselves and our cultural heritage'.[7] He is an 'uncanny prognosticator' of late modernity, his 'anticipatory modernity' foreseeing social and political concerns centuries in advance.[8] He is even credited with anticipating postmodern methodologies that question 'whose fiction-making activities are to be construed as legitimate' and how 'truth effects' are discursively produced. In short, this 'alternative' Shakespeare is a precursor of the late modern dissident political analyst bent on tracking and exposing 'truth' as 'somebody's truth'.[9] Destabilising the dominant order by unpacking discourses of legitimacy is hers, as it is Shakespeare's chief mode of operation. You have a question about the legitimacy of political authority, social hierarchy, domination or subordination? He's your man. And if all that is not enough food for critical thought, there's his unsurpassed cultural capital from which it follows, as many feminist Shakespeare scholars argue, that 'feminist revisions of his work, if accepted, could have real cultural – and therefore political – consequences'.[10]

Aligning with this 'alternative' Shakespeare does not entail attributing any particular viewpoint to him. After all, as Shakespeare scholar Jonathan Bate puts it, Shakespeare was quite content to dramatise important issues but 'leave the rest to his audience'.[11] To take a very pertinent example, Bate reads *Titus Andronicus* as a 'forerunner' to *Troilus and Cressida*, a play he describes as Shakespeare's 'most thorough going critique of the ancient world'.[12] That critique questions moral philosophy and finds it wanting. The Trojan Hector seeks to distinguish between 'the dangers of actions based on emotion ("the hot passion of distempered blood") and the propriety of those based on reason'. Hector believes the rights and wrongs of the Trojan war can be judged objectively. But his fate, that of going against his better judgment to indulge in a futile challenge of bravado against the Greeks, reveals that 'all moral judgments are relative'. In fact, Bate argues, that's what the play 'as a whole' proposes, leaving the playwright's own position unclear. Shakespeare's political beliefs are 'as elusive as his religion, his sexuality and just about everything else about him that matters'. And it is precisely because he was not an apologist for 'any single position' that his work lends itself to continual reinterpretation.[13]

Indeed, as Catherine Belsey observes, it is his very 'undecidability' that makes him ripe for recruitment and enlistment in any number of causes.[14] The cause for which I am enlisting Shakespeare is that of challenging the idea that a 'provoked' impassioned homicide is not murder. This returns us to the question: Why *Titus Andronicus*? Why start with a drama that for all its record-breaking array of slaughters does not feature a 'crime of passion' as conventionally understood? I do so for this reason: in my reading, the play offers an extended gloss on justifications for murder written at the very moment English jurists were forging a way to distinguish murder from the lesser crime of manslaughter. Furthermore, it is in this play that Shakespeare appears to query the traditional fiction deeply embedded in classical Roman and, by extension, early modern English law that some femicides can be ethically warranted.

Finally, I shall argue that the play not only foreshadows feminist critiques of the operation of provocation defences in wife-killing cases; it is itself a template for the kind of deep critical work required to dismantle the enduring legal fiction that some women warrant murdering. Remarkably too, the play offers guidelines for thinking about how to speak for women who have suffered violence at the hands of men. Astonishingly, in making his way through all the bloodshed, pleas for mercy and resorts to precedents for justifying murderous violence, Shakespeare still found time in *Titus Andronicus* to turn his attention to the question of how to give women a resistant voice.

Hot and cold-blooded murder – anger as outrage in early modern England

But let us begin with early modern developments in the law of murder to which *Titus Andronicus* can be productively read as an acerbic response.

There is no better point of entry to these legal developments than leading legal scholar Jeremy Horder's *Provocation and Responsibility*, his definitive history of the emergence of provocation as a defence to murder. This absorbing account is indispensable for unmasking the changing nature of the rage said to ignite in provocation cases. Starting in the sixteenth century, Horder provides a fascinating elucidation of the shift over the centuries from the early modern conceptualisation of anger as justifiable outrage to that of a partly excusable ungovernable rage. Most crucially, he explains how anger would retain what he calls 'a justificatory element' that enabled righteous anger to claim for itself a moral warrant, no less, for murder. For as he is at pains to point out, 'at the root of *provoked* anger' lies moral evaluation and judgment, specifically 'a judgment of moral wrongdoing by another that is experienced as demeaning or potentially demeaning to oneself'.[15] Tracing this conceit back to Aristotle, Horder shows how it was revived by early modern England's honour theorists and jurists before finding a lasting place in the law of murder. All this makes *Provocation and Responsibility* an invaluable resource for my inquiry into the continuing purchase of the traditional view that impassioned homicide is not murder.

But I begin my conversation with Horder with a spoiler alert. Looking ahead – it is vital to do so in order to grasp the power of the legal fiction that men's feelings, indicatively feeling angry when demeaned by a woman, should mitigate murder if he kills her – Horder concludes his book by advocating the abolition of the provocation defence. Refusing the excusatory distinction that developed over the centuries in the law of murder between revenge killing and killing in anger, he comes to the conclusion that there is 'no moral justification for acting on a desire to take retribution personally'. Notwithstanding its august foundation in Aristotelian ethics, outraged retaliation actually has 'insufficient ethical status to warrant reducing murder to manslaughter'. There is 'nothing morally understandable' about an angry exaction of vengeance to warrant 'the exceptional mitigation' of provoked killings from murder to manslaughter.[16]

What had led Horder to this conclusion? Crucially, it was what he saw as the disturbing operation of provocation defences in late twentieth-century intimate femicide cases that would clinch the case for him against the conceit that a provoked killing is a partially excusable homicide. At least, that was his view in 1992 when he published *Provocation and Responsibility*. In Chapter 6, we shall see that when, two decades later, he sat on a Law Commission charged with reviewing the operation of partial defences to murder, he would disavow the conclusions he reached in that book. Along with the other Commissioners, he would come to endorse the idea of a warranted excuse for murder, reinstating it in precisely the same kind of femicide cases that had once so troubled him.

For now though, let us start where Horder does, charting how the idea of a warranted excuse for murder came about via the development of a distinction between hot-blooded and cold-blooded killing. This distinction turned on the early modern understanding of killing in anger as justifiable retaliation. Beginning with the propensity of medieval juries to find ways of avoiding convicting defendants of capital murder, he documents how they would find ways to take a merciful view of provoked killings 'in hot blood'. For example, a jury in a 1341 case found a man who had found his wife *in flagrante* not guilty of murder by tailoring the facts to say he had acted in self-defence, a verdict unsupported by any evidence. When by 1400, judges came to instruct juries to differentiate been premeditated killing and hot-blooded killing, Horder shows that juries had been doing so in their own way for some time. In his telling, hot-blooded killing had by the 1550s come to be recognised as an established category of provocation sufficient to reduce murder to manslaughter, while by the late sixteenth century, the notion of 'heated blood' had become the 'key conceptual tool' for distinguishing cold-blooded murder from less serious spur of the moment killing prompted 'by the heating of the blood'. This distinction, he argues persuasively, became 'the foundation-stone' for the modern law of manslaughter, the moral basis on which manslaughter became regarded as a less serious crime than murder linking the concept of heated blood to that of 'human frailty'. By the end of the sixteenth century, the distinctive character of voluntary manslaughter as a less grave form of homicide was framed as 'what was and is still called a concession to human infirmity, a concession to the strong retributive impulse of great anger upon grave provocation'.[17]

What exactly was the early modern understanding of hot-blooded anger? According to Horder, it was anger in the Aristotelian sense of righteous indignation at injustice. He calls this 'anger as outrage', a conception of anger that was indebted to 'a change in ethical thinking about anger as a passion'. Importantly, this righteous anger would become embedded in the conceptualisation of provoked impassioned homicide.[18] This anger was what jurists had in mind when they started developing the categories of anger-inducing provocation sufficient to reduce murder to manslaughter. From the start, finding a wife committing adultery was singled out as the gravest provocation, Horder noting in passing that in seventeenth-century England the cuckold 'almost invariably' killed the male adulterer, not the adulterous wife.[19] That aside, what needs emphasising it that 'mitigation for *all* hot-blooded killings came to depend on the gravity of the provocation offered'.[20] That gravity, crucially, was to be determined by the man of honour who, according to contemporary honour theorists, upholds his 'natural honour' and retaliates in justifiable anger if it is besmirched. It is this fictitious man of honour who would make his way into the law of murder, featuring most dramatically in provocation by infidelity cases.

Honour, anger and the highest invasion of property

Continuing his quest to locate the origins of the provocation defence, Horder lights on *Maddy*'s case, decided in 1671. This case is significant because it was the first to provide 'unequivocal support' for the view that finding a wife in adultery was provocation sufficient to reduce hot-blooded killing from murder to manslaughter.[21] Coming home to find another man in the act of adultery with his wife, John Maddy threw a stool at him, instantly killing him. Indicted for murder, Maddy was arraigned at the Assizes in Southwark where he pleaded not guilty. The judge directed the jury to find a special verdict, namely, that Maddy had 'no precedent malice', premeditation in today's parlance. The case was then removed to the King's Bench which held unanimously that killing a man found 'in the very act' of committing adultery with his wife was 'but manslaughter, the provocation being exceedingly great'. Accordingly, the court directed the executioner to burn the defendant's hand gently, for there 'could not be greater provocation than this'. In the early modern era, finding one's wife *in flagrante* ranked, as Horder puts it, 'very high indeed' in the inventory of offences against honour. The court did however, insist on distinguishing this case from one where a man, on hearing of another man's 'familiarity' with his wife, said he would 'be revenged of him' and killed him. Announcing an intention to kill was still murder. He had to find his wife in the act.[22]

Maddy's case was approved in the foundational provocation case of *Mawgridge*, reported in 1707.[23] Mawgridge was not a wife-killer. He killed a man who had objected to him insulting a woman. The Queen's Bench considering his appeal against his conviction for murder saw this as 'a case of great expectation', turning as it did on the yet to be clarified distinction between murder and manslaughter. Delivering the judgment, Chief Justice Holt elaborated on 'the passion of malice' which he deemed central to a conviction for murder. Malice was 'a design formed of doing mischief to another'. It was not just a feeling. It was an action and 'a cruel' one at that. Killing without any provocation was 'express malice', for the killer acted 'designedly and purposely' and this was so crucially, even if committed 'of a sudden, and in the heat of passion'.[24] Sudden or not, it was murder. The case's main claim to fame however, was its setting down of the four rules, 'supported by authority and general consent' regarding 'what are always allowed to be sufficient provocations' to reduce murder to manslaughter. The most important rule was the fourth: finding your wife *in flagrante delicto* with another man, the Chief Justice famously laying it down that:

> when a man is taken in adultery with another man's wife, if the husband shall stab the adulterer, or knock out his brains, this is bare manslaughter: for jealousy is the rage of a man, and adultery is the highest invasion of property.[25]

The authority for this proposition was great indeed. It was Leviticus 20:10 translated in the judgment thus: 'If one committeth adultery with his neighbour's wife even he the adulterer and the adulteress shall be put to death'. Holt reluctantly acknowledged that this did not mean a man was 'justifiable' in killing a man he 'taketh in adultery with his wife'. For that 'savours more of sudden revenge, than of self-preservation'. But he stressed that the law 'hath been executed with great benignity' in such cases, resulting in manslaughter convictions not warranted by a strict interpretation of the law. For his part though, Holt regarded the killing of an adulterer as being as 'justifiable' as the killing of a would-be robber. After all, they were both invasions of property.

In Chapter 2, I will return to the all-important propertied aspects of the wife-killer's anger. For now let us stay with Horder who notes in passing that Holt's views about invasions of property demonstrate his 'patriarchal assumptions'. For Horder, these assumptions are not as significant as the judge making central to the doctrine of provocation Aristotle's doctrine of retributive justice in which judgments are made about the appropriateness of angry retaliation. Central to this doctrine is the figure of the virtuous man who has feelings 'at the right times on the right grounds towards the right people for the right motive and in the right way'. Indeed, the 'stirring of the right sort of passions in a man' and the performance of the right sort of actions is part of 'what it meant to be virtuous'. It follows that there are times when the virtuous, self-controlled man of honour *ought* to be angry. Here the passions have a 'positive ethical role to play'. With the 'guiding influence of reason, they assist men to act virtuously', reason ensuring 'a just and proportionate emotional response'. It is these Aristotelian doctrines, Horder argues, that informed 'the true ethical foundation' of law's mitigating concession in cases of 'homicide upon provocation in hot blood'.[26]

It pays to linger a little longer with Horder's account of the origins of the much-touted ethical foundation of the provocation defence, as it helps to explain how the defence would retain pride of place in the English law of murder for so long. For the Aristotelian man of honour, retributive justice in the face of grave provocation is a virtue that remedies 'unwarranted inequalities', injuries or injustices, including provocations. For Aristotle, as for early modern jurists, adultery was a perfect example of such an injury. The adulterer has perpetrated an injustice on the cuckold by inflicting a loss of honour on him via a loss of his property rights in his wife. Such an injustice 'cries out for rectification'.[27] However, early modernist jurists differed from Aristotle in a crucially important respect. Whereas he maintained that the requisite retribution had to be taken by the state, not by the injured person, they believed that citizens had the right to administer an ascending scale of retaliatory responses to provocations of increasing gravity. The man of honour will act justly, displaying 'the right amount of angry feeling' that is proportional to 'the affront in question'.[28]

It was to be this Aristotelian-inflected understanding of anger as justifiable outrage, Horder argues, that informed the *Mawgridge* court's framing of the justification for a manslaughter conviction in a provocation case. Honourable men who have been gravely provoked have 'somewhat over-reacted by killing in anger'. They have departed from the mean or right response by inflicting excessive retaliation but their action is not greatly excessive given the gravity of the provocation. While a murder verdict is appropriate for intentional killings that are gross over-reactions, even if they took place in the heat of passion, it is a very different matter if the response was to grave provocation. That could 'extenuate' the crime and make it manslaughter only. In other words, men who killed in anger in response to grave provocation had not gone '*too* far beyond the mean', and so a manslaughter conviction was thought to be warranted. But to be clear, grave provocation does not justify homicidal anger. It only extenuates it.[29] In bringing attention to the justificatory element of the Aristotelian theory of anger as outrage, Horder highlights how in the early modern, self-controlled man of honour, 'passions speak with the same voice as reason' just as they did for Aristotle. Indeed, allowing reason to intercede before acting on a desire to inflict retaliatory suffering for an injury involves no less than 'an ethical duty'.[30] This idea of an ethical justification for retaliatory violence becomes profoundly significant when we realise, courtesy of Horder's careful analysis, that it would survive what he calls 'the rise of excuse' at the expense of justification in the eighteenth and nineteenth centuries. This new Hobbesian conception of anger understood great anger as an ungovernable loss of self-control that overwhelmed the voice of reason. The 'modern question of excuse' would replace questions about justification, that is, about 'the moral warrant for retaliation' as the central question relevant for assessing mitigation by way of a manslaughter conviction in provocation cases.[31]

Nevertheless – and this is the central point – justification still has an important role to play. The categories of sufficient provocation reducing murder to manslaughter remains as 'justification-based restrictions on the scope of mitigation'. And crucially, it is the fourth category – catching a wife *in flagrante* – that exemplifies the tricky transformation from justification to excuse, one that holds fast to its justificatory element. Recall that for Chief Justice Holt, killing an adulterer was barely manslaughter because a wife's infidelity was about the highest provocation a man can get. Therefore, the cuckold's anger is reasonable and therefore justifiable. By contrast, when the question of self-control came to the fore over the next two centuries, courts would start speaking of killers succumbing to 'transports' or 'gusts' of passion. They were no longer seen as making reasonable decisions about how to act within the mean but instead as having succumbed to 'the irresistible impulse of ungovernable passion'. Certainly, the gravity of the provocation was still relevant but not for justification, not for determining the mean and right response. It was relevant now for excuse, that is, for explaining and thereby excusing how a man might lose self-control. Yet through all this, the supposedly supplanted idea that outraged action – say, killing an adulterous wife – is 'action on principle' somehow still survived.[32]

And this is why Horder's meticulous glosses on the Aristotelian-inflected notion of the honourable man's justifiable retaliation to affronts are so important. Most crucially, they register the indefeasible quality of the notion of a moral warrant for murder that, as we shall see, has played out in disturbing ways in 'provoked' femicide cases. Indeed, such has been the tenacious hold of the fiction that a homicide in response to grave provocation, indicatively a wife's infidelity, is morally warranted, that it comes to envelop Horder himself.

Misgivings about the 'peculiarly favourable' English law of murder

While Chief Justice Holt found it odd that the law did not regard killing a wife found *in flagrante* as justifiable, he was happy to lay down general rules distinguishing murder from manslaughter. Not all judges were. Listen to Judge Aske raging against them in his dissenting judgment in a 1655 provocation case. Disagreeing with the majority decision that found a man who had stabbed another to death in a dispute over a debt guilty of manslaughter, he went on to query the whole idea of distinguishing murder from manslaughter in intentional homicides. In his view, this was a wrong turning in the law that he attributed to 'the popish power' that had 'introduced the clergy to be given for manslaughter'. He was referring to the institution of 'benefit of clergy' which traditionally had allowed clergy to escape with lesser penalties for offences but had now been extended to any offender who could recite a biblical verse. In his view, this development had diminished the common law, 'regal power' and the law of God. These laws did not distinguish murder from manslaughter. They made 'no difference between hot blood and cold blood, as we do now distinguish'. Remarkably, he buttressed his argument with the claim that the distinction benefited men, not women inasmuch as if a woman killed, she would not 'have her clergy' for manslaughter. She would be hanged.[33]

Seventy years after Judge Aske railed against distinguishing cold-blooded murder from hot-blooded manslaughter, his misgivings were echoed in another equally significant provocation case. In 1727, John Oneby killed a man in a sword fight occasioned by heated words. What is of particular interest is that in deciding the case, Lord Raymond, the Lord Chief Justice, elaborated on the contemporary judicial understanding of an excusatory 'heat of passion'. A 'transport of passion', he said, should 'never make the killing of a man manslaughter only' unless it deprived a killer of 'his reasoning faculties from the time when it was raised until the giving of the mortal wound'. Lord Raymond did not consider it necessary to go back to the 'old law books' since it had long been settled that murder was the voluntary killing of a person by 'malice prepense'. But he did want to consider what 'malice' meant. He found that in 'common acceptance', malice was 'a settled anger (which requires some length of time)' against another person and a desire for revenge. It 'imports a wickedness' that 'cuts off all excuse'.[34] Referring to the authorities, the 'mighty' warrants laid down by such eminent judges as Lord Chief Justices Coke and Hale, Lord Raymond explained further that malice, an essential ingredient of murder, could be express or implied. In the case at hand, the defendant had express malice against the victim who, in the judge's view, had done 'nothing that could reasonably raise a passion' in him. Accordingly, he rejected the defence argument that killing taking place in 'a sudden fighting in heat of passion' was merely manslaughter. If there was 'sufficient time for this passion to cool, and for reason to get the better of the transport of passion', it was murder.[35]

Lord Raymond had still more to say about the English law of murder. In sharp contrast to the standard English view that foreign jurisdictions were too indulgent towards impassioned homicide, he found English law to be singularly favourable to men who succumbed to excessive anger and passion. The law of England, he said,

> is so far peculiarly favourable (I use the word peculiarly, because I know no other law that makes such a distinction between murder and manslaughter) as to permit the excess of anger and passion (which a man ought to keep under and govern) in some instances to extenuate the greatest of private injuries, as the taking away a man's life is.[36]

Foreshadowing the strict judicial approach that would be taken by nineteenth-century judges, he insisted that there must be such a passion as deprives a man of his reasoning faculties. For if reason has 'resumed its office'; if a man reflects, deliberates or considers before delivering the fatal stroke, the law would no longer 'under that pretext of passion' exempt him from the punishment for his heinous crime that he 'justly deserves'. It should definitely not lessen his crime from murder to manslaughter.[37]

For Horder, the significance of this passage lies in what it reveals about an important change in how the relationship between passion and reason was understood when people (read: men) become extremely angry. The *Oneby* case, he argues, is one of the first where we see the switch from justification to excuse. Great passions are now said to '*deprive* people of their reasoning capacities', leading them to lose their self-control, an effect captured in the 'transport' metaphor. Passion is no longer guided by reason in the moderating and mediating Aristotelian sense. It was now understood to have overthrown reason. An ungovernable 'fury of passion' – loss of control in modern parlance – replaced the early modern notion of reason-based anger as outrage. That is, passion was being transformed from a justifying emotion to an excusatory one, a development that can be tracked most clearly in intimate partner femicide cases.[38]

While Horder's insightful gloss on this passage is well taken, it is also significant for a reason he overlooks. English judges over the centuries have regarded as a foreign innovation the conceit that a hot-blooded crime of passion is less culpable than murder – that crime was committed by men elsewhere, indicatively 'hot-blooded' Latins. Lord Raymond, by contrast, laid its invention firmly at the door of the English with their 'peculiarly favourable' law permitting excessive anger and passion to extenuate murder. English courts, he warned, needed to guard against the 'pretext of passion' creeping any further into that law.[39] Certainly, passions were tricky. But difficult though it was for the law to fix the time span in which passion was supposed to have cooled, nineteenth-century judges would fixate on the requirement that a man's homicidal feelings had to be still hot at the time of the killing. This, it was felt, was the best means of holding impassioned wife-killers to account.

As we shall see in Chapter 3, for the most part, it would do just that. What needs emphasising here is that in insisting that a heat of passion killing was murder if premeditation could be established, Lord Raymond hedged passion's excusatory force. Just twenty years after the *Mawgridge* case enshrined an impassioned killing of an adulterer as 'mere' manslaughter, he insisted that 'malice' equally fell to be considered. But let us turn now to Shakespeare's take on the notion of justification-via-precedent for retaliatory justice that was contemporaneously preoccupying the early modern honour theorists and jurists parading through Horder's history.

Titus Andronicus – querying foundations

Written between 1588 and 1593, Shakespeare's *Titus Andronicus* is notorious for its sheer excess of interpersonal violence. Half the cast are dead by the end. On one critic's count, it features

> 14 killings, 9 of them on stage, 6 severed members, 1 rape (or 2 or 3 depending how you count), 1 live burial, 1 case of insanity and 1 of cannibalism (the serving up of 2 butchered sons to a mother in a pie) – an average of 5.2 atrocities per act, or one for every 97 lines.[40]

Such an exuberance of violence finds a parallel in the scale of men's homicidal violence against wives and women partners; the two killed per week in the UK by current or former male partners, the thousands killed over the 400 years since Shakespeare.[41] But that is not why I have chosen *Titus Andronicus* to kick-start this book's Shakespearean glosses on the notion of justifiable homicide. It is rather the play's querying of the notion of a culturally mandated warrant for murder. It is this questioning that is so germane to a history of the rage that culminates in wife-killing and is subsequently framed in criminal courts as understandable and, at the very least, partly excusable. No matter that there is no intimate partner homicide in the play. What is critical is that *Titus Andronicus* invites a re-examination of law's legitimation of retaliatory interpersonal violence whatever form it takes. Furthermore, it leaves us in no doubt that justifications or 'warrants' for murder are deeply gendered.

Once dismissed as a simple revenge drama, as nothing more than a gore-fest of retaliatory violence – *Titus Andronicus* is today widely interpreted as a scathing parodic indictment of classical Rome and its much-vaunted values. This follows from Heather James' influential interpretation of the play as performing an Ovidian critique of Rome, one pitting Ovid's 'irreverent counter-epic', the

Metamorphoses, against Virgil's 'imperial epic' in the *Aeneid*. As she memorably puts it, of all Shakespeare's plays this one 'cites the most Latin yet hacks up the most bodies' as the Ovidian plot 'unravels Virgilian values'.[42] Clearly, James did not let Shakespeare's 'undecidability' get in the way of interpreting *Titus Andronicus* in this way and neither have other Shakespeare scholars. Jonathan Bate argues that Ovid's parodies of Roman heroes not only provide a precedent for 'debunking' them; they are put to work to destabilise 'the entire humanist project of learning from the exemplars of the past'.[43] Coppéla Kahn, amongst other Shakespeare scholars, also sees the play as 'a serious critique of Roman ideology, institutions and mores'. Moreover, it is not only Rome 'as Elizabethan culture knew it that they play attacks, but also the humanist appropriation of Rome's textual legacy from grammar school through university in Shakespeare's England'.[44] 'Rome' is Elizabethan England, barely disguised. Read this way, the play creates 'an interpretative space' not only for examining the legitimacy of violence but for interrogating the dominant order of things in self-proclaiming 'civilised' societies like classical Rome and, by extension, early modern England.[45]

Many superb readings have occupied that interpretative space, none more notably than critical race Shakespeare scholar Francesca Royster's reading of the play's Rome as 'an analogue of Britain'. In her telling, the culture displayed there is 'proudly committed to Romanness, to Roman honour, to ancestral Roman practices and values' and is clearly related to the early modern rhetoric of English nationhood. There are other similarities. Classical Rome and Elizabethan England both feared invasion and infiltration by foreigners. In *Titus Andronicus*, the barbarians are no longer at the gate. They have infiltrated Rome's sacred sanctum. But the rot was already within.[46] While many critics have subscribed to this view, what is distinctive about Royster's reading is that it shows how whiteness is made racially visible and complicated in the play, thus providing 'a more complicated vision of Rome as the cornerstone of England's national identity'. Royster does not rest with registering the pairing of Tamora, the conspicuously white Goth queen with Aaron the Moor, the ultra-black villain. In a stunning move, she unpacks variations of whiteness represented in the bodies of the ultra-white Tamora and the 'temperate Roman whiteness' of Titus' daughter, Lavinia. In the eyes of Shakespeare's audience, she suggests, Tamora's whiteness cannot compete with 'the truly more normative and foundational whiteness of Roman (and Englished) Lavinia'. Shakespeare not only reveals how white supremacy in the Roman polity is 'normalised and patrolled through the bodies of women'.[47] More than that, he disrupts 'the seemingly intractability and permanence of whiteness', thereby dismantling it as 'a uniquely privileged cultural force'.[48]

Relatedly, Royster shows how whiteness plays out in the reversal of moderates and extremists in the play. As she explains, in early modern scientific thought, the Goths inhabiting the extreme North were seen as similar to Africans from the extreme South. Both were 'associated with extremes and with excess, hence distanced from the more moderate Romans'. To the Elizabethans, moderation and restraint were 'quintessential Roman virtues'. But in *Titus Andronicus*, Shakespeare contests this theory, presenting the Romans as the extremists. Try as the Romans might to attribute extremism to outsiders, the maligned others, be they too white Goths or too black Moors, see through this invidious scapegoating. To them, it is Roman piety that is barbarous. The antithesis between civilised Rome and the barbaric foreigners has collapsed entirely.[49]

Developing this argument, leading postcolonial Shakespeare scholar Ania Loomba observes how, by the end, the opposition between Roman civility and barbarism 'has been so rearranged that the Goths become crucial agents in the righting of Roman order'.[50] The evidence for this interpretation of the play as questioning the received idea that Rome stood for civilisation and the Goths for barbarism is overwhelming. Tamora, the Queen of the Goths condemns Titus' 'cruel, irreligious piety' when he orders the sacrifice of one of her sons. Another of her sons joins in with: 'Was never Scythia so barbarous'. Even Marcus, Titus' brother, implores him not to be barbarous: 'Thou art a Roman, be not barbarous'.[51] As for Aaron, the proud black Moor, he amuses himself by toying with Roman myths and using them against the Romans, going so far as to direct Tamora's sons to re-enact Ovid's story of Philomel's rape on the body of Titus' daughter, Lavinia. Mocking Rome's self-acclaimed superior white culture, he muses whether black is 'so base a hue'. He decides not. 'Coal-black is better than another hue', and certainly superior to white, that 'treacherous hue' that betrays itself with its blushing.[52] For all their self-aggrandisement, Aaron is under no illusions about 'the den of hissing vipers that is Rome'. He knows there is no line demarcating the civilised' from the 'unenlightened' others. Be they Romans, Goths or Moors, they all have 'debasing and dehumanising traits' and all 'ghoulishly relish revenge'.[53]

Aaron, the abject outsider, knows full well that classical Roman and, by extension, Elizabethan society, likes to project its own violent and destructive forces onto the outsider scapegoat, conveniently a primitive Moor such as himself. He happily obliges by playing the villain while holding up a mirror to the treacherous white-hued standard-bearers of Roman virtue. Crucially, Aaron turn the tables on the derisory practice, often featured in commentaries about impassioned homicide, of attributing murderous rage to black or otherwise minoritised subjects or foreigners, thereby deflecting attention from 'civilised' white men. In a most helpful way, Aaron directs our gaze to the violence committed in the name of Roman piety by the Roman war hero Titus Andronicus – 'surnamèd Pius', the 'good Andronicus, Patron of Virtue, Rome's best champion'.[54] Watch now as Titus, standing in for the moderate, even-tempered precedent-following man of honour so admired by early modern honour theorists and jurists, takes centre stage. Watch how through him, Shakespeare dramatises the impassioned man who kills in response to grave provocation, the man who contemporaneously was being built into the English law of murder.

Patterns, precedents and 'lively' warrants

Titus Andronicus has now found a place in the law and literature genre, critics recognising its articulation of the 'unstable relation of revenge to justice' and the use of excess and overkill to 'define the ethical' and, ultimately, justice.[55] As a theatre reviewer puts it, the play's 'nightmarish spectacles' of retaliatory violence are 'cathartic channels through which the spectator is at once horrified and compelled to think about justice'.[56] Certainly, justice and injustice are dominant themes throughout: 'This prince in justice seizeth but his own'; 'my lord, you are unjust'. Titus goes mad in search for justice. Searching by land and sea, he finds justice has been 'shipp'ed' from Rome by a tyrannical emperor. The goddess of justice having left the earth, he shoots arrows attached with petitions to the gods and even to the underworld, but he finds 'no justice in earth nor hell'. The Andronici 'go pipe for justice', leaving Titus no recourse, at least in his mind, but to take matters into his own hands.[57] Indeed, in troubling the belief that murder can itself be justice, *Titus* challenges the standard binarist assumption that justice is easily distinguishable from injustice. That assumption has been queried philosophically by legal scholar Eric Heinze and, as we shall see, devastatingly by the families of murdered women outraged by short sentences handed down to their killers.[58]

What is most interesting about scholarly reclamations of *Titus Andronicus* however, is what they have to say about its intricate structuring and patterning that are derived from classical allusions.[59] In all there are over 50 classical allusions, the key ones providing what have been called 'textual precedents' for the current situations of the characters. Crucially, these precedents 'authorise (quite literally) their subsequent actions', the sacrifices and slaughters that deplete the cast.[60]

The textual precedent that primarily concerns us here is Livy's tale of Virginius, the centurion who killed his daughter to prevent her rape. As Pascale Aebischer points out, Shakespeare has his protagonist twisting the original tale, 'wresting' it to suit his purpose by misremembering 'rash' Virginius as slaying his daughter after she had been raped – 'enforced, stained and deflowered'.[61] Titus 'makes do' with this his chosen 'textual exemplar' in order to give himself a 'reason mighty strong and effectual'. It is a 'pattern, precedent and lively warrant' – to kill his daughter Lavinia who had been raped and mutilated.[62] Distorted though Livy's tale is in Titus' re-telling, he believes that it provides him with a textual precedent to authorise and sanction Lavinia's murder. A 'great Roman precedent' becomes his 'deadly logical proof' that she must die, no matter that he does not really value his stated textual authority.[63] As the bearer of 'the language of the fathers, especially the texts of the fathers', Titus thinks it is appropriate to kill his daughter 'because Livy told the story of Virginius killing *his* daughter' thus confirming the pre-eminence of a past text that 'originates and sanctions actions'. Lavinia suffers 'death by the book'. But it's the wrong book. She had pointed to Ovid, preferring his rape revenge story where the victim, Philomel, survives, whereas Titus points to Livy's tale of a raped daughter warranting femicide.[64]

Titus wants the Emperor Saturninus to endorse his choice of literary precedent. Was it justifiable, 'well done of rash Virginius' to slay his daughter? Saturninus agrees it was. Titus, like Virginius, did indeed have a 'reason mighty, strong and effectual', a 'lively warrant' to 'perform the like'. The 'lively' in 'lively warrant' is glossed in Bate's edition of the play as 'striking'. Calling it 'the OED's first usage for this sense', he suggests that 'lively' plays perhaps on the more usual Elizabethan sense of 'living', as in Titus' earlier reference to Lavinia's 'lively body'. Bate notes the irony: Titus' 'lively warrant' becomes her death-warrant. Indeed, considerable critical commentary has converged on highlighting the irony of Titus' description of his warrant as 'lively'.[65] The corporeal effects of the 'lively warrant', understood as an authorisation or justification for an action, are deadly for Lavinia.

While it goes without saying that Titus' warrant is one exclusively reserved for male title-holders, it is the deployment of legal language – 'precedent' and 'warrant' – that has attracted the most attention. Some critics read the play as supporting the authority of precedent. Titus' appeal to 'precedent', 'the bedrock of the common law, in a play set in Rome, the home of civil law', suggests to Bate 'an intervention in the late Elizabethan argument about the relative weight' of civil law, by then associated with arbitrary government and common law. He sees Titus' argument from the common law principle of precedent as making him into 'the very voice of the English common law'.[66] In this reading, taken up by some legal commentators, the play is a gloss on juridical developments in the 1590s, the last decade of Elizabeth's rule, when the jurisdiction of the common law was being encroached upon by the Tudor prerogative courts. Within this interpretative paradigm, Titus is both a 'dramatic antecedent' to Sir Edward Coke, Jacobean champion of the common law, and a 'dramatic descendant' of Sir John Fortescue, the fifteenth-century 'apologist' for the constitutional supremacy of the common law.[67] Some readings go even further, presenting Titus as a moderate man, an Aristotelian hero in search of the ethical mean. However 'imperfect' his piety, he 'nonetheless nobly privileges the ethos of gratitude over unrestrained self-interest', even when he kills Lavinia. When situated within the Aristotelian ethical theory of the late 1590s, *Titus Andronicus* reveals a 'deeply moderate protagonist', a man provoked beyond endurance but whose 'deep', indeed 'almost organic sense of proportionality' and 'temperance of anger' are 'easy to overlook'.[68]

They are indeed easy to overlook. After all, this was a man who slaughtered one of his sons for filial disobedience, killed his daughter for dishonouring the family by getting herself raped and then served up two sons to their mother in a pie as revenge for the rape. And yet for scholars who view Titus as some kind of hero, Lavinia's killing is 'no savage murder'. Adopting Titus' viewpoint, they see it 'an act of love' that ends her terrible suffering and her 'shame', conveniently forgetting that Titus adds that his 'sorrow' ends when she dies. Embodying the principle of precedent, he is a seeker after the Aristotelian ethical mean no less, plausibly defending femicide on the basis of his lively warrant. Some go so far as to suggest that, in symbolic terms, the killing of Lavinia, Rome's 'rich ornament', is 'a necessary act'. Her mangled body symbolises the 'desecrated body of Rome' which 'had to perish so that a new, benevolent order might arise from the ruins of the old'. Shakespeare, they argue, 'distinguishes clearly between barbarous acts of violence and the sacrificial rites' that Titus enacts, seeing Lavinia's death as a 'legitimate form of sacrifice'.[69]

Reaching that conclusion is quite a feat given that, as we have seen, so many Shakespeare commentators have highlighted the evidence for reading the play as presenting the Romans as barbaric and their self-legitimating precedents for retaliatory violence as deeply problematic.[70] Far from supporting the Roman protagonist's killings as culturally and legally warranted, they read the play is a critique of cultural texts that distinguish between 'good and bad killing' and of the use of 'elevating' discourses, legal or poetic, that legitimate violence and grant it meaning.[71] It is a parody of its protagonist's 'aggressive imitations' of his precedent texts, a critique, not a celebration, of imperial Rome. Titus' slavish adherence to them in order to authorise his revenge is flatly condemned. Ovid's tale of Philomel should have provided Titus with an authoritative text to replace his 'obsolete Virgil'. Instead, his adherence to his Virgilian precedent and Rome's rigid code of pietas leads him to commit murders, which he calls sacrifices, that have 'emptied Roman institutions and values of meaning'.[72] Within this interpretative paradigm, Ovid's poem and Shakespeare's play condemn 'the systematic violence and subordination embedded in patriarchal culture'. Both deplore classical Rome's accommodating view of its own culturally mandated violence, its own version of honour killing.[73]

Challenging the depiction of Titus as epic hero, these critics see his killing of his daughter as clearly murder. Titus may claim to act on a classical precedent authorising him to remove her shame and 'stain' on the family honour – 'die, die Lavinia, and thy shame with thee'. But he actually has a selfish motive, that of ending '*his* sorrows' by killing her – 'and with thy shame thy father's sorrow die', lines often omitted in performance.[74] Moreover, he knows his act is outrageous. In adapting the Virginius story as a model for action, he describes that father as 'rash', and his own deed as an 'outrage', but still attempts to justify it:

> I am as woeful as Virginius was,
> And have a thousand times more cause than he
> To do this outrage.[75]

For these scholars, Titus is a pathetic figure who mistakes 'false shadows for true substances', a man 'so confined by an education that substitutes erudition for wisdom that he cannot even invent the form of his own revenge'.[76] Titus 'forces a grim pattern upon events', adapting the Virginius story to 'satisfy his perverted sense of honour', while Lavinia's death is nothing more than 'gratuitous'. Far from receiving Shakespeare's endorsement, his 'shocking' killing of Lavinia 'warns against the danger of becoming compulsively caught up in acting our deadly artistic patterns'.[77] For all his posturing about his honour-driven clinging to Roman piety and precedents, this was no man of honour. It follows that Lavinia's death was no honour killing.

'Speechless complainer, I will learn thy thought'[78]

Paralleling the debunking of the idea that Titus is any kind of man of honour is a move in Shakespearean criticism to transform Lavinia from an object to a subject, a move I will be replicating in my analysis of intimate partner femicide cases. Once she was presented as just a mangled body symbolising the fallen world of Rome; a 'mute presence' serving as 'a constant symbol of the appalling injustices that are inflicted on the body politic by an unaccountable and tyrannical lawmaker'.[79] Now she is transformed from a mere stage prop in Titus' revenge drama into a survivor and even a 'co-author' of her rapists' punishment. In this reading, Lavinia rejects Titus' repetitive narrative strategy and commitment to literary precedents to authorise his actions. Insisting on 'other narrative possibilities beyond her father's proscriptions', she attempts to create a future outside his 'preset stories'. She especially wants to derail the sacrifice narrative he learnt from Livy's tale of Virginius. Recognising that her survival depends on rejecting his 'repetitive strategies', she tries to move the Andronici males away from the expected sacrificial narrative in which she commits suicide. But she is no match for Titus' 'reiterative coping strategy' in which he inserts himself into pre-existing tales and finds 'stability in repeating them'. His enactment of Livy's sacrifice narrative puts paid to her efforts to tell a different ending, one in which she survives, even if only in the form of a bird.[80]

Nevertheless, several Shakespeare scholars suggest that Shakespeare is complicating the question of women's voice, one critic asserting that the play demonstrates the 'need for Lavinia's voice'. This, she argues, was especially the case in the context of the emergence in early modern England of a new understanding of rape as sexual assault. Now rape was no longer defined exclusively as 'bride theft' or abduction but as an assault on a woman. Accordingly, men had to rely on women to report it. Hence the play's repeated evocation of classical precedents illustrating men's need to rely on women as the authority of their own experiences of rape. Admittedly, this grants only a 'limited agency' to women, 'hardly something for feminists to celebrate'.[81] However, Shakespeare does grant Lavinia a voice, for example, when Marcus observes how she 'quotes the leaves' from Ovid's *Metamorphoses*.[82] For another critic, this means more than simply citing pages from the poem. By referencing her own rape in the 'ruthless' woods outside Rome, Lavinia is making 'the Ovidian forest speak', bringing to words the rustling of the many victims of rape in the classical poems, victims who are 'left without speech'.[83] Bate too sees the play as being 'deeply concerned' with giving back language to the silenced woman. When Titus tries to translate her gestures into language, to interpret and transform into speech the 'map of woe' that is her body, Bate sympathises with his desperate efforts to empathise with her pain and understand its cause.[84]

Feminist Shakespeare scholars are more pessimistic. When Lucas, Lavinia's young nephew, sees her mutilated body, he cries: 'This object kills me'. She is for him no more than an object, the emphasis being on the 'me' of his own distress at seeing her wounds. He's not the only one to feel this way. In the eyes of all the Andronici males, Lavinia's rape and dismemberment fashions her into 'a problematic sign'. She oscillates between virtuous daughter and violated object defying nomenclature. Titus insists on her position as daughter, correcting Marcus' use of the past tense: 'This was thy daughter' by replying 'so she *is*'. But Lavinia's 'problematic subjectivity' is further betrayed as other representations displace her suffering by emphasising her familial relationship to the men.[85] For these critics, Lavinia's tragedy is that she has 'an internal voice' but lacks the agency to speak it. Perhaps the most that can be read into her failed efforts at speech is that Shakespeare was troubling the value of women's silence, exposing its 'sinister effects' in 'the disquietude of quiet'.[86] A slightly more optimistic view is that the play construes a distinction between 'better and worse ways of speaking for a victim', better or worse ways of 'committing oneself to another's pain'. Treating her as an object, describing her 'in vegetative terms' as a tree or a piece of wood as the Andronici men do, is clearly way down the reprehensible end of the speaking-for spectrum. Responding to a victim, the play seems to suggest, should be 'a mode of recognition and a commitment to spend time' with her 'in order to alleviate her loneliness'.[87] That, at least, would be a lesson well worth taking when it comes to speaking for the victims of intimate partner femicide.

Still, there is no escaping the fact that Lavinia is treated as 'a mere prop in Titus' final show'.[88] Continuing to read against the grain of older scholarly assessments of *Titus Andronicus* as a simple revenge drama, Shakespeare critics have also clocked how its performance history has overwhelmingly endorsed Lavinia's death, most directors seemingly content to accept Titus' self-justification for murder. Theatre critics too have tended to support the murder, refiguring it as euthanasia or assisted suicide and, at any rate, warranted by classical precedents. But not all. What 'never ceases to amaze' Pascale Aebischer about Lavinia's death is 'the sheer endorsement Titus received from critics and performers alike for his wresting of her into another myth which prescribes her destruction'. This endorsement is oblivious to 'the obvious unsoundness of Titus' pre-text'.[89] Or, as another critic observes, Lavinia's death is 'refigured' by textual precedent into an explanation of her own slaughter. Both the knowledge and resolution of her violation are enabled by classical allusions that allow Titus to contextualise her murder as 'justice'.[90]

How fascinating it has been to follow critical Shakespeare scholars reading *Titus Andronicus* as a searching critique of justification-via-precedent for retaliatory violence. And what striking parallels there are between that critique and late twentieth-century-century feminist critiques of the operation of provocation by infidelity defences to murder. Shakespeare's Roman protagonist defends his murderous acts with reference to time-honoured Roman precedents that have become licences to kill. Late modern law reformers call out the time-honoured 'infidelity' defence that has allowed femicidal Englishmen to get away with murder for centuries. Shakespeare identifies Roman culture as endorsing retaliatory violence. The law reformers condemn the 'culture of excuses' informing the English version of honour killing. Within this interpretative paradigm, Shakespeare anticipates feminist challenges to a law privileging a man's homicidal reaction to what he perceives to be grave provocation.

Over the intervening centuries, femicidal men have had varying degrees of success when relying on those precedents to avoid murder convictions. For the most part, English criminal courts have refrained from calling femicide 'well done', as Titus claimed his killing of Lavinia was. But many courts, especially in the second half of the twentieth-century, would determine that wife-killing was not that bad either, a long line of common law precedents dictating that femicidal men be found guilty of 'mere' manslaughter. As for the victims of impassioned femicide, courts continued to reconfigure them into an explanation of their own slaughter, divesting them of subjectivity, agency and a voice as surely as Titus did Lavinia's.

Titus Andronicus as template for critique

Titus Andronicus provides a template for the kind of critical work that is still needed to contest two widespread beliefs; first, that self-entitled men who kill women in a self-justifying rage deserve law's compassion and second, that foreign 'others' are more impassioned, more homicidal. *Titus Andronicus* puts paid to both views. How astounding that, at the very same time that jurists were busy distinguishing murder from manslaughter with the help of Aristotle's theory of justifiable retaliation to grave provocation, Shakespeare wrote a play querying that very conceit. A revenge drama with a difference, *Titus Andronicus* unmasks the 'lively' warrant as a deadly precedent that is nothing more than a mandate for revenge. Not until the late twentieth century would a whole host of feminist legal scholars and activists register what Shakespeare had observed four hundred years earlier, namely, that there is something profoundly problematic about the idea of justification-via-precedent for retaliatory violence. In the following chapters, I track how provocation defences have fared in impassioned femicide cases over the centuries. There we shall also highlight the deleterious effects of the stubborn drive to attribute murderous rage to foreigners, an insidious othering practice that Shakespeare queries in *Titus Andronicus* and would continue to do so in his later plays, notably, *Othello*. It would be a long time before such critical attention would be drawn again to the fact that the English law of murder, as Lord Raymond so astutely observed, was 'peculiarly favourable' to impassioned Englishmen, permitting their excessive anger and passion to extenuate murder.

But let us conclude by returning briefly to Horder's *Provocation and Responsibility*, where we find him continuing his history of the provocation defence into the nineteenth-century. By then the notion of a justifiable killing committed by an honourable man acting on appropriate anger began to be displaced by the idea of excusable rather than justifiable homicidal rage. The anger of the provoked defendants was no longer said to be morally warranted. It was attributed to a loss of self-control or a 'fit of passion'. Yet as Horder shows, provocation cases would retain the 'justificatory element' that he so meticulously tracks back to the early modern era. Nowhere is this more apparent than in provocation by infidelity femicide cases. Chief Justice Holt's understanding of a man's justifiable, not merely excusable, rage in the face of infidelity as set down in the famous *Mawgridge* case would haunt criminal courts for centuries. And as we shall see, the early modern notion of a justifiable sense of being seriously wronged by grave provocation has survived the early twenty-first-century overhaul of the law of murder.

Horder's contribution to unmasking changing conceptions of the nature of the rage unleashed in impassioned homicides is invaluable. For the most part though, he does not appear to find it noteworthy that the provoked killings he discusses were committed almost exclusively by men. His deeming 'patriarchal' Chief Justice Holt's equation of adultery with robbery, for example, is no more than an aside. It therefore comes as something of a surprise to find him concluding *Provocation and Responsibility* by adopting 'a feminist perspective' from which he argues for the abolition of the provocation defence. Why? First, it had become an excuse for men to kill women. Second, the traditional assumption that the infliction of retaliatory retribution has an ethical basis was not sustainable because there is 'an alternative conception of anger' that has the better claim to be regarded as 'an expression of moral virtue'. He calls this alternative conception 'righteous indignation'. What sets righteously indignant persons apart is that they do not desire retaliation but rather to 'negate wrongdoing by an open condemnation of the wrongdoer'. Controversial though Horder thinks it might be to suggest that 'gender politics' are at issue here, he acknowledges that women express righteous indignation more often than they express outrage or lose their self-control, 'particularly in their dealings with male wrongdoers'. For men, on the other hand, 'it is all too frequently the other way around'. Moreover, once it is recognised that righteous indignation 'captures most of what is ethically appealing' about the expression of anger, the 'excusatory distinction between revenge killings and killings in anger vanishes'.[91]

And yet these striking gendered dimensions of the expression of anger are almost an aforethought and are not mentioned at all in Horder's discussion of Aristotle's musings about angry retaliation. By contrast, they are at the forefront of feminist philosopher Elizabeth Spelman's contemporaneous critique of Aristotle's musing on the propriety of anger. As she explains, Aristotle saw the task of thinking about the appropriateness of anger and other emotions as 'part of thinking about how we ought to conduct our lives'. His was not an inclusive 'we'. Women and slaves were 'naturally' excluded. Dominant groups, indicatively elite men who appropriate anger for themselves, regard anger as inappropriate in subordinated groups. Anything resembling anger in these groups is condemned as hysteria or, at any rate, as an unwarranted, furious outburst.[92] While these considerations fell outside Horder's analysis of Aristotle's thoughts about anger, in the final analysis he comes to register what feminist critics have recognised from the start. The 'red mist' rage whipped up in impassioned homicides is experienced almost exclusively by men.

.....

The seventeenth-century jurist Judge Aske could not have been more scathing about the accepted legal practice of distinguishing between hot and cold-blooded murder. Seventy years later, Lord Raymond did his best to rein in 'passion' as an excuse for murder. They both deserve credit for querying vengeful murders masquerading as impassioned homicides and expressing doubts about whether labelling an intentional killing 'manslaughter' can be defended on ethical grounds. But long before them, a young playwright penned a revenge drama that spectacularly dismantled the entire conceit of a moral warrant for murder even as early modern jurists were busy constructing one. That's quite an impressive dissenting tradition to build on when we continue our examination of the culturally mandated legal precedents hauled out over the centuries to justify or excuse so-called 'crimes of passion'.

Chapter 2

Othello – 'An honourable murderer, if you will'

LODOVICO
What shall be said to thee?

OTHELLO
Why anything;
An honourable murderer, if you will,
For nought I did in hate, but all in honour

Othello 5.2.289–292[1]

Introduction

We turn now to *Othello*, read here as a critical reflection on 'infidelity'-inspired femicide. *Othello*'s significance for historicising and querying the emotions attending intimate partner femicide cases cannot be underestimated, packing to the brim as it is with the early modern emotions, or 'passions' as they were then called, informing 'crimes of passion'. Possessive jealousy, shame, rage and self-pity on the part of an over-emotional man are all on display. So too, in Othello's self-serving final speech, is the overwrought wife-killer's appeal for compassion. But might a close reading of the play reveal Shakespeare questioning whether he is deserving of sympathy? Might he even be querying the criminal law's hallowed distinction between hot and cold-blooded murder and that distinction's equally venerated by-products? They are first, the conceit that a wife's sexual infidelity warrants violent retaliation and second, the belief that men's homicidal feelings towards an adulterous wife are understandable and so at least partially excusable. And what is to be made of his attributing such ludicrous femicidal rage to a racialised character, 'black Othello' as he is referred to throughout?

Chapter 2 makes the case for reading *Othello* as problematising both the perpetrators and the perpetration of impassioned homicide. It contains everything you need to know about a crime of passion and, if read from any of the post-humanist perspectives I will discuss here, everything you need to contest the conceit of a mitigating impassioned killing. Here's a quick snapshot of what's on offer. There's the dramatising of the workings of what philosopher Denise

DOI: 10.4324/9781003301974-3

Riley calls 'persecutory interpellation'.[2] That's as apt a description as one can find of the discursive trashing of impassioned homicide's victims by their killers and their counsel in the courtroom. Listen as Emilia tells her husband, Iago, that Othello has 'so bewhored' his wife, Desdemona, cast such 'heavy terms upon her' that 'true hearts cannot bear it'. Desdemona pipes in: 'Am I that name, Iago?' He replies: What name, fair lady? She demurs: 'Such as she said my lord did say I was'. Emilia reminds him: 'He called her whore'.[3] Then there's the racialisation of the impassioned killer as monstrous other. The racist epithets pile up: Othello is the 'thick lips', an 'old black ram', a 'barbary horse', 'a lascivious Moor', an 'extravagant and wheeling stranger of here and everywhere'. Why, Desdemona's father Brabantio asks, would a white Venetian woman run to 'the sooty bosom of such a thing' as him, a man whose judgment is 'collied' by inordinate passion?[4] Why, more pertinently, would Shakespeare cast his protagonist as a black Muslim and subject him to so much racist vilification?

For anyone bent, as I am, on dismantling the sympathetic figure of the impassioned wife-killer deserving of law's compassion, there's so much more to unpack in the play. The astonishing depth of its critique of obsessive male anxiety about 'unfaithful' women is highlighted in feminist and Marxist readings of the play as dramatising the operation of commodity fetishism in early modern capitalism. Here we see highlighted the slippage from love to loathing that is narrated in impassioned homicide's conventional scenarios of dispossessed love. Femicidal rage is exposed as founded on beliefs in the property rights of honourable Englishmen who are racialised as white and thus readily distinguishable from their supposedly barbaric others. Then there's the play's pervasive legal language, notably Othello's demand for 'ocular proof' of his wife's infidelity.[5] As if all this were not enough food for critical thought, Shakespeare foreshadows the main defences which would be raised in those trials. Finally, and perhaps most astoundingly, he gifts his proto-feminist character, Emilia, a speech slamming men's obsession with infidelity. 'These men, these men', she cries. Why such anxiety about a wife's adultery or suspicion thereof? It's such a 'small vice'. Would she do such a deed for all the world? She would.[6]

Chapter 2 brings this book into conversation with *Othello* and with a selection of key texts from the vast pantheon of Shakespeare scholarship. It is indeed vast. By the late twentieth century, it could already be said that the play's treatment of race had become so extensive as to make full citation impossible.[7] Twenty years later this is even more obviously the case. As the next generation of critical race scholars enriches *Othello*'s scholarly reception, they are ensuring that the play remains today what leading Shakespeare scholar Jean Howard calls 'a great test case for racial thinking'. As another reminds us, it is simultaneously a great test case for thinking about how its preeminent race questions are inextricably linked to what she calls, rather quaintly, 'women's issues'.[8] Feminist *Othello* scholarship defies any attempt at inclusivity or summation as surely as critical race and other post-humanist approaches to the Shakespeare text.[9] Accordingly, I will focus on those strands of critical Shakespeare scholarship that I regard as shedding the most light on the question animating this book: how to account for the extraordinary tenacity of the view that impassioned femicidal men deserve law's compassion. What does *Othello* and its critical reception bring to that table? What do they contribute to understanding the stubborn drive to distinguish cold-blooded murder from hot-blooded or heat of passion manslaughter, defended to this day as an understandable concession to 'human frailty'. As we shall see, a great deal.[10]

Jealousy, 'the rage of a man'

> *A jealousy so strong*
> *That judgment cannot cure*
>
> 2.1.298-300

At the dawn of the capitalist era – and much has been made of the late Elizabethan and early Jacobean period as a signal time, one intensely preoccupied with what has been retrospectively labelled 'nascent capitalism' – Shakespeare paid close attention to contemporary social anxieties. It is a critical commonplace that his work is packed with insights into the social changes wrought by the intensified economic exchanges of emergent capitalism in early modern England. Shakespearean scholars have explored the canon for their stunning critiques of the rapidly developing exchange-based market economy and consequent commercialisation and commodification of social relationships. How Marx, an avid Shakespeare buff, must have enjoyed reading *The Comedy of Errors*, the fetishised commodity form on staggeringly brilliant dramatic show 250 years before he theorised it in *Capital*. He certainly enjoyed the scathing indictment of capitalism's monetary ethos in *Timon of Athens*.[11] But what of Shakespeare's take on the affective dimensions of nascent capitalism, on the impact of the new economic imperatives on emotional life in early modern England? What has literary criticism made of that? One well-documented theme explored in the plays and the sonnets is that of capitalist angst about property and its potential loss.[12] Relatedly, Shakespeare's male characters suffered from sexual anxiety about losing 'their' women. Hence the recurring image of the cuckold, represented in Shakespeare as a man overwhelmed by paroxysms of anxiety when wrongly suspecting his wife of infidelity. So many obsessively anxious male characters worrying about wives testify to what one Shakespeare scholar calls his 'enduring, almost excessive interest' in competitive sexuality and the jealousy it provokes.[13]

Shakespeare's many returns to the question of 'extreme possessive jealousy in men' has received much scholarly attention, one of his modern editors suggesting he found it 'increasingly reprehensible' and deserving of 'severe punishment'.[14] Did he? Recall from Chapter 1 his notorious 'undecidability', his extraordinary opacity in the face of bids to pinpoint his views.[15] Did he really find men's jealous obsessions reprehensible? What might he have made of late modern criminal courts' indulgence of homicidal passion against wives no longer constituted in law as their husbands' property? We shall never know. What is arresting though is his linking of his male characters' emotional life to the rapidly changing political economy of early modern England, thereby opening up a fruitful inquiry into capitalism's impact on affect. As we shall see, Marxist readings of *Othello* as an inquiry into the operation of commodity fetishism throw an especially revealing light on passion's enmeshment with the emergent capitalist economy of Shakespeare's time.

Whatever Shakespeare's views were, this much is clear: in play after play – *The Merry Wives of Windsor, Much Ado about Nothing, Cymbeline, The Winter's Tale* – masculine fantasies of cuckoldry are parodied mercilessly. As for *Othello*, where else in English literature is there a more damning critique of a man's delusions about his wife's infidelity, delusions founded on a lost handkerchief that led hastily to murder? Male cultural fantasies about 'unfaithful' women are also hard at work in *The Merry Wives of Windsor* where Frank Ford, an absurdly jealous husband, whips himself up into a frenzy over his wife's suspected adultery and in *Cymbeline*, where discourses of conquering empire and vassal nation eventually take centre stage.[16] But how interesting that *Cymbeline*'s wager story takes up most of the first two acts. Here Posthumus tests the chastity of his fiancée, Innogen, and plots to have her murdered over allegations of infidelity trumped up by the Italian, Iachimo. Here too Posthumus delivers the notorious 'women's part in me' speech, described by Jean Howard as 'one of the most deeply misogynist speeches in the Shakespeare canon'. But he is also filled with remorse for ordering his wife's death, uttering words that form 'a remarkable exception to the more usual patriarchal assumption that sexual fidelity is the primary marker of a woman's value and virtue and that loss of chastity is an unforgivable crime'.[17] Hear him berate husbands like himself for murdering wives 'for wrying but a little':

> You married ones,
> If each of you should take this course, how many
> Must murder wives much better than themselves
> For wrying but a little![18]

Tellingly, he also hastens to divest himself of his Italian clothes, replacing them with the sort worn by an English peasant. His belated efforts to reclaim a properly temperate English identity notwithstanding, we should not forget that in Posthumus Shakespeare has yet another male character succumbing to a hellish 'infidelity'-inspired homicidal rage, but not one woman doing so in the entire Shakespeare canon. At least Innogen survived, unlike Desdemona, murdered by a husband just as deluded about his wife's fidelity, or Emilia, murdered by one who lost control over her.

Such an array of gullible male characters sucked in by their own or others' highly fanciful 'evidence' of waywardness in wives meander from *The Merry*

Wives all the way through to *Cymbeline*. At best they receive their creator's mocking scorn; at worst well-deserved punishment. In *The Winter's Tale*, one of his many returns to the abject figure of the obsessively jealous though delusional man, Shakespeare makes Leontes suffer profound guilt for having falsely accused his wife of infidelity and banishing her to prison. It is however, in *Othello* with its completed 'infidelity'-inspired wife-killing that he dramatises and, in the process, queries the culturally mandated belief that men who kill women they suspect of infidelity deserve compassion.

If you can believe Iago – and, concededly, there is good reason not to, he having lied his way through the play – *Othello* features two men succumbing to causeless jealousy. He and Othello both experience 'a similar torment, a monster of the imagination'.[19] Iago's unfounded belief that his wife, Emilia, is having an affair with 'the lusty Moor' derails him. It 'like a poisonous mineral gnaw at my inwards' such that

> nothing can or shall content my soul
> Till I am evened with him, wife for wife …
> Or, failing so, yet that I put the Moor
> At least into a jealousy so strong
> That judgment cannot cure.[20]

Famously, Iago warns Othello against succumbing to 'the green-eyed monster' which mocks the 'meat it feeds on'. Emilia takes up this refrain. Responding to Desdemona's perplexity at Othello's rage – 'I never gave him cause' – Emilia peremptorily dismisses the vapid 'cause'-based excuse that Othello would later make for killing his wife. 'Jealous souls', she says, 'are not ever jealous for the cause/But jealous for they're jealous/It is a monster/Begot upon itself, born on itself'. As for infidelity, she thought it but a 'small vice', nothing to get so puffed up about as men did.[21] Not that she is advocating adultery for women so much as making light of a relatively commonplace occurrence. In sharp contrast, Iago and Othello's fantasies about their wives' sexual infidelity are reinforced by 'paranoia about unrestrained female sexuality'. In such fantasies, women have 'little control over whether they will be cast as wives or whores' and they have to 'pay dearly'. Emilia questions why Othello must call Desdemona 'whore', but her voice is lost in 'the male drama of jealousy' and fear of cuckoldry, a fear that is 'a determining feature of male identity' in early modern English culture. Hence Othello's automatic (because learnt and thus thoroughly internalised) response: 'I will chop her into messes – cuckold me!'[22]

Many Shakespearean scholars have highlighted the sexed specificity of extreme jealousy in the canon. Some pursue this line of inquiry further, reading *Othello* as questioning the conventional view that a wife's adultery deserves death and her killer compassion.[23] In the play, men who kill wives they merely suspect of adultery – as many men who murder wives do – are ridiculed for their pettiness, for acting on 'Trifles light as air' which are 'to the jealous confirmations strong/As proofs of holy writ'. In the final scene, Othello seeks to excuse the murder of his wife as manslaughter by provocation committed by 'one not easily jealous, but being wrought/Perplexed in the extreme'. But most Shakespeare critics read Shakespeare as condemning his actions 'as both morally wrong and tyrannical', in short as murder.[24]

By contrast – and this point needs emphasising – law scholars are prone to sympathise with Othello. Placed on trial for murder in the late twentieth century by a North American law student, he was found guilty of that crime.[25] Far more frequently however, he is championed as the 'honourable murderer' he claims to be, and as such an automatic candidate for law's compassion. Noting that some critics would 'pardon Othello for having committed a crime of passion', one North American commentator explains the legal ramifications of Desdemona's death in the North American context:

> Most legal scholars, rightly I think, would have little difficulty convicting Othello under the Model Penal Code of the lesser offence of manslaughter committed under the influence of extreme mental or emotional disturbance for which there is reasonable explanation or excuse.

Shakespeare, he continues, leaves us 'torn between blaming Othello for premeditated murder and excusing the mental state that led to the crime'. He may '*logically*' be considered to be the innocent victim of Iago's machinations. While Lodovico, Venice's official representative, reminds Othello of his complicity in the attempted murder of Cassio, this is quickly dismissed. '*Naturally*, Lodovico cannot understand Othello's mental state as *we* do'. Shakespeare is 'ahead of his time in giving Othello's genuine mental stress quasi-legal and tragic substance'. Moreover, his outsider status as a Moor gives him 'possible mitigating excuse'.[26]

Let us leave aside, at least for now, the casual assumption that Othello's outsider status might give him mitigating excuse, presumably because it gives him permission to vent emotions deemed extreme by those with insider status. Here I want to focus on the antediluvian universalising 'we' of these pronouncements. Such a putative 'we' gives force to the view that everybody agrees Othello's crime is not murder. This 'we' is mirrored in the phallogocentric universalisms of the provocation defence as it has operated in the context of impassioned homicide cases. That defence, as we saw in Chapter 1, is said to be a concession to the 'human frailty' of those who kill in the face of grave provocation, indicatively infidelity. Never mind that it is overwhelmingly men who do so. Anyone might succumb. We all understand their mental stress. We all sympathise with them.

So entrenched is this view that it has even been expressed by a law academic who recognises that 'sexual provocation' claims for itself 'a constituency almost exclusively masculine'. He is critical of how opportunities for men to tell 'sympathetic stories' are enlarged when restraints on the provocation defence are abandoned. Noting that compassion for the man who kills his wife is founded on 'familiar Anglo-centric patterns of tragic narrative' with *Othello* drawing on 'salient points' of that story, he condemns the manner in which the wife-killer appropriates her life for his 'redemptive narrative'. The woman's death is transformed into his tragedy, reducing her murder to the 'moral ambiguity of manslaughter'. Yet this troubled legal commentator still believes that men who kill 'because they are unable or unwilling to distinguish between reality and the ideal have *some* claim to compassion'. He does not find this to be a 'particularly compelling claim' and concedes that given the 'disparity between the sexes in the matter of who kills whom, women may be more likely than men to conclude that this claim is an anachronism'.[27]

Indeed, we might. Certainly, feminist Shakespeare scholars do. Carol Neely, for example, takes it as read that Othello is guilty of murder. Approaching *Othello* in her self-fashioned 'Emilia critic' role – named after Emilia who called Othello a murderer, defying her husband's demand that she remain silent – Neely portrays it as 'a terrifying completion of the comedies'. There men's misogyny, foolishness and anxiety are mocked, transformed and dispelled – 'laughed to scorn' as in *As You Like It.* And through their 'wit', the women in the comedies transform the men 'from foolish lovers into ... sensible husbands, and at the end submit to their control'. By contrast, the men in *Othello* all have a 'possessive view of women', are 'jealous in honour, sudden and quick in quarrel'.[28] Where cuckoldry and sexuality find acceptance in the comedies – 'as horns are odious, they are necessary' – this is 'impossible' in Othello, where men's fragile self-identities are so conspicuously on display. Witness Cassio, utterly frantic on losing his post:

> Reputation, reputation, reputation! O, I have lost my reputation. I have lost the immortal part of myself, and what remains is bestial. My reputation, Iago, my reputation![29]

Othello is so dependent on the 'rich opinion' of others that 'feathered Cupid' potentially threatens his 'reputation'. Later he seems to find the fantasy that he has been cuckolded more difficult to bear than the loss of Desdemona. It has invalidated his military glories such that only her murder and his own suicide restore his pride in his 'occupation'.[30] Whether Othello was motivated by jealousy or, more likely, shame at the loss of his reputation that cuckoldry entails, he is guilty of murder and nothing else. At least he is in the view of the Emilia critic.

Shame, anxiety and 'the male order of things'

> *It is the cause, it is the cause, my soul!*
> *Let me not name it to you, you chaste stars:*
> *It is the cause. Yet I'll not shed her blood*

Nor scar that whiter skin of hers than snow
And smooth as monumental alabaster:
Yet she must die, else she'll betray more men.

5.2.1–6

Tis pitiful; but yet Iago knows
That she with Cassio hath the act of shame
A thousand times committed.

5.2.209–210

Such is the male characters' obsession with reputation that it has prompted Ewan Fernie to argue that *Othello* is actually a play about shame rather than jealousy. This argument has some force. After all, Othello's feeling that he has lost sexual possession of his wife is indeed 'intensely focused on himself, on the consequences for him'. Noticeably indifferent to Cassio, the supposed seducer, Othello's most overwhelming feeling is that 'he has himself been degraded and defiled'. Indeed, there is a whole 'sequence of male shames', starting with Iago who feels shamed and slighted and whose goal of shaming the man he believes shamed him drives the plot forward to its disastrous conclusion. Brabantio is so ashamed that his daughter has eloped and married a Moor that he dies. Roderigo is shamed by being passed over by Desdemona for Othello and rejected by Brabantio as unsuitable. There's also Cassio's dramatic shaming. Of course, women are shamed too – Desdemona by Iago's false allegations, Bianca by being publicly denounced as a 'courtesan'. But their shame 'pales to insignificance' next to that of the men.[31]

Moreover, men's shame is bound up with obsession about ownership, sexual ownership. Take Iago's fantasy that Othello has cuckolded him: 'I hate the Moor/And it is thought abroad that 'twixt my sheets/He's done my office'.[32] This imagined loss of sexual ownership produces a mixture of jealousy and shame in Iago:

> he feels Othello has violated him professionally and this has spawned the feeling that he has also violated his wife. Thus we have not jealousy *ex nihilo*, but shame and jealousy bred from shame. Iago almost chooses to believe he has been cuckolded ... because he is overwhelmed with shame already.[33]

While Iago's deep-felt professional shame is transposed into sexual shame, Othello's supposed sexual shame produces professional inadequacy, self-doubt and ultimately self-splitting, 'the self-splitting of shame' when he refers to himself in the third person – 'That's he that *was* Othello?'[34] Interestingly, while Fernie touches on the key theme of sexual ownership and its loss that is so central to *Othello* and to the provocation by infidelity case law, the shame-rather-than-jealousy thesis leads him straight into the blame-the-victim camp. Desdemona has provoked her own murder with 'the hapless fashion in which she consistently promotes suspicions of adultery' and her reminders that 'she is a desiring as well as desirable woman'. What 'an inviting eye' she has, Fernie seeming to agree with Iago that it 'sounds a parley to provocation'.[35] By contrast,

> Othello is morally degraded – we must never forget that he has killed his wife – but he is also a spiritual hero, one who shows up the cosseted and frightened self-deception of those who thrust off and misplace shame.[36]

Desdemona improperly 'desiring' and Othello a 'spiritual hero'? We must never forget that he killed her? Forgetting femicide's victims is precisely what so many non-feminist commentators do. In provocation by infidelity cases, the court's focus is almost entirely on the much put-upon defendant; the victim is of interest only to the extent that she contributed to her own death.

This critic is not alone in sympathising with this fictional wife-killer. Others have been 'moved to pay homage to Othello's courage and dignity', seeing his story as tragic rather than 'an unpleasantly sordid tale of battery and murder'. Such is the 'persuasive power of the heroic ideal'. None of the male characters on stage at the end question the honour code to which Othello appeals in justification of his actions. None challenge a code that dictates 'vengeance for an act of adultery'.[37] And few if any of Othello's late modern legal commentators do either. Nor have they noticed that Othello's is no Aristotelian judgment, the kind that, as we saw in Chapter 1, befits an honourable man acting in anger but always in moderation. Othello can protest as much as he likes that he is 'an honourable murderer' and that all his actions were done in honour. But as he himself concedes, passion had his best judgment 'collied' or blackened as might be expected of a racialised other. His was an ungovernable passion stemming from 'a jealousy so strong' – or a debilitating felt sense of shame – that judgment could not cure.

Meanwhile, Neely, the Emilia critic, watches Emilia move from 'tolerating men's fancies to exploding them', even coming to see them as cannibalistic: 'They are all but stomachs, and we all but food/They eat us hungerly, and when they are full/They belch us'. From this perspective, if the play's ending is tragic, it is the women's tragedy, not Othello's. Obsessively self-justifying to the end, seeing himself as ill-fated, even as a victim, Othello does not cut a tragic figure. Whether his uncontrolled emotions are specified as jealousy or shame, he is nothing but a pathetic wife-killer.[38] Moreover, he is one, as Mark Breitenberg puts it, who has succumbed to a 'circularity of patriarchal logic' in which women enact how they have already been constructed insidiously in the wife-killer's mind. *Othello* stages unjustified male rage in order to 'foreground male jealousy as a discursive energy that does not require a referent'. No referent required – just note the preponderance of false accusations. Masculine anxiety towards women's sexuality is 'both prior to and considerably in excess of any "referent" such that it seems to be the very condition of romantic love rather than an unfortunate effect'.[39]

One of the strongest cases against Othello and his emotional indulgences is made in Edward Snow's stunning psychoanalytic analysis of 'the male order of things' in the play. Avoiding the trap of succumbing to the pervasive felt need to excuse extreme emotions in men, he sets about unpacking Othello's sexual anxieties.[40] Starting with his famous 'it is the cause speech', Snow sees this 'incantation' of an obscure unspecified cause as an 'intense, distracting assertion'. More broadly, the repression of male anxious sexual fantasies and fears about women's threatening sexual demands pervades 'the entire world' of the play. The play's very first line – 'Tush, never tell me' – suggests that while Othello ostensibly seeks the truth, a 'texture of disavowal' determines the limits of what he wants to be visible. Just such a texture of disavowal has enveloped the discursive constitution of wife-killers and their emotions ever since, making Snow's brilliant critique of Othello's free-floating euphemisms that obscure what is really at stake all the more insightful. As he observes, even the 'apparent moment of insight and repentance' when Othello finally grasps that he 'threw a pearl away' by killing his wife, fails to provide critical clarity. Instead, it invites the audience to 'become complicit in the definition of Desdemona as a valuable object, a private possession that was his either to keep or dispose of'. Furthermore, Emilia's defence of Desdemona's chastity is also problematic in that it 'only makes it more difficult to bring into focus the pernicious effects of chastity itself, as a doctrine men impose upon women'. What is needed, or so it is argued here, is a critique of 'the pathological male obsessions beneath' Othello's supposed 'just grounds' for killing her and of his and the play's 'resistance to demystification'.[41]

But while sexual repression is pervasive in the play, it is 'uncompromisingly lucid' in its treatment of jealousy 'not as a given but an object of inquiry'. That inquiry leads Shakespeare to a startling finding which has considerable resonance for my enquiry into the tenacity of the view that a wife-killer's extreme emotions warrant compassionate consideration. When Othello refers to his wife's 'filthy deeds', he is not so much expressing rage over her supposed infidelity as 'post-coital male disgust with the "filthy deed" of sexuality itself'.[42] Furthermore,

> This pathological male animus toward sexuality is a 'cause' Shakespeare pursues relentlessly through the play, into the roots not only of Othello's jealousy but the social institutions with which men keep women and the threat they pose at arm's length. Time and again in *Othello* language condemning adultery both masks and draws authority from an underlying guilt and disgust about sexuality itself.[43]

So, crucially, it is the sexual act *per se* rather than adultery that is the 'act of shame' Desdemona has 'a thousand times committed with Cassio'. She has 'sinned' as a wife rather than an adulteress and it is 'more as a husband than a cuckold' that Othello becomes obsessed with her 'ritual execution'. Here Snow calls attention to the 'fantasy of the wedding night' which is 'submerged in the actual murder' where it has been 'refined to become a ritual of disavowal and undoing'. Othello's cry – 'Yet I'll not shed her blood' – is 'a resolve not to repeat his earlier mistake'. Othello attempts to recover what he lost when he 'deflowered' his wife, all the while denying what he 'thereby discovered and released in her and in himself as well'. He wants to annihilate 'something that has been sexually engendered in him' and, indeed, in all men – 'she must die, else she'll betray more men'.[44]

Snow has less to say about Othello's otherness, which he references as his 'Moorishness'. But what he does say is revelatory. Othello's Moorishness

> merely forces him to live out with psychotic intensity the metaphors of self-contempt that every civilised white man can be brought to experience in his sexual relations with a woman.

By way of explanation, he adds that:

> Augustine remarks that we are all Ethiopians, black in our natural sinfulness but allowed to become white in the knowledge of the lord ... The possibility of Desdemona's infidelity causes him to see himself (as if for the first time) as black and to regard that blackness as a measure of sexual corruption as well as social disgrace.[45]

More needs to be said about the loaded pairing of blackness and whiteness in *Othello*. For now, it is important to register Snow's insight that a key component of Othello's jealousy is a generalised 'patriarchal conscience', one shared by 'every civilised white man'. That conscience tells him his wife's alleged affair with Cassio is 'only a repetition of what she first did with him', and that 'he himself has released in her the boundless appetite she now satisfies with Cassio'. Such fantasies, Snow contends, have little to do with Desdemona's 'mundane reality as a specific woman' and everything to do with the 'underlying male fear' of 'thralldom to the demands of an insatiable sexual appetite in women'. Hence the play's tragedy is her inability to escape 'the restraints and Oedipal prohibitions that domesticate woman to the conventional male order of things'. Othello is caught up in 'the disavowals and repressions of the civilised world of Venice'. What erupts in his jealousy is not 'primitive, barbaric man but the voice of the father', the outraged voice of 'the patriarchal social order'. Just like Hamlet – a white character who vies with Othello for pre-eminence in the canon – Othello becomes possessed by 'the father's perspective'. Just like Desdemona's father, Brabantio, Othello determines to silence her in order to 'undo the breach' in patriarchal order that 'her sexuality has created'. And he does so safe in the belief that he is 'acting in the name of men, as minister of their justice and their faith'.[46]

What an intriguing reading it is. But just when you might think scholarly glosses on Othello's 'cause' could not get any richer, there are eminent Shakespeare scholar Patricia Parker's to consider. Complex though it is, it pays to follow her close linguistic analysis of the play's final scene because it deepens our understanding of the perverse logic that informs the still widespread belief that killing a wayward wife is excusable. Parker begins by noting how the 'judicial resonance' of Othello's repeated 'cause' – 'it is the cause, it is the cause' – summons 'the judicial language' that is so pervasive in the play. Here it is invoked to 'authorise a husband as final judge and executioner of a too open, too "liberal" wife' who must die else she'll betray more men. The 'satisfying of a justice' is clearly evident in Othello's response to Iago's suggestion that he strangle Desdemona in her bed, 'the very bed she has contaminated' – 'good, good, the justice of it pleases'. There is more to Parker's reading. The cause that Othello cannot name to the 'chaste stars' hides 'a language that has lurking within it the threateningly open "case" of an unchaste woman, through a complex interlingual pun on *cause*, *case*, *chose* and *thing*'. This thing is 'the obscene, unnameable "case" of a woman whose opening provides the justifying "cause" of her death'. It follows that killing a wife is the 'foregone conclusion' of 'a predetermined justice'.[47]

Teasing out this complex play on words, Parker notes Shakespeare's linking of property with propriety; that is, between men's proprietary rights over women's and their need for women to act with propriety. The logic at work in impassioned femicides is 'the proprietary logic by which assault on a woman is "caused" by the beauty that in this perverse reasoning occasions it'.[48] Thus does Parker arrive at the same conclusion reached by feminist legal scholars researching impassioned femicide cases – accordingly to the perverse logic of Othello's sympathisers, Desdemona, like so many other slaughtered wives, brought it on herself. Accordingly, the justice of it pleases because, in the final analysis, she was 'the cause'. Like thousands of non-fictional women who followed in her wake, this Shakespearean wife has provoked her own demise, her apparently insatiable sexuality derailing yet another sexually insecure and repressed man, one not immediately recognisable to early modern England's men of honour. Or was he?

Anxious cuckolds, fetishised women

O curse of marriage
That we call these delicate creatures ours
And not their appetites!

3.3.272-274

I will chop her into messes! Cuckold me!

4.1.197

Defying her husband's order to 'get you home', Emilia finally speaks out against Iago. Her political awakening began however, when she saw Othello hit Desdemona. For feminist scholars, it is such 'a familiar story, a story of domestic abuse' in which 'male power, male appetite, possessed, authored and mastered women's lives by mastering the narratives that wrote their history'. So much of the play has been about male possession – 'male possession reconfigured as demonic possession, pursued to an appalling performative conclusion that monstrously inverts them'.[49] Property, ownership, loss – these are key themes in *Othello* as numerous Shakespeare scholars have noted, none more succinctly than Kenneth Burke. Othello's stake in Desdemona, he suggested in a much-cited passage, is essentially about ownership:

> a tragic trinity of ownership in the profoundest sense of ownership, the property in human affections, as fetishistically localised in the object of possession, while the possessor is himself possessed by his very engrossment.[50]

In this reading, the jealousy plot instantiates the capitalist sense of ownership. Othello attempts an act of enclosure and declaration of private property but is overwhelmed by a sense of impending and unbearable loss. Cuckoldry 'triply threatens' him: 'with the loss of Desdemona's love; with the supremacy of Cassio, his lieutenant over him; and with the loss of his reputation and the scorn of other men'.[51] This gets to the heart of the matter: male anxiety in *Othello* is inextricably bound up with the burden of ownership and its ever-threatening obverse – fear of loss in the deepest sense, the loss of property in human (read: women's) affection.

A more detailed examination of the propertied dimensions of the anguish experienced by Shakespeare's male characters living in fear of cuckoldry usefully begins with Douglas Bruster's *Drama and the Market Place in the Age of Shakespeare*. Noting the massive increase in the sale and purchase of commodities and 'the market-orientated ascription of unreal and inordinate value to material objects, something we have come to call the 'fetishisation of commodities', he suggests that 'The Age of Shakespeare' could well be characterised as 'the Age of Commodity Fetishism'. Jacobean drama and Shakespeare in particular, he argues, rendered operative and even concretised concepts such as 'fetishism' and 'reification' to an extent 'as unprecedented as it was alarming'. Moreover, with the commodification of the personal, women were more often portrayed as commodities, with marriage frequently seen as a marketplace transaction, a development that 'along with the commodification of chastity worked to their detriment'. Property received 'new emphasis conceptually'. The self's relation to property came to assume 'a cardinal role in the theatrical construction of an early-modern, bourgeois subjectivity' as a sense of inner worth once based on tradition and hierarchy starts to give way to a sense of self in terms of market value.[52]And what takes centre stage in Jacobean drama, turning up on the slightest pretext, is the medieval myth of cuckoldry.

Bruster explains that the myth was based on a delineation of exchange in which women were used 'in a system of male-to-male exchange as the literalised, objectified version' of 'symbolic capital', described as 'a disguised form of physical "economic" capital'.[53] Within this system, the cuckoldry myth has a 'structural logic' that works as a metaphor of 'gendered labour and economic relations' that can be traced back to Greek anthology where it made its 'first explicit appearance as a trope for labour'. This labour is simultaneously gendered and sexualised. Husbandry, for example, is labour performed by the husband, the one who tills and cultivates the soil, Shakespeare using the term to emphasise its link to property, labour and sexuality. *Othello* draws on the pun of having a livelihood and occupying one's wife. 'Farewell! Othello's occupation's gone', he moans, referring to his lost possession of his wife but also echoing Iago's vicious double entendre: it's 'fit that Cassio have his place/For sure he fills it up with great ability'.[54]

Bruster has more. Intrigued by why merchants are so often cuckolds and cuckolds so often merchants in Jacobean plays, he suggests that to be a merchant is 'to risk loss, to render commodity up to chance. Consequently, the business of commerce produces inescapable anxiety'. That is why merchants gained, in literary presentations, a special reputation for anxiety, an anxiety 'latent within the concept of property itself'. But when it comes to fear of cuckoldry, any male character can experience acute anxiety. In *Othello*, for example, the commodification of the cuckold scenario reveals male subjectivity to be absolutely dependent on 'an invidious gender tension ... a project of identity construction based in the market and directed toward objectifying the female'. And naturally, this market-driven identity construction is 'a property-centred social transformation'.[55] *Othello* brings all these key themes together – possession of commodities in a rapidly developing and anxiety-producing anonymous exchange economy; the misplacing or loss of property; acute anxiety about cuckoldry understood as a most unwanted male-to-male commodity exchange and, inextricably related to all that, loss of identity suffered by property-obsessed male characters busy fetishising their objects of desire.

No fetishised object has attracted more critical attention than Desdemona's handkerchief, a standout being Paul Yachnin's Marxist reading of *Othello* as showcasing the operation of commodity fetishism in early modern capitalism.[56] Placing Othello's fetishising of the handkerchief – that infamous 'ocular proof' of Desdemona's adultery in the context of early modern England's trade in textiles, Yachnin illuminates the slippage from love to loathing that is narrated in scenarios of dispossessed love that subsequently explodes in impassioned femicides. While all the characters except Othello see the handkerchief as marketable goods, he views it as a wondrous object, an object of great emotional intensity signifying love, or more exactly, anxiety about lost love. To understand the particular mystery of Desdemona's handkerchief from Othello's perspective, it is necessary to recognise that its properties are 'continuous with the properties of love', or more exactly, possessive love:

> Were Desdemona an object like the handkerchief, Othello could possess her, but so could anyone else, and in any case she would then be a 'common thing' like the handkerchief, certainly not the inimitable treasure for which Othello happily sacrifices his 'unhoused free condition'.[57]

On the other hand, if she is not an object, then she is a self-possessed subject, 'free to give herself away to another'. But if she is her own private property, then 'her defining attribute – her honour – becomes as detachable as her handkerchief'. As Iago says, the handkerchief, 'being hers/She may, I think, bestow't on any man', leaving Othello to despair: 'She is protectress of her honour too/May she give that?'[58]

What a dilemma for Othello for whom it becomes impossible to 'unburden heterosexual love of the contradictions involved in the patriarchal ownership of women, who are also required to be owners of themselves'. Love turns to loathing, here captured in a material object, the famous handkerchief, the loss of which is calamitous. It is proof of Desdemona's infidelity – 'if she lost it/Or made a gift of it, my father's eye should hold her loathed'. It becomes 'ocular proof' against her, something that 'the desirable thingness of the handkerchief has already inscribed as inevitable in heterosexual relations'. Cuckoldry for Othello and, by extension, all men is thus 'destiny unshunnable, like death'.[59] This brings Yachnin to a stunning conclusion:

> It is the fate of every man to invest his all in the vexed figure of Woman, she who is unique because she is a rare object and 'common' because she is a subject ... the vexing constitution of Othello's selfhood on the basis of heterosexual mutuality is no different from anyone else's – it is only that his terminology is strangely revealing.[60]

Strangely revealing indeed, not least of the process Yachnin calls 'the production of woman-as-fetish' and which I have called elsewhere 'dis-affectionate fetishism' in which subjects are transformed into objects that come to embody lost love.[61] Long after women obtained the status of legal persons and were no longer, at least at law, deemed to be mere objects, property items, men have continued to explode in homicidal rage against women as love turns to loathing. The obsessive possessiveness that had its origins in early modern Englishmen's fetishising of their objects of desire displayed in *Othello* has had a tenacious and pernicious legacy.

Racialising property in women

> *Zounds, sir, you're robbed, for shame put on you gown!*
> *Your heart is burst, you have lost half your soul,*

Even now, now, very now, an old black ram
Is tupping your white ewe!

1.1.84-87

Shakespeare studies locating the origins of men's sense of entitlement over 'their' women in early modern England's rapidly commodifying economy have much explanatory power when it comes to understanding their anxiety about the loss of ownership that adultery entails. There is however, a complicating factor as early modern scholar Natasha Korda reveals in another astute reading of the handkerchief. While early capitalism produced women as commodified objects of exchange and desire, it also provided opportunities for women to own property themselves. Accordingly, they could then be the subjects, as well as objects, of property. Not simply 'trafficked' as passive objects of exchange between men, they bought and sold property, held trusts and became creditors. This too produced tensions, 'numerous cases' in Shakespeare's time involving husbands resorting to violence 'if their wives refused to hand over money set aside for their own use'. Wives' property was then 'the source of considerable strife within marriage and of ideological conflict in the culture at large'.[62]

And Korda reveals another complicating factor related to Desdemona's handkerchief. Discourses about the under- and over-evaluation of material objects and possessions in early modern England were highly racialised, dominant groups projecting attachments to material objects and anxiety over their loss to racialised 'others'. Africans in particular were stigmatised for their excessive attachment to 'trifles' or what were termed 'for the first time in the early modern period as *fetissos* or fetishes', a term used frequently in travel narratives. These narratives, Korda argues, influenced *Othello*'s depiction of Othello's jealousy which expressed itself in his overvaluation or fetishising of the handkerchief and undervaluation of his precious 'pearl'. The early modern conception of jealousy, so Korda's intricate argument goes, associated it with greed and covetousness arising from the institution of private property with its attendant anxieties about dispossession. Best then to project this anxiety onto subjects 'excluded from the prerogatives of possession' such as Africans. Depicting them as particularly susceptible to jealousy deflected attention away from the jealous dispositions of covetous early modern English capitalists living in fear of becoming, or being seen to become, cuckolds. Not that projection allayed their anxieties. Worryingly for 'civilised' European householders, projecting onto 'barbarian cultures' a perceived inability to determine value and to overvalue 'trifles' recalled their own excessive attachment to household objects. This too was a source of anxiety. Thus, *Othello*'s handkerchief 'brilliantly weaves together' the 'civility of the luxury commodity or status-object and the alienating strangeness of the African fetish'.[63]

We need not read further into Korda's riveting account of the way Shakespeare dramatises the complex propertied underpinnings of possessive jealousy – how he twins Othello's overvaluation of that notorious fetish, the handkerchief, with his under-valuating of his wife for having lost it.[64] It is enough to register that the contradictory subject-object constitution of the 'vexed figure of Woman' that Paul Yachnin contends derailed Othello's selfhood is even more profoundly contradictory than he thought. More broadly, all these readings go some way to illuminating two of this book's key interlinking themes. Most notably, they highlight crucial links between the fetishising of commodities central to the capitalistic sense of ownership and the continuing production of woman as possessed object of desire even in late modernity when women are *de jure* fully subjects. Admittedly, a chasm separates Othello's eloquent lament: 'O curse of marriage that we call these delicate creatures ours, and not their appetites' from the wife-killer's reductive, tirelessly repeated cliché, 'If I can't have you, no one can have you'. What is clear nonetheless, is that the fetishistic reduction of a wife to an object can be traced back to the early modern period, directly linking the fictional Othello to late modern wife-killers.

While this might seem to be more than enough property-focused food for thought, there is still more to consider. It is the early modern law against fraudulent conveyancing mimicked in lines in Othello relating to the conveyance or seducing of women for their money. It has been suggested that this overlap partly explains why the language of commercial credit is often deployed in 'the context of desire', a situation that arose because daughters were regarded as property. A daughter, 'insofar as she owed obedience to her father, could be compared to a debtor, and her elopement fraud against him'. Thus, Brabantio, Desdemona's father, accuses Othello who has eloped with his daughter of fraudulent conveyance – 'O thou foul thief, where has thou stowed my daughter?' In this reading, fraudulent conveyance becomes a metaphor:

> not just for the abduction of young ladies, but also for obscuring the issue of the commodification of women and the related issue of race: the status of a child fathered by a Moor on a Venetian lady he has abducted.[65]

In short, being robbed by an 'old black ram' who eloped with his very white Venetian daughter only served to exacerbate Brabantio's anguish at his loss of his proprietary interest in her.

Black passions, white anxieties, humoural complexities

> *Now, by heaven,*
> *My blood begins my safer guides to rule*
> *And passion, having my best judgment collied,*
> *Assays to lead the way*
>
> 2.3.200-203

A great deal has been said about Shakespeare's mapping of extreme passions onto black or otherwise 'othered bodies'. Look at those ridiculously jealous Italian characters parading their way through the canon – Claudio in *Much Ado about Nothing*, Leontes in *The Winter's Tale*, Iago in *Othello*. But whichever foreigners English writers picked to project their own anxieties onto, early moderns were in no doubt that sexual jealousy was a furious passion that was most prominent in men.[66] How prescient that view has turned out to be. Here however, I want to focus on the early modern English insistence that it was foreign men who fell into extreme passions when faced with the fear of losing 'their' women.

What, exactly, were the passions that overrode Othello's judgment? The early modern understanding of the passions was informed by classical humoural theory that held that 'the passions' – rage, anger, fear, grief, envy – disrupted rational thinking. Moreover, they were regionally inflected. The ideal body, so this theory goes, was one that achieved 'temperance or humoural balance'. Passions threatened that balance.[67] Where were these bodies most likely to be found? The problem facing early modern English writers was that classical humoural theory located these ideal balanced bodies in temperate and warmer climates in the south, not in the north where they resided. So, they set about positioning themselves as the more evenly tempered and foreigners as more prone to excessive jealousy. To take us through this complex and contradictory process, I turn to Mary Floyd-Wilson's account of the origins of the propensity to racialise foreign men as more impassioned and more irrationally anxious and murderous than temperate Englishmen.

It is her argument that while humoural theories helped shape the derisory othering practice that located extreme passions in foreign men, they did so in more complex ways than has been previously realised. *Othello*, she argues, reveals a 'much more vexed relationship to regional identity' than traditional humoural theory allowed. Her starting point is Desdemona's arresting defence of Othello against the charge that he was a jealous man:

> my noble Moor
> Is true of mind and made of no such baseness
> As jealous creatures are ...
> ...I think the sun where he was born
> Drew all such humours from him.[68]

The idea that the heat of the African sun would dry and cool the body's humours was a commonplace in classical, medieval and early modern humoural theory about somatic differences between regions and culturally and geographically acquired traits. Desdemona was appealing, Floyd-Wilson argues, to the 'conventional ethnology' that if Othello lacks humours, he must not be jealous and that his lack of humours is what distinguishes him from people of cooler climates. However, this theory created a problem for the English because, as she explains, 'to be white and British in the early modern period was not a badge of superiority'. Instead, they were cast on the margins as 'uncivil, slow-witted and more bodily determined than those people living in more temperate zones'. Britain's northern location had excluded it from the superiority of temperance and moderation, positioning them as 'other' to the normative middle attributed to the Mediterranean's temperate climate. But being estranged from this middle was not a place that self-respecting English men of honour wanted to be. So, they set about reinterpreting their classically derived natural philosophy to make it more favourable to them and in the process developing the idea of 'a distinctly English temperament'.[69]

In this fascinating reading, *Othello* testifies to the emergence of a revisionist racial discourse that clashed with still dominant classical and medieval 'geohumouralism'. Floyd-Wilson tracks this interpretive move through what she calls *Othello*'s 'racialised twist'. Arguing against the play's legacy which has identified Moors with jealousy and jealousy as a barbaric passion, she maintains that while Othello's passionate fury affirms an emergent racist stereotype, it had its origins in England's 'prior obsession with an Italianate and urban form of dramatic jealousy'. This type of jealousy was understood 'primarily as a state of paranoid suspicion born out of a corrupt inwardness' that the English typically associated with Italians. It was the Italians, not African or Moors, whose complexions had 'degenerated most severely' and who were afflicted by 'pathological inwardness'. Witness Iago, the 'hyper-civilised Italian' with his 'hyper-civilised state of suspicion', 'jealous for they're jealous' as his wife Emilia put it.[70]

But in 1604 when *Othello* was first performed, discourses about the passions were in flux. Things had got particularly complicated with the publication in London in 1600 of Leo Africanus' *The History and Description of Africa*, widely regarded as a key source for *Othello*. This history contradicted the classical humoural view of Africans and Moors as having a cool, dry and melancholy temperament. *His* Africans were passionate, given to extreme jealousy. In certain African groups, he reported, the men 'beare a most savage minde, being so extremely possessed with jalousie, that whomsoever they finde but talking with their wives they presently go about to murther them'.[71] Taking his lead, English writers started distinguishing impassioned Southerners, including African and Italian men, from more easily provoked but more easily pacified northerners, indicatively Englishmen, thereby overturning humoural theory's longstanding attribution of dispassion and constancy to blackness and Italian self-control and temperance to their temperate climate. *Othello* dramatises this metamorphosis but, crucially, it does so while sustaining 'a conflict between an emerging racial stereotype of a volatile, jealous African and the older 'geohumoralism' that, as Desdemona noted, believed the southern sun drew all jealous humours from him.[72] The play's 'racialised twist' thus registers an important shift in the early modern understanding of regionally inflected jealousy. Transforming jealousy into 'an exotically tragic passion' now projected onto black or Moorish Africans, reinforced the emerging view that the northerners, indicatively Englishmen, experience heated passions easily. But they feel them only fleetingly before regaining their equanimity, thereby contributing to the establishment of a 'more virtuous model of English feeling'.[73]

There is certainly strong evidence to support the view that at the time *Othello* was written, early modern English writers were busy forging a theory of jealousy they could live with and that the play stood at the crossroads of these developments. Consider, for example, *The Blazon of Jealousie*, Robert Tofte's translation and annotation of Benedetto Varchi's 1545 *Lettura ... della gelosia*. Published in London in 1615, Tofte uses Varchi to create what Natasha Korda calls 'a specifically English version' of contemporary continental theories of jealousy, one which placed them in the moderate middle. As she explains, jealousy arises for Varchi from four possible causes: Pleasure, Passion, Property and Honour, and the first three are clearly 'shaped by the paradigm of private ownership'.[74] For example, pleasure, the first cause of jealousy, is a desire for exclusive possession while the second cause, passion, 'at once incites a desire for and precludes exclusive ownership'. As he explains, 'we covet to enjoy or possesse that which we most love' while simultaneously 'wonderfully fearing lest we should loose possession thereof'. And which possession springs first to mind? It is 'our Mistresse' whom we fear might become 'a secret sweet Friend unto another man'. When he gets to the third cause of jealousy, Property, Varchi becomes more explicit about the relationship between passion and property and, once again, it is men's property rights in women that are exemplary:

> Thirdly, Jealouise springeth from the Propertie or Right that wee have, when we (enjoying our Lady or Mistresse) would have her soly and wholy unto ourselves; without being able ... to suffer or endure, that another man should have any part or interest in her.

Robert Tofte agrees. Warning against succumbing to extreme passions, he castigates those men 'so obsessed with this as their own that they cast off wives and mistresses for a mere suspicion'. The 'poor women being in no fault at all' are prey to men's 'fantastique and jealous Conceite and Humours'.[75]

Which men were these? We find Tofte's answer in his comments on Honour, Varchi's fourth cause of jealousy. He agrees that Honour is the 'Reputation and Credit' of a man and that it is rated so highly that he would rather 'lose all his wealth, yea, and his dearest life too' than have it eclipsed. But what did he make of Varchi's view that a man's honour is determined by 'the fashion and manner of his Country' and that 'they say' that it was 'the Southern Nations and such as dwell in hot Regions' who are very jealous, they holding it

> a great disparagement and scandal to have their Wives or their Mistresses tainted with the foule blot of Unchastitie: which thing those that are of

> contrary Regions and such as live under the North Pole take not so deep at the heart.

Apparently in agreement, Tofte notes that it was once the Persians who deserved being singled out for jealousy. They were so jealous of their wives that they 'never allowed them to go abroad but in Wagons close shut'. But 'at this day the Italian is counted the man that is most subject to this vice, the shallow complexioned fellow with a black beard'.[76] He is the fellow who is the most prone to be suspicious about 'Women's matters'. Implicitly, it is Englishmen living in the northern sphere, who do not obsess so much over the foul blot of 'Unchastitie'. Their sense of entitlement to their possessions, wives included, was legitimate provided it did not become extreme.[77] And here we get to the heart of the matter. Jealousy *per se* is not problematic, only its 'Excesse'. As Varchi explains,

> if any shall be Jealous with discretion (and not without great and important cause), observing a true and temperate decorum in the Time, the place, the person, and only the cause … especially if it shall concern his own reputation and credit, or the good name of his Mistress, or Wife, he is not discommended at all.

Again, Tofte could not agree more. Too many jealous men had acted 'over-rashly' resulting in their 'utter overthrow', losing sight of 'the golden Meane' bequeathed by 'that Prince of Philosophers', Aristotle.[78]

We are returned to the notion of acting within the Aristotelian mean as befits the man of honour, say one confronted with the highest provocation a man could face, his wife's infidelity. This moderate man is not to be found in *Othello*. But the sallowed complexioned Italian is, telling all and sundry that he suspects his wife has been unfaithful with Othello. Making an appearance too is the newly minted racial stereotype, the excessively jealous man from a hot southern land, the man who could now to be expected to act 'over-rashly'. Here is Leo Africanus' African man with his 'most savage mind', 'so extremely possessed' with jealousy that it sets him on a path to 'murther'. What a contrast to the moderately jealous Englishman who is jealous with discretion if he becomes suspicious about his wife. As for Tofte's poor innocent woman prey to a man's fantastic and jealous conceit, she too is here. She is of course Desdemona, killed for 'mere suspicion'. Whether she was completely 'innocent' though, is a moot point. By preferring black to white, picking a 'sooty' Moor over the 'wealthy curlèd darlings of our nation', behaving provocatively, recklessly bantering in public with her fellow-Italians, she brought it on herself.[79]

By 1621 when Robert Burton published his *Anatomy of Melancholy*, it was understood that while women's jealousy was 'sufficiently curbed', 'the rage of men' who succumbed to jealousy was 'more eminent' and 'frequently put in practice'. By now too, the finger could firmly be pointed at 'those jealous husbands' who 'tyrannise over their poor wives in Greece, Spain, Italy, Turkey, Africa, Asia and generally over all those hot countries'. These 'southern men' were 'more hot, lascivious and jealous' than those living in northern countries where 'young men and maids familiarly dance together', something Italians could not abide. They would not suffer their women to be 'near men'. The English, by contrast, permitted their wives and daughters to go to the taverns with friends and suspected 'nothing' such that England was 'a paradise for women, and hell for horses: Italy a paradise for horses, hell for women'.[80]

As it turned out, England was no paradise for women then or since if rates of intimate partner femicide are any guide. But early modern English writers had worked hard to perform the 'racialised twist'. Revising the received humoural ideas about regionally inflected passions they demonised Africans and Latins as murderous outsiders, while positioning themselves as men of moderation acting within the mean. Shakespeare showcases it all. By inviting his audience to hear *Othello* in light of their traditional biases against Italians and newly created ones against Moors, he produced 'an endless relay of "othering" centring on the improbable desires of an Italian bride who proudly prefers black to white'.[81] Just such an endless relay of racial othering, albeit one populated with different nationalities depending on the biases of the time, has been a feature of the English version of 'honour killing' committed by femicidal Englishmen to this day. But what to do with a white Englishman, hot blood coursing through his veins, who fails to act within the mean and commits a 'crime of passion'? That was a problem that no amount of humoural revision could erase. He would tax English criminal courts for centuries.

Black Othello – standing in for the category of the husband

> *O, the more angel she, and you the blacker devil!*
>
> 5.2.131

The intersecting crucibles of gender and race so crucial to the formation of white English national identity has been extensively explored by critical race Shakespeare scholars, notably Kim F. Hall. Her superb exploration of how ideologies of fairness and the language of darkness and light were racialised in early modern England reveals the process by which blackness helped to create 'a value for whiteness'. Fairness, she argues, became a medium for shaping the subjectivity of white English men and women, Shakespeare's Desdemona being a classic case in point. Complicating this argument is the suggestion that Othello too, was white – a white man's caricature of a black man. But this only serves to underline the importance of registering whiteness as a raced identity as we saw Shakespeare doing in *Titus Andronicus* and now as Hall shows he did in *Othello*.[82] But I turn now to consider how Shakespeare fashions his 'black Othello', as Iago pointedly refers to the play's protagonist. Othello's blackness pervades the play, perhaps most famously when Iago tortures Brabantio with an image of his daughter enmeshed with Othello: right now, an 'old black ram' is 'tupping your white ewe'. Seeing his daughter as property, Brabantio views Desdemona's elopement as utterly improper. How could she, Brabantio asks Othello, have 'run from her guardage to the sooty bosom' of such 'a thing' as you?[83] Such a transgressive act, making a black man the protagonist, has attracted a great deal of scholarly attention. Some studies though, strain to keep the focus on the play's double-troubled problematising of racial othering and sexual oppression.

Take Michael Bristol's reading of the play as 'carnivalesque', bordering on farce. It is a charivari that while firmly focused on Othello's blackness, must be seen as a 'text of racial *and* sexual persecution'.[84] Within this 'comedy of abjection', one that competes with a reading of the play as a 'grand opera of misdirected passion', Desdemona is 'an impossible sexual object'. She is a 'female artefact created by a male imagination and objectified in a boy actor's body'. This, he argues, is 'just as artificial and as grotesque a theatrical manifestation as the black-faced Othello who stands in for the category of the husband'. As for Iago, Bristol attributes to him the view that envy and jealousy are not aberrations in early modern England's 'erotic economy', but are rather 'the fundamental precondition of desire itself'. Within the 'envy jealous system' where men are social agents and women objects of exchange, Iago successfully manipulates pervasive misogynist fantasies of 'an exclusively male world' in which women are completely oppressed. For a Jacobean audience however, Shakespeare still needed to racialise his protagonist, letting him stand in for the category of the husband. A suspicion that the passions leading him to kill his wife expressed 'all too accurately an element present in the structure of every marriage', a horror scenario dissolving the ideal of companionate marriage 'back into the chronic violence of the envy-jealous system', would be 'unendurable'.[85]

However, having offered a plausible explanation for Shakespeare's racial othering of the wife-killer, Bristol surmises that the play's original audience may not have been much bothered by Othello's blackness. The social consequences of problematic 'racist sensibilities', he muses, had not yet become visible. By contrast, he thinks late twentieth-century audiences may have found it harder to receive the play as a 'derisory ritual of racial and sexual persecution'. Why so? Because by then 'the social experience of racial difference' had become 'such a massive scandal'.[86] This leaves the feminist critic pondering how the 'sexual persecution' Bristol detected as one of *Othello*'s focal concerns ultimately drops out of his image of a scandalised late modern *Othello* audience. Admittedly, sexual violence was not to rise to the ranks of massive scandal until the early twenty-first century, a decade or so after he published his article. But wife-killing certainly had, my point being that Bristol exemplifies here a tendency of some Shakespeare scholars to allow the pivotal race question in *Othello* to over-determine readings of the play. Lest we forget: while it is absolutely essential to register that Othello is a racialised character blackened by racist language and that the play is, as we have seen Jean Howard proclaim, a 'great test case for racial thinking', it is simultaneously a great test case for thinking about impassioned femicide.[87]

Another Shakespeare scholar, Michael Neill, manages this double-vision well. He suggests that drawing attention to the play's anxiety-producing death bed scene as a 'site of racial transgression' and to the bed itself as 'a site of forbidden mixture' helps to locate the play's 'continuing power to disturb' in its racial *and* sexual transgressions. In the early modern period, adultery and 'disproportionate desire' were specifically linked to the question of race. Adultery was conceived as 'quite literally a kind of adulteration', or pollution, while the polluting propensity of blackness imagined as 'a symptom of the monstrous', was a cultural given.[88] It follows that acknowledging Othello's blackness as well as the metaphorical blackness associated with Desdemona's suspected adultery highlights the play's condemnation of possessive passions. Given *Othello*'s demonstration that jealousy is 'itself an extreme and corrupted (adulterate) form of sexual excitement', only murder with its 'violent rapture of possession' can end 'desire's downwards spiral'.[89]

While Neill leaves it implicit that it is a specifically male cultural anxiety that the play addresses and that it is a man, not a woman, who experiences violent possessive rage, the sexed asymmetry of domestic homicide does not pass Shakespeare or his feminist readers by. In her analysis of sixteenth- and seventeenth-century literary representations of English intimate partner homicides, Frances Dolan notes that although husbands murdered wives far more frequently than wives killed husbands, popular representations of murderous wives vastly outnumbered those of murderous husbands.[90] In her reading, *Othello* anticipates the post-1650 literary pattern of paying far more attention to murderous husbands. Shakespeare does so 'in part' by making his protagonist black in order to prepare his audience to question abuse of authority by the early modern husband. Iago dupes Othello by drawing on the 'deeply entrenched, reactionary cultural interest in insubordinate wives', an interest which associates women's self-assertion with betrayal, adultery and violence in order to incite Othello into experiencing his wife's alleged infidelity as 'a fatal assault'. For Dolan, seeing how Iago deploys the pervasive fiction of the treacherous wife highlights 'the endlessly interesting question of why Othello so readily distrusts Desdemona'. By demonising and racialising the tyrannous, possessive husband, presenting him 'as foreign, duped and dark', Shakespeare certainly deflects blame onto racialised difference between the spouses, thereby 'somewhat' distancing them from 'the conflict in most English marriages'.[91] Still, in Dolan's view, he deserves credit for getting his audience to start querying Englishmen's violence against their wives.

That might be a stretch and not only because it falls into the trap of attributing intentionality to a playwright whose views are notoriously difficult to pin down. Moreover, far from inventing a black protagonist, Shakespeare joined the bandwagon of notoriously pilfering early modern writers, grabbing his storyline from the Italian playwright Giovanni Cinthio, right down to his impassioned Moorish soldier.[92] Still, whatever Shakespeare's motivation in retaining Cinthio's black protagonist as wife-murderer, the play's presentation of Othello as simultaneously exotic and an embodiment of universal male subjectivity recalls powerful critiques of the operation of so-called 'cultural defences' in late twentieth-century Anglophone jurisdictions. Defence deployments of 'culture' in North American courts in particular have received sustained critical attention following a spate of controversial late twentieth-century cases in which minority ethnic men invoked cultural traditions to excuse homicidal and sexual violence against their wives. Their 'backward' cultures, their defence counsel argued, led them to violent acts that would never be tolerated by the dominant culture, a sentiment echoed in Lodovico's astonishment at Othello's striking of his wife – 'this would not be believed in Venice'.[93]

Yet as Leti Volpp, a leading critic of late modern cultural defences notes, the idea that a minority ethnic man would react more violently to the belief his wife was unfaithful is 'belied by the very encoding of the manslaughter/provocation doctrine' in Anglo-American law. This doctrine, as she explains, is 'explicitly premised upon a *violent* reaction to this knowledge'. Indeed, adultery is '*the* paradigmatic example' of mitigating provocation in western jurisdictions.[94] Or, as the early twenty-first century English law reformers put it, the defence of 'provocation by sexual infidelity' is 'our own version' of honour killing. Making the protagonist in his intimate partner homicide drama a racialised other presaged the English propensity to project murderous rage against women onto foreigners, thereby deflecting attention from theirs. But sympathising with enraged wife-killers caught up in a violent rapture of possession is an ingrained cultural judgment of English and foreign men, Volpp's – and perhaps Shakespeare's? – point precisely.

Othello as template for critique

The gift that keeps on giving, *Othello* addresses the question, still not resolved to this day, about what constitutes murder and what manslaughter in an intimate partner femicide case. Recall that in Chapter 1, I suggested that *Titus Andronicus* provides a template for critiquing the notion of justification-via-precedent for retaliatory violence. Now I propose that *Othello* provides a template for the more specific task of querying the justifications and excuses for wife-killing that would be hauled out over the centuries. Othello escaped justice by committing suicide but what of latter day Othellos charged with murdering their wives? Would their emotional turmoil mitigate murder if they killed their wives?

Imagine if Othello himself was put on trial for murdering his wife. His defence lawyer would make the case for a manslaughter conviction, and there is plenty of material in *Othello* to draw upon. Most obviously, there's Othello's self-serving plea that he was an 'honourable murderer' – 'For nought I did in hate, but all in honour'. The speech, a masterpiece of dissembling self-justification, is a gift for the defence team:

> When you shall these unlucky deeds relate,
> Speak of me as I am. Nothing extenuate,
> Nor set down aught in malice. Then musts you speak
> Of one not easily jealous, but being wrought,
> Perplexed in the extreme: of one whose hand,
> Like the base Indian, threw a pearl away
> Richer than all his tribe.[95]

Nothing extenuate? Here Shakespeare appears to invoke the exculpatory script being worked up contemporaneously by jurists busy distinguishing extenuating provocations that might lead to a manslaughter conviction from fully justifying grave provocations, indicatively finding one's wife in the act, warranting an acquittal. Othello himself is ambivalent about his crime, fluctuating between seeing it as honourable and just but also as 'unlucky', committed by a man 'eaten up with passion'.[96]

Arguing extenuating circumstances for men whose 'best judgment' had been derailed by passion is the defence lawyer's area of expertise. However, Othello's counsel would face an uphill battle given the abundant evidence supporting the prosecution case that this was no spur of the moment hot-blooded killing. It was a premeditated, calculated murder. Othello had made clear his intentions to kill Desdemona and Cassio, her alleged lover, when he asked Iago: 'How shall I murder him?' He would have him die a slow death, 'nine years a-killing'. As for Desdemona, she could 'rot and perish and be damned tonight, for she shall not live. No, my heart is turned to stone'.[97] His own words surely condemn him: 'I will chop her into messes! Cuckold me!' as he rails against the image of her in bed with Cassio:

> *OTHELLO:* I will chop her into messes! Cuckold me!
> *IAGO:* O, 'tis foul in her.
> *OTHELLO:* With mine officer!
> *IAGO:* That's fouler.
> *OTHELLO:* Get me some poison, Iago, this night. I'll
> not expostulate with her, lest her body and beauty
> unprovide my mind again. This night, Iago.
> *IAGO:* Do it not with poison, strangle her in her bed –
> even the bed she hath contaminated.
> *OTHELLO:* Good, good, the justice of it pleases, very good![98]

Given all the evidence against him, it might be best for the defence to cut their losses and plead guilty to murder. Or perhaps they could rely upon a diminished responsibility defence, referencing Othello's bizarre 'Goats and monkeys' address to Lodovico, on his arrival in Cyprus: 'You are welcome, sir, to Cyprus. Goats and monkeys!' For his part, Lodovico found Othello 'much changed' from the man he knew in Venice. Is this, he asked, 'the noble Moor whom our full senate' had called 'all in all sufficient? This the nature/Whom passion could not shake?'[99]

As well, there is evidence, if you can believe Iago, that notoriously unreliable witness, that Othello suffered from epilepsy leading to a loss of consciousness when confronted with 'evidence' of his wife's infidelity.[100] At the very least, demanding that Desdemona die 'else she'll betray more men' indicated a very confused state of mind. As he said himself, he had farewelled his 'tranquil mind'.[101] Perhaps it might be suggested that he suffered from so-called 'Othello Syndrome', a defence we shall see making an occasional appearance in late modern cases. Or might his counsel risk a cultural defence, explaining his crime as a product of a more patriarchal, more misogynist alien foreign culture. After all, though he asks that his crime not be extenuated, he goes on to racialise himself as either a 'base Indian' or a 'base Judean', it's unclear which.[102] At any rate, he ends up, at least in his own mind, as a 'turbaned Turk' and a 'circumcised dog', Shakespeare here referencing the revised humoural theory that located extreme passions in African and other 'southern' nations.[103] How could the Moor of Venice help from descending into a furious passion? It was geographically preordained.

Most likely it would all be to no avail in a criminal court today. As we shall see, sexual infidelity has been excluded as a trigger for loss of control in a new loss of control defence to murder in England and Wales. Moreover, alleging that a wife was adulterous did not save wife-killers from the gallows in those nineteenth- and early twentieth-century courts taking a strict approach to the law. There had to be 'ocular inspection of the act', the very same ocular proof that Othello demanded of Iago: 'Villain, be sure thou prove my love a whore/ Be sure of it, give me the ocular proof'.[104] There is none. Desdemona was 'innocent', her killing scenario a far cry from that required by the modern law of murder to warrant a conviction for manslaughter.

Desdemona was 'innocent'. What though of wives who *are* unfaithful? While other early modern playwrights featured adulterous wives, there's scarcely a cuckold in the entire Shakespeare canon.[105] Once again, this is stunningly prescient on Shakespeare's part. Over the centuries, English case law has produced relatively few adulterous wives, but a host of suspicious husbands and quite a few dispensing with wives without any real suspicions at all. Reading the cases, it becomes abundantly clear that the predominant motive for wife-killing is the woman's desire to exit the relationship, whether or not she leaves for another man. Astonishingly, Shakespeare even foreshadows this, the most common type of intimate partner femicide, when he has his proto-feminist, Emilia, contemplating leaving Iago on discovering his duplicity. Watch as this once 'naively collusive patriarchal abject' woman finally makes 'staggering discoveries' about male powers, defies silencing to assert the truth and finds her voice to rewrite Desdemona's ending as murder, 'redeeming her contaminated death from slander'.[106] 'O villainy, villainy!' she cries, as Iago tries to silence her: 'I charge you get you home'. Emilia refuses to go:

> Good gentlemen, let me have leave to speak
> 'Tis proper I obey him – but not now.
> Perchance, Iago, I will ne'er go home.[107]

Iago tries again – 'Zounds, hold your peace!' – but Emilia is determined to find her voice. In doing so, she anticipates late modern feminist outrage at men's fatal violence against women. Iago tries once more: 'Be wise and get you home'. Emilia won't go, instead berating Othello for being so stupid as to suspect his wife on such spurious grounds as a missing handkerchief:

> O murderous coxcomb, what should such a fool
> Do with so good a wife?[108]

Condemning Othello as a murderer and refusing to obey her husband, Emilia pays the ultimate price, Iago finally silencing her with his sword.

.....

It has proved to be more difficult to silence late modern Emilia critics who have joined their fictional predecessor in writing Desdemona's death and those of thousands of victims of intimate partner femicide as murder. Whatever Shakespeare's views of the matter, his play, read as Desdemona's, not Othello's tragedy, raises questions that have continued to vex criminal courts until this day. Should 'being wrought, perplexed in the extreme' excuse femicidal men? Or should vengeful wife-killing masquerading as warranted femicide meet with the full force of the law? Shakespeare certainly trashes the pathetic figure of the overwrought wife-killer. Yet such is his and *Othello*'s renowned undecidability that the play leaves plenty of scope for those still disposed to sympathise with the impassioned femicidal man who throws a pearl away.

Chapter 3

'Unlucky deeds' – Passion's progress in the nineteenth-century courts

When you these unlucky deeds relate,
Speak of me as I am. Nothing extenuate

Othello 5.2. 340–341

Introduction

We turn now from the fictional Othello, the prototype of the emoting wife-killer, to intimate partner femicide cases. How did the courts respond to killers who argued, on the basis of received authority, that their homicidal fury against 'unfaithful' women was justifiable or at the very least excusable? Social historian Martin Wiener provides a thorough examination of this question in *Men of Blood: Manliness and Criminal Justice in Victorian England*, his history of the Victorian response to serious crimes. Based on a wide array of sources, *Men of Blood* not only provides a close analysis of violent crime committed by 'men of blood' who turn out to be predominantly wife-killers. More than that, the book is itself a case study of what an offender-centric legal history – one that speaks for and identifies with the killers – brings to an analysis of impassioned homicide. It brings a great deal, not least a persuasive argument that while Victorian judges and Home Office officials took an increasingly punitive approach to serious crime, especially wife-killing, their response was shaped by conflicting emotions inflamed by 'cross-currents of ambivalence and contradictions'. In particular, intolerance of men's violence against women was countered by revulsion against the gallows and, crucially, by an acceptance of 'excusatory explanations of "provocation" by bad wives'. Wiener's impeccably researched history certainly leaves readers in no doubt that 'the mix of discourses surrounding these cases could be highly complex, simultaneously performing many different forms of cultural work, and legal outcomes could vary a good deal'.[1]

What though of the cultural work performed by *Men of Blood*, a book that is openly sympathetic to wife-killers, especially those convicted of capital murder? What does lamenting the fate of men convicted of murdering their wives in trials conducted in the shadow of the gallows do? What follows from that?

DOI: 10.4324/9781003301974-4

Might it lean historians towards accepting unquestionably the condemned man's account of having been driven to kill a provocative wife in an excusable, if not justifiable rage? What might happen if we were to switch the lens and approach the cases from her perspective? What if the voices of the victims were inserted into the mix of recorded courtroom discourses about murder, manslaughter and mitigating passion, enabling them to join the conversation until now dominated by killers, lawyers, judges and offender-centric histories? Chapter 3 begins the process of rewriting the dominant historical narrative that pits provocative women against 'put-upon husbands', as Wiener refers to them.[2]

Reorientating the reader away from the fate of the killers and towards the victims of impassioned homicide, the following chapters contest a narrative that is in thrall to the centuries-old assumption that impassioned or 'hot-blooded' femicide is a lesser form of homicide, especially if the victim is a wife. Telling her side of the story necessitates reaching down into the records to bring up the bodies. This is labour-intensive and deeply traumatic work. However, building a critical mass of slaughtered women is essential in order to constitute intimate partner femicide as a killing field in its own right. This, in turn, is essential for making the strongest possible case for rejecting infidelity or any kind of 'provocation' as mitigating murder. Furthermore, taking this victim-centred approach accords with Italian philosopher Adriana Cavarero's understanding of ethical narration that I outlined in the Introduction. Ethical narration, she argues, tells the story of the 'who' rather than the 'what' of human existence. In the courtroom and in offender-centric history, it is the killer's story that gets told, allowing him to monopolise the role of what Cavarero calls a 'narratable self' while the victim is reduced to an annihilated 'what'.[3] Reversing this order of things, I will strive wherever possible to elevate the victims into narratable subjects while willing others into a ghostly presence as silent witnesses to their own demise. Conversely, the femidical killer who strides the stage in offender-centric histories, demanding compassion and understanding at his dispatching of a provocative wife, will be written out of the narrative.

Giving voice to the vanquished and downtrodden is hardly a novel approach. Victims of various forms of men's violence may have only come into their own with the advent of twenty-first-century 'MeToo' and other victim's-rights movements. But social historians, cultural theorists and postcolonial scholars amongst others, have long sought out ways of writing history from the bottom up by delving deeper into the records to record the subjugated voices of marginalised groups, women included. To my knowledge though, this approach has not been taken in the killing field of intimate partner femicide, one that is far larger than that of state-sanctioned executions of femicidal men. Naming the victims, reclaiming something of the victims' lived experience and final moments, not only serves to memorialise their lives. It provides a counterpoint to conventional offender-focused histories that have drummed them out of history. But while I deprive the defendants of their identities, the fate conventionally reserved for their victims, I do not lose sight of the all-important courtroom discourse. For notwithstanding our fundamentally different orientations and political agendas, offender- and victim-centric historians converge on viewing the criminal justice system, and more particularly, the trials of femicidal men, as 'a site of intense cultural contestation'.[4]

In *Men of Blood*, that cultural contestation is presented as taking place over changing gendered roles. By contrast, I read the nineteenth-century intimate partner femicide trial as a rowdy discursive field in which the participants – judges, juries, defence lawyers, prosecutors, defendants and, occasionally, their intended victims – engaged in heated discussions about whether a man's impassioned homicidal reaction to his wife's 'provocative' conduct warranted a conviction for murder.[5] Analysing these trials, many but not all discussed in *Men of Blood*, I will pay particular attention to Victorian-era judicial discourse on the subject of mitigating 'passion' in order to highlight the changing relationship between law and passion. Of particular interest are the judicial efforts to rein in passion's excusatory force by reinforcing strict rules set down in previous centuries for determining what constituted an exculpatory 'crime of passion'. For it is here that we see the first concerted legal attempt to challenge the conceit that passion should mitigate murder.

All in the heat of passion – 'very feeling' cases

I see, sir, you are eaten up with passion.

Othello 3.3.394

Let us begin by recalling *Mawgridge*, the famous 1707 case proclaiming that finding a man *in flagrante* with one's wife warranted knocking out his brains because jealousy was the rage of a man and adultery the highest invasion of his property. By the late eighteenth century, if not earlier, the target of men's homicidal rage at allegedly adulterous wives had shifted from interlopers to the suspect wives. In the 1790s, several wife-killers were dispatched to the gallows, juries deliberating for very short times before delivering murder verdicts. In one 1791 case, the killer claimed his wife had spent the night with their neighbour. Witnesses testified that while the neighbour was 'a very good man', the victim, Winifred Charles, was a 'very sober, religious, hard-working woman', making this 'one of the most cruel murders that ever occurred'. A murder verdict was so inevitable the judge did not even bother summing up the evidence.[6]

By contrast, detailed legal argument was presented in another wife-killing case a few months later. The victim, named as a Mrs Dingler, had separated from her husband, only to finally succumb to his repeated overtures to return. A conversation then ensued wherein they accused each other of infidelity, leading him to stab her to death. Just before dying in hospital, she forgave her killer and wished, like Desdemona, to 'exculpate him of any murderous intent'. Outlining the factors reducing murder to manslaughter, the prosecutor told the jury that the law was always attentive to 'the frailties of humanity'. If the circumstances were such as to 'raise a sudden, natural gust of passion' and a man killed 'under the impulse of that passion', that might only amount to manslaughter. Indeed, if there was anything in the case that could excuse 'a natural and sudden gust of passion' he was sure the jury would take it into account because it would be 'for the honour of human nature'. However, if it appeared that the killing was 'not at all called for by any provocation from the poor woman, but indicated a savage and bloody intent', it would be murder. In 'common cases', those 'between man and man', the distinction between murder and manslaughter frequently arose and just as frequently resulted in manslaughter verdicts if the killing was occasioned by a blow exciting 'a sudden gust of passion'. But 'between man and wife, and between man and woman', he felt that distinction would hardly ever arise.[7]

While this prosecutor won his murder verdict, his prediction that distinguishing murder from manslaughter would hardly ever arise in intimate partner femicide cases turned out to be spectacularly wrong. For these were the very cases where the distinction was most thoroughly played out. As we shall now see, nineteenth-century judges and juries were frequently at loggerheads about which verdict impassioned wife-killers deserved, their disagreements turning, crucially, on how much excusatory weight should be given to the impact a woman's behaviour had on a man, especially her 'infidelity'. Being dead, the victims were not heard in the courtroom. But delving into the trial records we find witnesses, women neighbours especially, challenging defence narratives about dissolute, unsavoury women provoking men to kill them.

In 1819, Ann Holmesby's husband stood trial at the Old Bailey for her wilful murder. He bludgeoned her to death with an axe, claiming he had long suspected her of being unfaithful and had finally caught her *in flagrante* with another man. The case is in many ways a fitting starting point for a study of the nineteenth-century cases, not least because of the Shakespearean overtones of the killer's defence that it was 'all in the heat of passion'. Her alleged taunts about preferring the other man had put him in such 'a great rage' that it led to a macabre re-enactment of Othello's equally drawn-out slaughter of Desdemona, albeit with some scene reversals. Othello kisses his wife *before* he smothers her, saying:

> O balmy, balmy breath, thou dost almost persuade
> Justice to break her sword! Once more, once more:
> Be thus when thou art dead and I will kiss thee
> And love thee after. Once more, and that's the last.[8]

He then explains why she had to die, smothers her, has a conversation with Emilia, overhears Desdemona deny he had harmed her (she having somehow survived being smothered), before checking that she is finally dead. On learning she wasn't unfaithful, he kills himself. By contrast, Anne Holmesby's husband kissed her *after* he killed her, saying in decidedly un-Shakespearean terms: 'God bless you my dear, you was once my comfort, I have been the death of you, and you will be the death of me'.[9] He was right on both counts. As the judge told the jury, the law would have 'humanely provided a palliation for his crime' had he killed her at the moment he caught her in the act, but not when 'the passions had time to cool'. The jury agreed, rejecting the heat of passion defence and declining to recommend him to mercy.

The case is significant inasmuch as it is one of very few where the defendant's fate is not lamented in *Men of Blood*, Wiener finding Ann's alleged adultery to be unproven and his nearly chopping off her head 'repulsive' and 'highly premeditated'.[10] Certainly, the evidence against the defendant was damning. Witnesses had heard 'nothing about any other man', and Ann's young brother testified he heard him say he had 'done for her and should be hung' before threatening to kill witnesses who dared to incriminate him. And Anne's view of the crime? Unlike Desdemona's exculpatory defence of Othello – Anne's last word was 'murder'.[11]

When Frances Wood's husband beat her to death with a hammer in Nottingham in 1826, she also cried 'murder'. He claimed he saw no alternative to killing her, telling a witness: 'what could I do when I caught them in the act'. In court he claimed he had found her in bed with a man and, not in his right mind, was 'actuated by jealousy'. The jury took 'a very short time', to return a murder verdict, the judge having directed them that her alleged infidelity 'could not form a ground of justification' unless he could prove he discovered the man in 'a criminal intercourse' with his wife 'at the moment he committed the act'. Even then that would not excuse, only mitigate the crime. In any event, there was no such evidence beyond the defendant's testimony. Furthermore, his talking incoherently did not constitute insanity and his wife's infidelity was no excuse for using a deadly weapon. Her killing was, as Frances had foreseen, murder.[12]

Age was no barrier to a husband alleging infidelity as an excuse for wife murder, but it could increase a judge's scepticism. The husband of 66-year-old Sarah Baker killed her in Wiltshire in 1828. He claimed to have acted in a 'fit of passion' believing her to have been unfaithful. A 'fit of passion' might fairly describe the judge's reaction to the defence's suggestion that a husband may legally proceed to chastise his wife. That was not the law of England, he imploded. Even if there was a law giving men the right to inflict moderate chastisement on their wives, which he doubted, there was no licence for 'immoderate or unreasonable chastisement'. As for the idea that a mere suspicion of a wife's adultery would reduce murder to manslaughter, he demanded to see the authority for that opinion. No such precedent justifying femicide existed in English law. Certainly, the law made the killing of a man 'in some degree excusable' when he received a 'violent provocation', but this principle did not apply here. Indeed, even if the defendant killed his wife after finding her 'in the very commission of the act' which, the judge added, 'he only suspected to have occurred a year before', it would be manslaughter 'at the least'. Furthermore, considering the victim's age, the judge dismissed the allegations against her as completely unfounded. He left it to the jury to decide whether the defendant had been justified in attacking his wife on his 'lightly entertained' suspicions or whether his response had been 'brutally excessive'. The jury immediately finding him guilty of murder, the judge delivered the death sentence in what *The Times* described as a 'very feeling address'.[13]

Hannah Abbott – 'My life was at stake as well as his'

These were, after all, 'very feeling' cases that affected everyone involved, even on occasion prosecutors. In 1828, the same year that Sarah Baker was murdered, a man appeared at the Old Bailey charged with wounding his wife, Hannah Abbott, with the intention of killing her. He was hanged, much to the shock of those who had petitioned for his reprieve. Wiener sees this as yet another regrettable example of 'the judicial offensive' in the 'war on violence' and, more specifically, of the judicial 'attack' on the provocation defence. Why hang a man for attempted murder, an offence that had only been made a capital crime in 1811 and had hardly ever been applied? But he confines his reaction to a footnote where he laments this 'unexpected hanging'.[14] By contrast, Vic Gatrell, an offender-centric historian concerned with the popular reception of hanging in England, does not hold back. To make his case for the condemned man, he accepts as fact the mercy petitions and affidavits that sought to 'invalidate' Hannah's testimony by slamming her as unfaithful and worse, a prostitute, thereby cementing the historical case against her and for her husband. She had defied her husband by working at a public house so she could meet men. She neglected her children which were probably not her husband's. She had sex with a stranger, contracted a venereal disease and gave it to her husband – these, Gatrell assures us, were 'things everyone knew'.[15]

But were they? And were they true? Hannah Abbott's story begins at the committal hearing she attended after releasing herself from Bartholomew's hospital. Not yet fully recovered from the injuries she sustained in the attack, she had nothing positive to say about her husband and preferred not to comment on his 'general conduct'. Pressed, she told how he had beaten her many times. We learn too that when he slashed her throat with the knife he had sharpened the previous day, she rushed out of the house for help. Before being hospitalised, she insisted that someone first check if he had killed her children. In court, Hannah was an impressive witness, precise in her answers and quick to correct clerical errors. The magistrate at the committal found her to have answered 'very satisfactorily' questions about her needing to work as a charwoman at the local public house to provide food for her children. He had no truck with her husband's story about finding her there, sitting too close to a waiter singing songs about cuckolds. Hannah denied it and the pot-boy confirmed that the waiter did not sing any songs. There was nothing indecent about Mrs Abbott's manner of sitting.[16]

Giving evidence at the Old Bailey trial, Hannah said she had been afraid to go to bed on the near fatal night. On her return from work, she had hidden in terror in the privy until he broke the door down. Under cross-examination, she was asked whether her husband was 'weak in his mind'. She said she didn't think so. Was he 'very much given to jealousy'? Not in the least, she replied. He only 'pretended so'. He had imputed infidelity to her. She insisted there was 'clear proof that it was quite false'. Pressed yet again whether she knew whether he was 'very weak in his understanding', she again denied it, swearing she never knew of 'any deficiency in his mind more than wickedness'. He was, she testified, 'excessively wicked'. But did she not realise his life was now at stake? She did. Taking a stand rarely heard in the courts, most women not surviving men's homicidal assaults, Hannah was defiant: 'My life was at stake as well as his; I never considered my life safe with him – I do not want him executed; it is my wish to save his life, but my own as well'. Witnesses testified that the defendant was depressed, labouring under 'an infirmity of mind' and an unfounded belief in his wife's adultery such that his neighbours pitied him. So did the jury which, after finding him guilty, recommended him to mercy because he believed his wife was unfaithful, but there was 'no proof to that effect'.[17]

As for mercy petitions and affidavits sent to the Home Office on behalf of the condemned man's neighbours and fellow workmen that so convinced Gatrell of Hannah's blame-worthiness, the archive contains more documents. Her statements are there too. Pressured into writing a letter for his reprieve, she was clearly ambivalent about the outcome and more intent on expressing her outrage at her husband perpetuating lies about her. He claimed she had not visited him in prison. She said she had. Furious about other allegations made against her in letters published in the *Morning Advertiser*, she asked the editor to publish, 'as an act of justice', her letter to her husband. Her keen sense of injustice is evident there as she castigates his 'wicked conduct', especially his throwing cruel and unjust aspersions on her character. He said they had a happy home with their three children. She says it never was. Had he forgotten he denied they were his children and accused her of having a different father for each one? More damningly, she implies he was responsible for the death of her new-born fourth child. He said she prostituted herself. She denies it but says he had wanted her to 'go on the town' so that they could live comfortably. She would 'sooner suffer death'. She refused to visit him again. His beatings she could forgive, but not what he had said of her character. He should have said all these derogatory things at the Guildhall committal hearing so that she could have 'publicly denied them'.[18]

Hannah had told more of her side of the story in her petition to the Home Office for a reprieve. Presenting 'certain facts' which might mitigate his crime, she gave her version of the story, repeated by neighbours at her husband's trial, of her having been paid for sex with a stranger she met in a London street. She said she had made up the story because she was tired of him falsely accusing her of infidelity. When these allegations continued unabated, she admitted responding to his outburst of jealousy by taunting him with a threat to go 'with half a dozen men'. She was so sick of him accusing her 'without cause' that she had refused to submit to his 'embraces'. But now she regretted making up the story, an 'act of retaliation', and hoped he would be reprieved. It was to no avail. He went to the gallows, the Home Office deciding it would be 'dangerous to society' to spare him.[19] Hannah and her children were left destitute. But ever resourceful, she left hospital after a five-week stay and before she was fully recovered, so that she could arrange for a philanthropic institution to admit her children while she looked for work. The records allow us to follow her from the hospital to a workhouse and then to her last known address in Turnmill Street.[20] Hannah Abbot had saved her life, such as it was, and lived to tell the story of an unsafe marriage to a violent man, a story that would be told in the courts over and over again by the neighbours and families of those who did not live to tell theirs.

Hannah survived. Dinah Quigley did not. But she lived long enough after her husband's attack in Liverpool in 1868 to record a dying statement documenting how she had run to a neighbour's house to escape his beatings. While admitting to sometimes giving her husband cause to beat her by having 'a glass of ale too much', she insisted she had been sober on the fatal night. So there was no cause for the beating that was to kill her. Convicted of murder, her killer was eventually reprieved. Wiener was astonished that a reprieve for a man burdened by a wife he describes as a 'drunkard as well as an adulterer' had been so hard to obtain. Surely the fact he did not use a weapon and that she took four days to die were mitigating factors?[21] Not in the view of the jury or the court reporter commenting on the 'shocking phases' of the fatal assault on Dinah under the headline, 'Brutal Wife-Murder in Liverpool'.[22]

'Ocular proof' versus 'exceedingly wild work'

> *Villain, be sure to prove my love a whore,*
> *Be sure of it, give me the ocular proof*
>
> *Othello* 3.3.362–363

As the century progressed, judges continued to hold fast to the line that, as one put it in the 1832 *Pearson* case, even 'strong misgivings' as to a wife's fidelity would not warrant the inference that a man was 'justified in any such feeling' without proof. Jane Pearson's husband beat her to death after abusing her at length, calling her a whore. Rachael Whitehead, a boarder in the same house, had often heard him threaten Jane. He had threatened to kill Rachael as well. The judge took the opportunity to spell out the law. Echoing, though without citing *Othello*, he insisted that there must be 'ocular inspection of the act'. Only then might a man be convicted of manslaughter, not murder. In the instant case, there was nothing in English law to 'warrant the inference' that the defendant was 'justified' in feeling jealous. He said he was 'excited' by his wife's infidelity, but there was no proof. Furthermore, even if she had been unfaithful, the fatal blow had to be given in 'the moment of passion'.[23] The jury took ten minutes to find him guilty of murder.

This view was reaffirmed in the famous 1837 *Kirkham* case two years later.[24] While *Kirkham* was not a femicide case – the defendant killed his son when his wife left him because the son tried to protect his mother against his violent father – it provided another opportunity for a judge to clarify the law in cases turning on a wife's alleged infidelity. Notwithstanding evidence that the killing was premeditated – he was overheard to say he would be his son's 'butcher' and had decided on the 'day of execution' – the jury returned a manslaughter verdict.[25] The judge clearly had misgivings. English law, he said, has 'at once a sacred regard for human life and also a respect for man's failings, and will not require more from an imperfect creature than he can perform'. The court did mean men's failings, it being 'well known that there are certain things which so stir up a man's blood that he can no longer be his own master' and law 'makes allowance for them'. For example, if a man 'being stung and excited inflicts a fatal blow' he would only be guilty of manslaughter provided the provocation was sufficient and recent, the law assuming that what he did was done 'in a moment of overpowering passion, which prevented the exercise of reason'. The contrast was between the 'cool' man who acted on malice and one who acts on 'sufficient' provocation 'while it is fresh'. He 'must be excused if the provocation was recent and he acting on its sting, and the blood remained hot'. If not it was murder. After all, 'though the law condescends to human frailty, it will not indulge human ferocity. It considers man to be a rational being and requires that he should exercise a reasonable control over his passions'.[26]

It could not be emphasised enough: the concession to 'human infirmity' (read: men failing to master their emotions) was a limited one as the court explained in the 1869 provocation case of *Welsh*:

> When the law says that it allows for the infirmity of human nature, it does not say that if a man, without sufficient provocation, gives way to angry passion, and does not use his reason to control it—the law does not say that an act of homicide intentionally committed under the influence of passion is excused or reduced to manslaughter.[27]

For nineteenth-century judges, human ferocity trumped human frailty nearly every time. Furthermore, 'ocular inspection' or discovery of a wife *in flagrante* was required to plead provocation by infidelity. Consider for example, the 1837 case of *Fisher* in which a man who killed a man he heard had committed an 'unnatural act' with his 15-year-old son. His counsel took the line that while killing an adulterer found *in flagrante* with a wife was 'the very lowest degree of manslaughter', the provocation here was 'far beyond that of adultery'. But it was not that far beyond, at least in the view of the judge who worried that there would be 'exceedingly wild work taking place in the world if every man were to be allowed to judge in his own case'. English law was clear: 'every killing of another is itself murder' unless there was 'an instant provocation' to justify a manslaughter verdict. Certainly, killing an adulterer found *in flagrante* would be manslaughter, 'and that in the lowest degree; for the provocation is grievous' and could not be borne 'in the first transport of passion'. But the impassioned killer must see the act done. A man could not take the law into his own hands and inflict vengeance on the basis of hearsay. And yet having laid down a strict view of the law, when the jury returned a manslaughter verdict and a recommendation to mercy, the judge obliged, handing down a one-year sentence.[28]

The question of whether a man could be justified or at least partially excused for killing an unfaithful wife was raised again in the case of the man charged in 1839 with the capital offence of wounding and stabbing his wife, Phoebe Miller, with intent to kill her. Clearly terrified of him, she was so reluctant to testify against him that she was threatened with transportation for contempt of court. He claimed he had found her in bed with another man after a party celebrating their wedding anniversary. He had tried to kill the man, believing himself justified in doing so. Remarkably, his defence counsel conceded that while 'persons' in his 'situation in life' might believe that a man making such a discovery would be wholly justified in killing either or both of them, they were mistaken. That was not the law. The defendant's actions were nevertheless 'in some degree excusable' and 'in pity to human frailty', the judge agreed. While appreciating the defence move to disabuse 'ignorant minds' of the view that a man who found his wife *in flagrante* would be justified in killing him, he found that the defendant had acted under circumstances 'of very great provocation'. Accordingly, 'every allowance ought to be made for his excited feelings'. Indeed, 'in proportion as a man's mind was pure and honourable, so would his passion be greater under the influence of such a grievous wrong'. The jury convicted him of common assault and recommended him to mercy. Agreeing with the verdict, the judge handed down a three-month sentence that gets the stamp of approval in *Men of Blood*.[29]

Things were about to change. According to Wiener, juries and 'English public opinion' became less inclined as the century wore on to excuse men's lethal responses to alleged infidelity, 'however tragic'. Acquittals disappeared and murder convictions increased as tolerance for killing 'even' an unfaithful wife diminished.[30] So was passion losing its excusatory force in wife-killing cases? It would seem so if several mid-century cases where defendants were convicted of murder are any guide. Consider this 1843 case featuring a twist on the standard adulterous wife tale. The defendant claimed he had killed his heavily pregnant wife, Elizabeth Buckley, near their St Helen's home because she had 'viciously insulted' and struck him. His telling her about seeing a former 'sweetheart' had made her jealous, prompting her to 'browbeat' him. Demanding she 'hold her noise', he cut her throat, while 'under heated and excited feelings'. It was an 'instantaneous passion'. A neighbour, Jane Rigby, told a different story. Elizabeth had dismissed the rumours about her husband's interest in other women. Though not liking how he looked at them, she had treated these reports as 'a joke'. For her part, Jane had told Elizabeth not to mind rumours, taking her queue straight from the *Othello* playbook: 'Unless you see a thing, never mind; if you don't know the consequences of jealousy, I will tell you: it damns many a soul, and commits many a murder'. It was not Elizabeth but her husband who had not considered those consequences, the judge laying down the law that neither words nor blows could reduce murder to manslaughter if they were 'merely' the product of the wife's 'passion of anger'. Nothing had occurred 'to take the offence out of the category of murder'. The jury agreed but recommended the defendant to mercy because of the suffering Elizabeth was said to have caused him.[31]

With a wife's 'passion of anger' thrown into the mix, the emotional register of intimate partner femicide went up another notch. In 1844, a man whose first wife had died under suspicious circumstances, stood trial for murdering his second wife, Ann Sherwood, at their Newcastle home. He claimed she had verbally abused and hit him which 'so excited and enraged' him with 'a feeling of jealousy' that he suddenly slashed her throat. Siding yet again with the defendant, Wiener tells a story of a browbeaten jury tricked by the judge into returning a murder verdict. In his telling, the conviction led to a 'vigorous' though ultimately unsuccessful reprieve campaign, one fuelled by the traditional sympathy, that Wiener shares, for a man suffering from a wife's 'long time querulousness'. Overlooking the testimony of Ann's niece that the defendant was extremely violent when intoxicated and had threatened to kill his wife, Wiener accepts as fact the defendant's account of Ann's 'unbecoming' conduct, especially what he calls her 'obscene verbal and gestural abuse' that implied she had committed adultery. Also overlooked in an account bent on emphasising judicial harshness is that although this judge did press for a murder verdict, he also hinted at how a jury could potentially return a manslaughter verdict should similar facts arise. For example, if the victim's blows were accompanied by words and gestures producing 'a degree of exasperation equal to that which would be produced by a violent blow' that could, the judge said, reduce the crime to manslaughter – just not in this case.[32]

By the mid-nineteenth century, unsubstantiated allegations of infidelity had little traction in the courts. Again and again, judges impressed it upon juries that in English law, entertaining suspicions about a wife would not save a man from the gallows. Ocular inspection of adultery, as Othello had insisted on, was essential for a successful provocation plea. Consider for example the much-cited 1848 case of *Kelly*. The defendant had been charged with murdering

Agnes Hill, a woman to whom he felt 'strongly attached'. His counsel conceded Agnes Hill's life had been 'sacrificed', but the defendant's 'strong feeling of affection' for her was 'not the less strong because illicit'. He had been 'excited to jealousy' and 'goaded to frenzy'. Unimpressed though he was with this tale of impassioned homicide, the judge begrudgingly acknowledged the received view:

> It is said that if a man were to find his wife in the act of committing adultery and kills her that would be manslaughter only because he would be supposed to be acting under an impulse so violent that he could not resist it.

However:

> to take away the life of a woman, even your own wife because you suspect that she has been engaged in some illicit intrigue, would be murder; however strongly you may suspect it, it would most unquestionably be murder … I state this without the least shadow of doubt. We must not shut our eyes to the truth.[33]

The jury quickly returned a murder verdict, though with an 'earnest recommendation to mercy' that was to no avail.[34] Another jury took only 15 minutes to convict Caroline Mobbs' husband of her murder in 1853 at their London home, his brutal killing a bridge too far to warrant a lesser verdict. Neighbours testified that Caroline was 'a quiet, well-behaved and strictly sober woman' and that her 'savage ill-treatment' at her drunken husband's hands 'almost' exceeded belief. Calling him 'General Haynau' in reference to an infamous contemporary wife-beater, they said he would throw her out at night then use that as a pretext for beating her. On more than one occasion she sought refuge at the house of her neighbour, Julia Engling, telling her: 'That wretch has been beating me again. I'm sure I don't know what I shall do. Will you allow me to sleep on your stairs?' It emerged too that Caroline had wanted to get legal protection but 'an indefinable terror' had stopped her. She was going to apply for a separation maintenance on the fatal day. According to the judge, there was not a 'single circumstance of palliation' for a man who was in the habit of exercising 'the most gross and unmanly violence' against his wife. He had insinuated infidelity but there was no proof. That did not stop his friends writing to the Home Office defending him and attacking Caroline's character as a 'drunken worthless woman' and an adulterer who had infected her husband 'with a loathsome disease'. Allege away. It made no difference. The Home Office dismissed their entreaties on the startlingly novel ground that 'the lives of many women are at stake', a stunningly evocative victim-centred statement recalling Hannah Abbott's moving testimony that her life was at stake as well as that of her assailant.[35]

'A violence to his feelings'

> *...but, being wrought,*
> *Perplexed in the extreme*
>
> *Othello* 5.2 343–344

Sympathy for overwrought wife-killers could still prove decisive. Amelia Ansell's husband shot her dead in Portsmouth in 1856 with a pistol he kept near their bed. Neighbours testified that Amelia, 'a timid woman', was terrified of the defendant. They heard her crying 'Help, help – murder, murder!' and then a pistol shot. The defendant's account was inconsistent. She had killed herself. It was an accident. Neither scenario was plausible given his invitation to one neighbour to 'come and see what I've done to my poor wife'. He was also overheard telling Amelia that the pistol was for her if she didn't 'behave well'. As for him throwing himself on Amelia's dead body in so 'violent a state' that three men had to hold him back, the judge was dismissive: 'exclamations made by a man after he had committed a crime' did not hold much weight. But the jury, impressed by his war record, his 'most excellent character for humanity and good conduct' and his kindness, acquitted him of murder.[36] The jury also sympathised with Mary Anne Turner's husband when he stood trial for her murder in Rochester in 1858. He said he killed her in a 'very excited state' caused by suspicions of her adultery. In gaol awaiting trial, he was said to be 'very much distressed in his mind', while in court his challenge to the alleged adulterer to admit his guilt was delivered 'in an excited manner'. His was not the only emotional turn. In a 'most feeling address to the jury', his defence counsel said the crime was committed 'while he was in a state of intense excitement' at 'an injury' he believed he had sustained at the hands of an adulterer. So, all things considered, justice would be 'amply satisfied' if he was found guilty of the lesser offence of manslaughter. The judge disagreed. Suspecting her of infidelity provided no 'legal justification' for killing her 'even supposing his claims about her infidelity were true'. Admittedly, he had killed Mary Anne while under 'an almost overpowering feeling of excitement', but whatever feelings the jury might entertain on the subject, they were bound to do their duty. The jury baulked, returning a manslaughter verdict, much to the displeasure of the judge who sentenced him to penal servitude for life.[37]

Emotions played out differently when Sarah Francis' husband stood trial for her murder in 1859. The Newport courtroom was 'densely crowded', many of them young women who remained throughout the proceedings. No allegation of infidelity was raised, Sarah's 'provocation' simply being her refusal to resume living with her husband and allegedly 'scoffing' and insulting him when she repelled his advances. What, his counsel asked, 'could be more harrowing to his feelings than to hear her sing and mocking at him in his agony. Was it not enough to drive any man to frenzy?' Not in the view of the judge who, while agreeing that women could be 'exceedingly provoking' and that 'mere words and gestures' had 'the power to excite a man's passions, and by laughter and insult to excite and irritate him', insisted that this could not reduce the crime to manslaughter. The jury agreed, taking ten minutes to return a guilty verdict and declining to recommend him to mercy.[38] Judge and jury had also been on the same page about the fate of Jane Banham's common law husband and required only 20 minutes to convict him of murder in 1856. No hint of adultery had arisen in the case where, as in so many hundreds of femicides to follow, a woman paid with her life for having left her relationship. Jane had taken her children to live with her father. When she refused to return, her husband took what he called his revenge and killed her. Sobbing and beating his forehead throughout the trial was to no avail. Assessing the 'steps from earnest affection to deadly thoughts', the judge asserted that 'disappointed affection' was 'no palliation of a deadly wound'. When the death sentence was read, the defendant was carried out 'apparently fainting', while the 'dense crowd' in attendance 'dispersed in silence', evidently in agreement with the verdict.[39]

Sometimes however, judges concurred with juries in viewing a suspicious femicidal man sympathetically. In 1862, Alice Isott was shot dead by her husband when he found her sitting near another lodger who was lying on a bed drunk. The shooting was clearly premeditated, the killer having practised at a shooting gallery and bought bullets. That didn't stop the defence from arguing that the case was about 'one of the most powerful passions which operate upon human nature'. Whatever the defendant had seen had 'raised in him a paroxysm of anger and jealous fury'. The judge explained that a man could not be excused for killing an adulterous wife. After all, 'death was not the legal punishment for adultery, and the law did not allow a private individual to take the execution of justice into his own hands'. But if a man found his wife in adultery that would be 'such a violence to his feelings' as to reduce his killing her to manslaughter. While this case is interpreted in *Men of Blood* as demonstrating a jury's refusal to heed a judicial instruction to find the defendant guilty of murder, I read it otherwise. The judge had left it to the jury to consider whether the circumstances of the case would justify a finding of the 'minor offence' where a man 'in a fit of jealous rage, founded on prior suspicions *and* on what he saw', killed her. The jury decided they did. However, the crime being 'closely akin to the crime of murder', the judge then sentenced him to penal servitude for life. After all, it was necessary to 'protect society from such acts of outrage'.[40]

From mid-century crowded emotionally charged courthouses became a feature of wife-killing trials, popular feeling now entering the mix. When jury recommendations to mercy followed a conviction for murder, defence lawyers frequently organised mass petitions requesting reprieves for condemned men, and it is significant that, as Wiener notes, of five cases listed by the Home Office between 1860 and 1895 where 'popular feeling' had to be considered in granting a reprieve, no less than four were killers of 'unfaithful' wives.[41] One much celebrated case, to which we shall return, resulted in a reprieve for the man convicted in 1864 of murdering his allegedly adulterous wife, Sarah Hall. It was secured by a petition with nearly 70,000 signatures attached.[42] He was not the only femicidal man to benefit from an outpouring of compassion. That same year, Mary Ann Phillip's common law husband was acquitted of her murder. He had cut her throat, claiming she admitted to having been with different men. The prosecution argued it was premeditated murder, he having been heard on a previous occasion that he 'would do for her' for being unfaithful. After retiring to consider their verdict, the jury returned to ask whether they could return a manslaughter verdict if the defendant killed her 'in a moment of passion arising from jealousy'. 'Certainly not', the judge replied. The only evidence to support a manslaughter verdict was the defendant's claim, made only when he had 'time to think about his defence', that Ann had cut his throat first. A defiant jury acquitted him of murder, evidently seeing Mary Ann as Wiener does – as 'a persistently bad wife' – and her killer as a man burdened by a woman described in court as 'very abandoned'.[43]

Jury dissents from judges' directions occurred in other cases. In 1864, Mary Ann Atkinson survived her husband's attempt to kill her by cutting her throat when she refused to return home from another man's house. Charged with feloniously wounding, he was found guilty of the lesser offence of wounding with intent to do grievous bodily harm and recommended to mercy 'on account of the great provocation' he had received. Handing down a six-year sentence, criticised in *Men of Blood* as 'particularly heavy', the judge maintained that whether he was provoked by 'her lightness of conduct or some other cause', he should not have beaten her. She had behaved 'most grievously', getting her revenge against her husband by committing adultery, but it was not for the jury to judge that 'immoral act'. The defendant was not 'authorised to use any violence against her'. Perhaps not authorised, but in the jury's view, beating a woman accused of 'lightness of conduct' did not warrant a conviction for a more serious charge.[44]

Juries continued to disagree with judges over what men were authorised to do or what, more exactly, they could at least be excused for doing. Charged in 1867 with the manslaughter of his wife, Mary Vicary, in Norfolk, her husband complained that she had spent his money on alcohol. The judge pressed for a conviction, memorably stating that being 'in a passion at the time was no defence; if it were, we should all be at the mercy of passionate men'. Certainly Mary had been, the judge noting she had been 'beaten and kicked' repeatedly during the fatal attack and had been on many prior occasions. The jury found him guilty but recommended him to mercy. Handing down a five-year sentence, the judge said he felt 'really sorry' for such a hardworking man but it was 'necessary that people in your class should be taught what I fear they don't understand – that they have no right to beat their wives'. One blow was excusable but not repeated ones. How a man could 'thus treat a woman and that woman his wife, and the mother of his children', the judge could not imagine.

Such was his outrage that he told the jury that while he had never disregarded a recommendation for mercy before, this time he would.[45]

Feelings ran very high when Maria Death's common law husband was convicted of murdering her at their Wood Green home in 1869. Shortly before he killed her, witnesses heard her say: 'Fred, you know what you have said to me; I am afraid for my life'. He shot her before battering to death the man he thought she was seeing. Witnesses were too reluctant to intervene in what they saw as a routine domestic dispute. *The Times* reporter agreed with the judge that the only possible verdict was murder. It was a 'shocking crime' and a 'cruel murder', Maria's fears for her life trumping the defendant's story that he had been 'impelled' by a 'paroxysm of rage' when she allegedly confessed to infidelity. As for the defence case that her alleged confession warranted a conviction for manslaughter, that was 'nothing short of immoral'. Most damningly, they were not married and 'all the sanctions of morality' would be abandoned if a man had 'all the rights of a husband over a woman with whom he had formed an unlawful connection'. He was not deserving of the same protection as a lawful marriage. That would be like saying that 'one unlawful passion is a sufficient excuse for another, and it would tend to render all crimes excusable if there were only sufficiently numerous'. The reporter continued:

> It is an unhappy fact that adultery and murder are often found together, and it would be a disastrous doctrine to admit the one as an excuse for the other … if we are invited to sympathise with him, we must also express our compassion for this unhappy woman who has degraded herself to live with him.[46]

While expressing compassion for the victim of a femicidal man was a relatively novel idea, others thought the killer deserved some too. As one critic put it, had they been married, 'thousands of people would have commiserated with him and have considered him partially justified'. It was therefore 'a morbid caprice' to say he ought to be hanged because they were not married. After all, he 'considered her his wife, she had children by him and it appears that he had used her well'. Furthermore, 'the very fact of the savageness of the murders' proved that he was 'wrought to such a state of jealousy, by being betrayed' that he lost control. Just like Othello, he was 'wrought, perplexed in the extreme' and therefore deserving of compassion. Hundreds of his neighbours and fellow workmen concurred, signing a mercy petition stating that the killings were unpremeditated, committed in a moment of 'uncontrollable frenzy' and under 'great and sudden provocation'.[47]

Confessing or fleeing?

> *She's gone, I am abused, and my relief*
> *Must be to loath her. O curse of marriage*
> *That we call these delicate creatures ours*
> *And not their appetites!*
>
> *Othello* 271–274

The evidence for Maria Death's infidelity was equivocal. It was in many cases. Femicidal men and their allies obsessed about infidelity, or said they did, some even getting up a 'mock passion' to beat a woman's brains out and then escaping a murder conviction, much to the disdain of a *Daily News* reporter.[48] Yet despite the frequent invocation of 'infidelity', court records indicate that far more frequently women had fled from their violence and not usually to another man. The 1871 case of *Rothwell*, one of many departure cases to come, would frequently be cited by defence lawyers as authority for opening the door for a wife's alleged admissions of adultery to count as sufficiently grave provocation to reduce murder to manslaughter.[49]

Betty Rothwell left her husband because of his violence, taking her four children with her. At his trial for her murder, Agnes Longfellow testified to overhearing Betty tell him she had left because of his 'damned threats'. He had often threatened her 'bloody life for going to the dancing-rooms'. He had asked her to forgive him and return home but she refused, saying she would not give up her new man and would have 'no more children of thee'. So he struck her. She died of her injuries in the Oldham workhouse a week later. Her story ended there but his lived on in the judgment. Addressing the jury, the presiding judge Lord Blackburn said there had to be 'heat of blood and provocation' but where there are 'no blows', there must be a provocation 'at least as great as blows'. What might that be? While words would not usually suffice to reduce the crime, 'under special circumstances' – always already those involving a wife's adultery – they might do so if a husband 'suddenly hearing from his wife that she has committed adultery, and he having had no idea of such a thing before', killed her. Would such words, uttered just before the fatal blow, provoke in 'an ordinary man, not a man of violent passionate disposition' in such a way 'justify him striking her' as he did. Taking the hint, the jury cleared him of murder.[50]

Judges remained reluctant to extend *Rothwell*'s concession to confessions. Well into the twentieth century, they rejected defence pleas to extend it to cover cases of murdered fiancées and unmarried partners. Even so, frequent citations of the case helped to reinforce the notion, one certainly 'disastrous' for women, that her confession might excuse him killing her. In the meantime, men kept killing women who left them. A spate of cases in 1872 saw juries returning quick verdicts of murder. The first stands out as a highpoint of judicial and, indeed, juror resistance to the notion that a man could kill a woman who left him. The victim, Mary Anne Moore, was so terrified of her alcoholic husband that she fled to her father's house near Ashford. Neighbours testified they heard him threatening to kill her, the separation having enraged him. Anger at her refusal to come home was not, the judge said, 'a sufficient motive' for murder 'in the mind of a sensible man'. But what about the effect of such a refusal on 'the ill-regulated mind of a passionate man'? Same difference: the jury took just 20 minutes to return a murder verdict.[51] Nor did allegations of adultery always ensure a manslaughter verdict. A crowded Lincolnshire courtroom heard that Jane Horry's killer had shot her, believing her to be unfaithful. The judge told the jury they could recommend him to mercy if they thought he was suffering from 'overpowering feelings of jealousy', but they declined to do so, rejecting the defence argument that his jealousy, 'whether justly or unjustly conceived' had so overwhelmed him that he lost self-control. As the judge told the condemned man, 'even if she were guilty, it was a terrible and awful thing to shoot her'.[52] Betsy Handcock's husband stabbed her to death, claiming she had been unfaithful with men in their Warwick neighbourhood. After hearing witnesses testify that there was no cause for his jealousy and that Mary Ann, terrified of his threats and violence, would beg not to be left alone with him, the jury returned a murder verdict without even bothering to retire.[53]

But outpourings of sympathy for men who killed departing wives remained the order of the day. In 1874, Charlotte Poplett's husband killed her after she left to live with another man. As the evidence showed the crime was clearly premeditated, a murder verdict was inevitable. Neighbours petitioned successfully for a reprieve, citing his long provocation by an alcoholic wife. Judge Bramwell, praised in *Men of Blood* for having shown 'greater sympathy for put-upon husbands than most of his colleagues', told the Home Office that the man was clearly guilty of murder. Nevertheless, it seemed 'strange' to him that at law, 'a slight blow should reduce such an act to manslaughter', while this woman's conduct, goading the man 'to desperation', did not. He thought her conduct should be investigated. The killer was 'a man of good character and conduct, the woman quite the reverse', and her leaving him was 'without any justification'.[54]

Four years later a man vowed he would cut his wife's head off if she refused to return to him. Instead, he cut her throat in Epping Forest. Twenty-three-year-old Hester Revell had left him and taken her children to live with her family, his alcoholism having become intolerable. The judge condemned the killing as a deliberate act and not at all 'the effect of passion under a sudden provocation'. Convicted of murder, he received no recommendation for mercy. And yet he is presented in *Men of Blood* as a man to be pitied, having suffered at the hands of a violent woman whose 'repeated blows', astonishingly in Wiener's view, did not constitute legal provocation. Repeated blows? She had grabbed his collar and torn his coat during a quarrel over his drinking.[55]

'Innocent suspicion'

> *Think'st thou I'd make a life of jealousy*
> *To follow still the changes of the moon*
> *With fresh suspicions?*
>
> *Othello* 3.3.180–183

Kate Mumford was seven or eight months pregnant when her husband killed her in Dover in 1879. His counsel argued that he was driven 'to madness' by her taunts about committing adultery, including saying the unborn child was not his. As if it needed any reminding, he told the court that it was 'the law of England that if a man detected his wife in the very act of adultery, he might kill both her and the adulterer'. Furthermore, *Rothwell* was authority for saying that killing a taunting, adulterous wife would be manslaughter. The judge vehemently disagreed that *Rothwell* was authority for such a proposition. A man must first hear about his wife's supposed infidelity on the fatal night 'so that with no time for his passion to cool' he was put into 'a state of frenzy'. As the defendant had admitted his suspicions pre-dated his attack on Kate, the jury could not to be 'carried away by any feelings that might be awakened' by allegations of infidelity. Convicting him of murder, the jury unanimously recommended him to mercy on account of the victim's 'previous provocation', such was the continuing cultural power of the infidelity tale no matter how implausible, strenuous judicial efforts to confine its reach notwithstanding.[56]

In 1882, Caroline Taylor's husband killed her on suspicion of adultery where 'there was no cause for it'. At his Old Bailey trial, a medical witness, Forbes Wilson, explained that 'being suspicious without proper cause' is not evidence of insanity, taken by itself. After all, 'perfectly sane men often have a suspicion of their wives having committed adultery'. That was 'a very common form of innocent suspicion', the kind that afflicted Othello. But should that 'false belief' mitigate murder? Not in the view of the jury which convicted him of murder. With no recommendation to mercy, he hanged.[57] Other suspicious killers fared better. The 1880 murder trial of Amelia Litchfield's husband had created 'considerable excitement in the town' of Northampton. He was regarded as a man of very good character, while Amelia had a reputation for drinking with other men. As the defence told the story, 'his life was blasted, his home desecrated and his name degraded' by Amelia's conduct, prompting him to kill her in 'a mad fit of jealousy'. The jury's manslaughter verdict was met with 'considerable applause' in the courtroom.[58] When Hannah Beckett left her husband for another man the following year, he was in such despair that he cut her throat. 'If I can't have her', he had exclaimed in that endlessly repeated memorable phrase, glossed here as: 'If I can't have her, Harry Ogden shan't'. The jury took just 15 minutes to return a manslaughter verdict. Concurring entirely with the verdict, the judge handed down a four-day sentence resulting in an immediate discharge.[59]

Allegations of a wife's infidelity did not usually have such a mitigating effect. Selina Smith's husband was found guilty of her murder at his 1884 Durham trial but was recommended to mercy. That she had eloped with his half-brother and former lodger in their house was seen as especially egregious. Something must have been said on the fatal night, the defence argued, to cause his 'sudden fit of passion'. The jury reluctantly convicted him of murder, recommending him to mercy on the ground of 'great provocation'. The judge understood that they had 'every desire to discover something' which could reduce the crime to manslaughter. However, the law required the 'full verdict' of murder, notwithstanding the 'many painful circumstances' that, as he told the accused, he would not 'harrow up your feelings by recounting them'. Though known to be a harsh judge, he supported the mercy recommendation, convincing the Home Office that the murdered woman's conduct rendered it 'a fit case for commutation'.[60] Compare what the judge had to say about Ellen Norman's husband when he was convicted of her murder in Fulham the following year. It would, he said, be an injustice to Ellen's memory if the jury felt there was any basis for his accusation of 'improper familiarity' on her part.[61] Or compare what happened when a man stood trial in 1887 for killing his wife, Ann Bloxham, in Leicester. Although she was described as a 'bad, drunken, dissolute woman' who, according to her killer, was 'wholly responsible' for her own death, no hope was entertained for him.[62] The jury took three minutes to find him guilty of murder. Some commentators condemned such a 'brutal crime', while others felt clemency was in order to avoid another 'judicial murder'.[63]

Clearly, Victorian-era opinion about excusable homicidal reactions to 'provocative' women had not yet settled. Sharply divided views were again on display in the 1892 Old Bailey trial of a man for murdering his common law wife, Mary Elizabeth Swift. Her sister testified that Mary had not given him cause. Others testified about their frequent quarrelling. Neighbour Lily Warner had tried to protect Mary and her children, on one occasion stepping between them, only for him to assault her as well. Lily had often heard him threatening to kill Mary. She heard him say 'I mean to cut her throat' on the day Mary visited her dying mother. Another lodger, Eliza Stewart, had overheard him say: 'Oh you blue-eyed beauty, if you have ever deceived me I will walk with a firm step to Newgate for the woman I love'. He did just that and was executed within the prison walls despite a strong recommendation of mercy on the grounds of Mary's alleged provocation and a petition with 1400 signatures attached requesting a commutation of his death sentence.[64]

On the other hand, reliable evidence of a wife's infidelity almost always spared a homicidal man from the gallows. Ellen Round's husband was convicted of manslaughter at his 1894 Old Bailey trial and sentenced to just 12 months hard labour. He fit the bill of a wronged man, having shown 'extreme emotion' when told Ellen was dead – 'even his wrists flushed the colour of a boiled lobster, scarlet'. Ellen had taken up with a man whom the jury thought 'deserving of very great censure'. His testimony at the committal hearing had been met with repeated 'loud hisses' while Ellen, the 'faithless wife', was seen to have erred by telling her husband 'I cannot leave this man'.[65] The following year, Emma Harris' husband won a reprieve from his conviction for murdering her near Exeter when she left him for his younger brother. The Home Office was swayed by recent cases where 'the provocation of infidelity on the part of the wife (where it has been of a specially aggravated character) has been allowed to tip the scales in favour of mercy'. Leaving for a man's brother met that standard, the crowded court having cheered the cross-examination of the brother so loudly that the judge cleared the room.[66] Alice Allison's husband was also reprieved after his conviction at his 1896 Old Bailey trial for murdering her. The testimony of a Holloway medical officer may have helped convince the jury to recommend him to mercy. The killer, he speculated, may have suffered from 'a sudden attack of homicidal mania', his delusions 'leading him to suppose that he was justified in entertaining ill-will towards his wife'. He had 'an exaggerated idea of jealousy' when he killed Alice, which might seem insane but 'some people do become ridiculously jealous at a trifle'.[67] Othello comes to mind.

Conflicting views of the excusatory force of mere suspicion played out again in another 1896 trial, one immortalised in Oscar Wilde's 'Ballard of Reading Gaol', published during the reprieve proceedings. Laura Woolridge's husband cut her throat when she asked for a divorce. Having recommended him to mercy, the jury petitioned the Home Office for a commutation of the death sentence, claiming the judge had misled them into returning a murder verdict. Declining to intervene, the Home Office dismissed the case as indicating no more than the possessive jealousy manifested in 'the old phrase so often presented to the Home Office of if she would not be his wife, she should be no one else's'.[68] It was indeed an 'old phrase' and already hackneyed by the time Sophia Watt's husband stood trial for her murder in 1898. Sophia had left because of his violence and obtained a judicial separation from him. He shot her then battered her skull with the pistol when she refused to return. Conceding that there were no grounds for his belief that she had been unfaithful, his defence counsel tried to argue, citing *Rothwell*, that Sophia's alleged taunts about another man constituted provocation reducing the crime to manslaughter. Dismissing that argument, the judge said he 'utterly failed to find a single particle of evidence to show that the deceased was other than a moral, chaste, good woman, or that there was any ground, except the prisoner's statement', for believing otherwise. The jury immediately pronounced him guilty of murder, an outcome decried in *Men of Blood* as resulting from unpalatable judicial strictness. For the pro-offender historian, it was surely to be lamented that judges continued to patrol the boundaries of exceptions to the rule that a man must find his wife in the act of adultery or, failing that, kill her immediately upon hearing her taunting him about it. Such judicial intransigence unjustly blocked the excusatory force of men's rage at 'bad wives', as Wiener calls them, un-italicised, throughout *Men of Blood*.[69]

Offender versus victim-centred histories of homicidal passion

There is though much to admire about Wiener's analysis of the Victorian criminal justice response to wife-killing. Not least is his compelling account of judges laying down the law, but often meeting resistance from juries supported by a petition-signing public demanding reprieves for condemned men. Another great strength of *Men of Blood* is its documenting of the cultural shifts taking place in nineteenth-century Britain that informed the criminal justice response. None was more important than the so-called 'civilising offensive' or 'state-driven pacification' that was accelerating in Europe against 'barbaric' or 'uncivilised' behaviour. While male-on-male killing declined, 'domestic or intimate killing' increased, matched by a trend towards greater punishment for serious crimes that was informed by an increasing intolerance of 'unmanly' behaviour. With violence against women, particularly wives, increasingly condemned in Victorian discourse, the received notion of the 'man of honour' was replaced with that of the 'man of dignity' who was expected to exercise self-restraint even with their wives. Relatedly, 'provoked' killings committed in defence of honour or reputation were 'losing their traditional excusable character' as the nineteenth century progressed. A 'new culture of sensibility' opposed to expressions of male aggressiveness, especially towards women, brought about significant cultural changes, 'respectability, Englishness, manliness and womanliness high among them' though distinctions were still made between more and less excusable acts of violence, with the Victorian 'war on violence' bearing down disproportionately on working-class men.[70]

Wiener explains that this process was not always straightforward, legal outcomes in these cases varying considerably. While wife-killer prosecutions doubled between the 1850s and 1870s, and those convicted of murder were almost twice as likely to be executed as all others charged with murder, most wife-killing cases continued to be prosecuted as manslaughter, sometimes resulting in very short sentences.[71] Conversely, the rarity of husband-killers is openly acknowledged, a rarity earning one jealous husband-killer a place in London's wax museum. Compare the 78 trials for husband murder he found in England and Wales between 1841 and 1900 against at least 701 for wife murder and another 283 trials for 'wife manslaughter'. No less than 42 of 43 murder trials motivated by a legally married spouse's established adultery placed men – not women – in the dock while the defendants in another 23 trials where the main motive had been a legally married spouse's unsubstantiated belief in the other's adultery were all men.[72] Wiener's readers are left with no illusions about who was killing whom in Victorian Britain's domestic cases.

Importantly too, he highlights the English propensity to racialise impassioned wife-killers by distinguishing stiff upper-lipped Englishmen from more impulsive foreigners, especially the French. English wife-killers, he notes, were treated far more harshly than other killers, intolerance of intimate partner femicide increasingly noted as a marker of British identity and superiority. As he shows, late Victorian newspapers frequently complained of less civilised European and American judicial practices resulting in what the British saw as ridiculous acquittals of men and women. French juries in particular, they complained, 'shut their eyes to the law when sentiment is involved'. In a tone reminiscent of the early modern humoral theory I discussed in Chapter 2, one 1884 English newspaper reporting the case of a French woman acquitted of murdering her husband noted that she was from southern France. Those people, it said, are 'nearer akin in the warmth of their temperament to the Italians than to the people of Normandy or Eastern France'. Their revenging of 'private quarrels in this red-handed fashion' was to be condemned. Or, as a defence lawyer cited by Wiener puts it: 'it would be deplorable if we came to look upon passion and sentiment as any excuse whatever for crime, after the fashion of Frenchmen and Mexicans'. The evidence supports his claim that by the close of the century, national identity had become 'increasingly identified with "reasonableness" and "coolheadedness" and the killing of unfaithful wives stigmatised as "un-English". While Frenchmen, Italians, Spaniards, Greeks might be quick to anger and to act violently, 'good Englishmen were expected to resist such impulses'. As Wiener explains, these others were seen as 'misogynistic in a way that Englishmen were not, or at least no longer'. "Englishness" involved self-control and, more specifically, restraints upon violence against women. Crucially, wife killing had 'arguably become more symbolically significant to English life, law and even national identity than ever before'.[73]

In short, Wiener argues persuasively that with the treatment of women becoming a 'measure of civilisation', the law-abiding, self-disciplined and 'woman-respecting Englishman' emerged as 'a cultural ideal', one to be contrasted with the archetype of the impulsive foreign other. As we will continue to see, this propensity to dismiss impassioned 'domestic' killings as un-English still blinds many commentators to the fact that provocation by infidelity wife-killing cases are, historically and still today, precisely the English version of impassioned 'honour killing' that they like to project onto foreign 'others'. Impassioned crime, in their view, was always committed elsewhere, in 'certain other countries', by Frenchmen in the nineteenth century, by Italians or Moors in Shakespeare's England.[74]

Less convincingly, Wiener claims that with the 'protection of women' assuming a place at the heart of 'civilisation' – that is, 'Englishness' – the 'evocative figure of the female victim advanced to centre stage'.[75] She certainly does not move there in *Men of Blood*. Indeed, it soon becomes apparent that the sexed asymmetry of killers and killed acknowledged in the book is of no moment to an historian primarily concerned with the fate of men 'burdened' with unruly wives. He concedes that by the late Victorian era 'unfaithful-wife' murderers, as he calls them, were given 'more sympathy and were less likely to hang than other equally deliberate killers'. But he is still concerned that they were dealt with 'more harshly than has been assumed' as the century wore on, particularly if infidelity was not clearly established.[76]

It is this perceived injustice that *Men of Blood* sets out to rectify. Siding throughout with defendants against what are described throughout as drunken, nagging, 'shrewish or, worse, dissolute wives', Wiener hears in jury recommendations for mercy and public petitions for reprieves for condemned men a 'more democratic voice', one 'unafraid to point out lack of worldly understanding in august judges'. It is a voice 'speaking for ordinary husbands', a voice he concedes (in parenthesis) that 'hardly' spoke for their wives. Femicide victims are unnamed in a history filled with compassion for distraught men who, like Othello, committed 'unlucky deeds'. Without citing *Othello*, Wiener describes one as having loved 'not wisely but too well' a woman whose alleged adultery even he finds questionable. Men's unsubstantiated beliefs in 'their' women's adultery parade their way through a book that is seemingly indifferent to the truth of the allegations and in any event, concurring with juries that even a sniff of 'wifely' adultery was intolerable provocation to a man.[77] Sympathy flows freely for overwrought, 'put-upon' men convicted of murdering what are persistently described as 'even' drunken or otherwise debauched women. '*Even*' that unnamed, presumably derelict woman, '*even*' this nagging disposable woman, is written off into shameful oblivion, that oft-repeated adverb signalling utter disdain for men of blood's victims. Oblivious to testimony given again and again in the courts by women's neighbours disputing defendants' accusatory tales of 'provocative' wives, Wiener remains staunchly in the defendants' corner.

The deleterious effects of this pro-offender bias are most vividly on show in Wiener's article about the 'sad story' of George Hall. This was the condemned wife-killer who earned a reprieve from his death sentence following a petition campaign supported by 69,000 Birmingham inhabitants, described by their mayor as 'not easily excited' and having 'great reverence for the law'. Hall had attracted a public profile with an impassioned courtroom speech after the sentence of death was pronounced. Protesting that his wife, Sarah, had been unfaithful shortly after their wedding, he asked: 'Is there a heart of a man in a Christian land' who would 'sanction the condemnation of a poor man under such circumstances?' The speech caused women in the gallery to sob 'aloud'. Everyone was 'visibly affected'.[78] Wiener is too, explaining in a footnote that he did not title his article 'The sad story of George and Sarah Hall' – 'though we might see it that way' – out of respect for contemporary opinion. There was, he said, 'a marked absence of sympathy for Sarah, along with a lack of interest' in her point of view. The 'popular feeling' according to one newspaper report, was that she had 'got nothing more than she deserved', she having left George on the night after their wedding, returning to her mother's house. Wiener agrees. He acknowledges that little is known about Sarah and that she, like all femicide victims, was 'silenced before the criminal case opens'. But that is as close as this offender-centric historian gets to considering that her story, one he speculates could perhaps have become a 'feminist story' containing a 'possible "defence" for her shocking departure', was never told.[79]

Returning to *Men of Blood*, we find it concluding with what at first sight appears to be a puzzling final claim. It is that late twentieth-century feminist movements had much in common with the Victorian era 'civilising' mission to curb the violence of working-class men.[80] That's a conclusion nowhere directly foreshadowed in the book. In fact earlier, the Victorian moralist's approach to containing men's violence against their wives is marked as fundamentally different from that of the late twentieth-century feminist campaigner's focus on saving women's lives. The ahistorical conflation of late modern feminism with nineteenth-century Victorian moralism in the conclusion makes sense however, when it is recalled that *Men of Blood* was written from a perspective that valorises impassioned homicidal men and their excusatory defence narratives over 'punitive' judges and disposable 'nagging' wives. No wonder late modern feminists critical of lenient sentences handed down to wife-killers get tarred with the same brush as 'punitive' judges browbeating juries into returning murder verdicts and dispatching them to the gallows. Accordingly, it needs emphasising that taking a victim-centred approach, at least the kind advocated in my work, is not to endorse capital punishment. It is not to advocate the execution of men who execute their wives.[81] It is rather to insist with early nineteenth-century assault victim, Hannah Abbott, that women's lives matter and to stand with her in refusing to make excuses for men who assault and frequently kill them. Recall that Hannah did not want her assailant executed, but nor was she prepared to lie under oath that he was mentally impaired. He only pretended so. Did she not know that his life was at stake? She did. She did not want him executed, but nor was she prepared to excuse his near fatal attack.

So compelling is *Men of Blood*'s gripping tale of emotionally wrought men driven to distraction and homicidal rage by 'provocative' wives, so thorough its documentation of harsh judges browbeating reluctant juries into returning murder verdicts that it takes some time to clock the cultural work that it performs. Like all offender-centric histories, it works implicitly if not insidiously, to bolster the hegemonic view – still widely held today – that men burdened with 'bad wives' deserve law and society's compassion. For all its emphasis on the complex and often contradictory emotions aroused in and by 'crimes of passion', *Men of Blood* leaves in place the fiction that men have possessory rights over women, including a right to act on homicidal rage against 'provocative' ones. By contrast, the victim-centred approach I have taken reads the cases against the grain of that excusatory narrative. Highlighting the evidence of women who had lived in close proximity to the victims, I read it as a testimonial to their lives such as they were, lives lived in such abject terror of 'their' men that they fled their impoverished, alcohol-fuelled homes, sometimes returning to their families, sometimes co-habiting with other men, some vowing never to return and many paying the ultimate price. It is only through this victim-centred approach that their voices, silenced first, by their slaughter and second, by their killers' self-serving defence narratives, get heard.

Certainly, *Men of Blood*'s account of punitive judges pressing reluctant jurors into returning murder verdicts as a means of controlling working-class men is well supported by the evidence. Recall the judge telling Mary Vicary's killer that 'people of your class' need to be taught that they have no right to beat their wives. Moreover, petition-signing campaigns on behalf of condemned men that were supported by thousands, sometimes tens of thousands of people – women included, as Wiener points out – is strong testament to popular feeling. Clearly, many people felt that hanging a man for dispensing with what was portrayed as a dissolute, drunken and fickle wife was unduly harsh. Nevertheless, the strict law-adhering directions nineteenth-century English judges gave to juries can be read otherwise. Is it any wonder judges became increasingly cynical about defendants' inconsistent and frequently far-fetched provocation by infidelity tales? Witness testimony made it clear that in most instances, these were departure, not adultery cases. Some judges went so far as to express compassion for the victims, however 'degraded' they appeared to be. Along with Home Office officials, they understood the broader implications of indulging men's homicidal passions. Recall the Home Office rejecting a mercy petition in 1853 on the ground that the lives of many women were at stake. Herewith the beginnings of an approach that in querying men's excuses for killing women opened up a space for making femicide victims legible as a class of victims. Dismissing mere suspicion of infidelity as a ground for murder, rejecting any excuse for wife-murder short of finding a wife *in flagrante*, going so far as to question men's proprietary rights over women, Victorian judges anticipated by 150 years late twentieth-century reform movements that, in the name of the victims, would revolutionise the legal and cultural understanding of putatively impassioned homicide.

English Othellos

Notwithstanding strenuous judicial efforts to rein in defences to murder, the traditional notion that finding your wife in adultery is the worst form of provocation imaginable survived. No matter that such cases were extremely rare. No matter that Wiener found only one Victorian case – that of a miner who killed his 'notoriously unfaithful wife', Mary Ann Hazelhurst in 1887 – that fulfilled the formal legal requirement, 'ocular inspection', for reducing murder to manslaughter.[82] No matter how far the actual circumstances of wife-killings strayed from fulfilling that requirement, judges and juries alike held fast to the 'unwritten law' that killing an adulterous woman was not murder. Over the course of the nineteenth century, the 'lively' precedents that rendered femicide 'well done' as Shakespeare's Titus Andronicus maintained, morphed into the more circumscribed excusatory explanations tendered by defence counsel to reduce femicide to manslaughter. Still, enduring compassion for femicidal men meant that the traditional distinction between hot and cold-blooded killing along with all its deleterious cultural baggage, indicatively its casting of blameworthy women against emotionally taxed husbands loving not wisely but too well, remained in place. Not until the early twenty-first century would law reformers mount a serious challenge to the conceit that killing your wife while in a 'red mist' rage was less than murder.

Shakespeare's *Othello*, as I suggested in Chapter 2, can be read as querying that conceit. Othello himself comes to see his killing of his wife as murder. But was *Othello* read that way in nineteenth-century England? It makes a fleeting though revealing appearance in *Men of Blood*. Noting that Victorian productions either tended to 'purify' or 'primitivise' Othello, Wiener cites a review of an 1875 London performance by a 'fierce' Italian actor who plays the role as a 'barbarian whose instincts, savage and passionate are concealed behind a veneer of civilisation'. Wiener cites this as evidence that 'the figure of the jealous wife murderer was a powerfully repelling one for respectable Victorian audiences'. Yet somewhat contradictorily, he then claims that a wife's infidelity, 'it was generally agreed', was the 'worst kind of provocation'.[83] That's the problem with generalisation. It fails to register whose perspective is being universalised. Certainly, the reluctance of some 'respectable' all-male juries to convict wife-killers of murder no matter how implausible their tales of adulterous wives, indicates they did not view these defendants as especially repellent. Vigorous petition-signing campaigns designed to save them from the gallows also suggest they were less than abhorrent figures. But in many cases juries were quick to return murder verdicts. Hence the contradictory and ambivalent response to wife-killing, a response fuelled by conflicting emotions that were as intense as those unleashed in the killings themselves.

Othello is barely mentioned in the wife-killing trials. One instance though is in an obscure 1840 case where a three-month sentence was handed down to a man found guilty of manslaughter for killing his eighty-year-old-wife, Mary Mayo. He denied assaulting her but two witnesses who saw him knock her down testified to his violent temperament when drunk. As for Mary's denial that her husband had struck her, the judge cited *Othello* as authority for querying its plausibility:

> When Desdemona was discovered to be dying from the effects of the violence inflicted upon her by her husband, Shakespeare … represents the dying wife as falsely accusing herself instead of him … showing the opinion of one who knew human nature well, that the circumstance was not so improbable as the learned counsel had argued.[84]

That judge, like Shakespeare, knew the victim's fear and self-blame. It was however, in the reaction to the much-publicised 1863 *Townley* case that *Othello* made its most arresting entry. George Townley, a member of a respectable Manchester family, killed his fiancée, Bessie Goodwin, when she broke off their engagement, viewing her as if she were an adulterous wife. Medical witness Forbes Winslow testified that Townley had told him he had a 'perfect right to deal with her life' as he had with any other property and that he had killed her to 'recover and repossess himself of property which had been stolen from him'. The doctor had tried to explain to him 'the gross absurdity' of this viewpoint, but nothing could dissuade him from this 'very insane idea'. The judge told the jury that if his 'real motive' was jealousy or a desire for revenge that would be murder. After all, these were 'the very passions which the law required men to control'. What, he asked, 'would be the consequences to society if men were to say to every woman who treated them in that way that she should die, and carried out these views by cutting her throat?' The defendant's claim that he exercised 'the same power over a wife as he could lawfully exercise over a chattel' was 'the conclusion of a man who had arrived at results different from those generally arrived at and contrary to the laws of God and man'.[85] But was that conclusion really so different? Didn't English law regard a wife's infidelity as an invasion of property? Certainly, nineteenth-century courts steadfastly refused to extend men's proprietary rights to women who were not their wives. Nevertheless, those rights have continued to underscore excusatory defence narratives proffered in intimate partner femicide cases to this day.

Townley was convicted of murder but reprieved. His escape from the gallows was cited by George Hall's supporters the following year. Compared with Townley, they said, Hall had 'every claim' to the Home Office's merciful consideration, 'and few can doubt which of the two would be the more dangerous character' if both were set free. Obviously, it was Townley. Hall, by contrast, had been 'wrought up to desperation by injuries that might have maddened the best and calmest of men'. Who could 'read the tale of this domestic tragedy without a sentiment of compassion for the murderer'? Hall's 'pathetic' courtroom appeal after his conviction had 'reached the hearts of many who were not present at the trial', tens of thousands signing the petition for his reprieve.[86] Townley's case was seen as quite different, a contributor to *The Times* going so far as to imagine Othello in his place with Forbes Winslow as a witness in his defence. He could just see what Dr Winslow would say of Othello:

> The rapid ebb and flow of passion, the incoherent utterances, the sudden revulsion which led the Moor to seize Iago by the throat, but above all, the utter perversion of moral sentiment which he manifested even after the death of Desdemona, would doubtless be quoted as decided symptoms of mental aberration. All the ravages of the green-eyed monster on a fiery but affectionate nature, all the inconsistencies of one 'who dotes yet doubts, suspects yet strongly loves' would probably suggest to the pathologist the idea of that curious disease which has been called 'insanity of the feelings'.[87]

The doctor would then insist that there was only one way a man 'tortured by the agonies of remorse and self-convicted of smothering the most devoted of wives' could say he did 'naught in hate, but all in honour'. There was only one way he could speak calmly of himself as 'one not easily jealous' when he knew his jealousy had been kindled by the 'lightest breath of suspicion'. It was to say he had become 'incapable of reasoning correctly on a moral subject'.

But nothing, *The Times* commentator continued, could save Othello from being seen as a murderer 'in the eyes of the English law'. Any compassion for him as the 'victim of Iago's diabolical arts' would not save him from 'a just doom'. Were it otherwise, women's lives would be at the mercy of passionate lovers 'and dramatists would not have to borrow their plots from the romance of distant lands and bygone ages'. True, Dr Winslow's testimony for Townley might have tended to acquit Othello on the ground of insanity. Indeed, the two cases were analogous save for the alarming fact that Townley was an Englishman, 'a man of very quiet and refined manners, a good linguist and an accomplished musician'. But anything less than a murder verdict for Townley and for Othello, would have been 'a grievous miscarriage of justice'. How could the defendant not be criminally responsible 'simply because' he felt he had been so wronged as to 'justify all that he had done'? One might feel compassion for 'the nervous excitement produced by a cross in love on a desponding temperament', but not forgiveness. Law must not be made 'subtle or flexible enough to exclude an act like this from the definition of murder'.[88]

How fascinating to read this cynical view of an imaginary medical expert trying to exonerate a defendant on the ground of 'insanity of the feelings'. That Townley was a 'refined' Englishman who had succumbed to passion, and not some foreigner, had only made matters worse. In all other respects he was just like the perversely over-emotional, amoral outsider that Shakespeare created. He deserved the same fate. Otherwise, women's lives would be endangered, leaving them at the mercy of 'impassioned' men.

•••••

The offender-centric historian interprets the increasingly dim view taken of wife-killers by nineteenth-century criminal courts as indicative of a punitive trend on the part of a harsh judiciary bent on controlling violent working-class men. Alternatively, I read it as a highpoint of judicial resistance to the notion that impassioned men who kill their wives should get away with murder. Over the next few decades, judges would continue holding the line that wife-killing, however impassioned, was murder. But mid-twentieth-century reforms to the law of murder would open the way for trivial provocations, indicatively, a wife's allegedly taunting words, to secure a manslaughter conviction for her killer. Not until the early twenty-first century would a new wave of law reformers insist that sympathy swing back from impassioned men to their slaughtered victims. Not until then would the voices of the victims, only faintly audible in the courtroom and in conventional legal history, finally make an impression on the English law of murder.

Chapter 4

Passions contained – 'Othello's crime was murder and nothing else'

Villain, be sure to prove my love a whore,
Be sure of it, give me the ocular proof

Othello 3.3. 362–3

O perjured woman, thou dost stone my heart
And makest me call what I intend to do
A murder, which I thought a sacrifice!
I saw the handkerchief.

Othello 5.2. 63–66

Introduction

There was a time when impassioned homicide was called murder in England and Wales. Chapter 4 continues the story of the English version of a 'crime of passion' through the early decades of the twentieth century when passion's roller-coaster ride as a legally mandated excuse for murder was at one of its lowest ebbs. What was a low point for passion's excusatory prowess was a high point of marked judicial intolerance of wife-killers at this time. Keeping a close check on what constituted mitigating provocation, judges steadfastly refusing to extend it beyond the classic case of finding a wife in adultery. As a consequence of their concerted attempts to rein in men's excuses for killing their wives and women partners, executions of femicidal men proceeded apace. Not that all impassioned attacks on women involved allegations of infidelity. In the first half of the twentieth century, men fell into homicidal rages against women who drank too much or asked them to stop drinking; 'nagged' them, talked to other men or refused to hand over money.[1] On the other hand, defence narratives about 'unfaithful' women goading men to kill them were not confined to capital murder cases. After all, cuckoldry, real or imagined, was too potent a transgression to be so contained, and 'infidelity' tales made their way into wounding and attempted murder cases.

Chapter 4 forgoes conversations with historians in order to focus more intently on the players inside the criminal courts. It listens to how they framed

DOI: 10.4324/9781003301974-5

intimate partner femicide and the homicidal rage said to have ignited it. Where possible, the victims' voices are inserted into the mix of courtroom discourses. Once again, the defendants are unnamed, occasionally appearing in footnotes to identify cases. As for the inevitable, impossible to evade question about the sexed distribution of defendants and victims in impassioned homicide cases, suffice it to say that, as in previous centuries, very few women killed their male partners in twentieth-century Britain. Moreover, those who killed unfaithful men were rare indeed, Ruth Ellis being a classic case of the exception proving the rule. Appellate and lower court judges were only too well aware of the sexed asymmetry of domestic cases, framing their rulings on 'provocation by infidelity' exclusively in terms of a suspicious male defendant. Not until mid-century would a court consider the prospect that, in an age of purported marital equality, a woman might consider killing an unfaithful husband. Well might she have considered it, but she rarely followed through. Husband-killing remained a rare occurrence, a footnote to the main event that concerns this book, namely, the excusatory force of hot-blooded homicide which is committed overwhelmingly by men against women.[2]

'Frenzies', 'fits of passion', 'impulses of rage'

As we have seen, nineteenth-century wife-killers were convicted of murder if all that they had to rely on was an 'innocent suspicion'. Judges were adamant: that was no warrant for murder. Juries did not always agree, frequently hedging murder verdicts with recommendations to mercy. These pleas and petitions for reprieves had a mixed success rate, executions of wife-killers increasing exponentially from the 1870s well into the 1890s. Approximately half of the men hanged in England and Wales between 1900 and 1950 had murdered wives or women partners.[3] The killing context remained the same as before – dire poverty and alcohol-fuelled violence that sometimes forced women to turn to prostitution to supplement their families' meagre earnings. Women who fled back to their families, or sometimes to a new man, enraged men. So did women who stayed, but annoyed them by 'nagging', not handing over money or staying out late. The killers' tales that the homicides were accidents, committed in self-defence or by someone else were so utterly implausible, flying in the face of witness testimony and their own prior admissions to neighbours or police, that most were convicted of capital murder. Convicted men were rarely reprieved, except occasionally on the basis of their age. Yet men as young as nineteen were executed, juries' recommendations for mercy failing to win them reprieves. Such was the condemnatory attitude of judges and Home Office officials towards femicidal men in the first half of the century.

Outside the courts, attitudes towards men who unburdened themselves of their wives while in a homicidal fury remained in flux. How the killing narratives played out, how killers and victims were portrayed in the courts, the press, mercy petitions and Home Office papers bears a close analysis. I begin with a study of passion's progress in cases decided in the first ten years of the new century. In that decade, 79 or approximately half of the total number of men hanged in England and Wales killed their wives or women partners.[4] Another three directed their homicidal rage at their wives or other female relatives, collateral damage in the rage against women partners. But even these killers could evoke sympathy. One man who suspected his wife of adultery, killed his five-year-old daughter saying she 'can't be brought up a prostitute now … I did it to save my old woman from putting her in bed with other men'. While convicting him of murder, the jury recommended him to mercy at his 1901 Old Bailey trial 'on account of the somewhat honourable motive he had of saving the little girl from a life of prostitution'.[5] Somewhat honourable or not, he hanged.

In 1905, a man was sentenced to death for almost decapitating his adult daughter, Elizabeth Rickus, when she refused to disclose her mother's whereabouts after her parents' separation. She had tried to calm him down by giving him cups of tea, but to no avail. Saying 'revenge is sweet' on being told she was dead hardly assisted his defence, the jury finding him guilty of murder in less than an hour. Yet he was strongly recommended to mercy on account of the provocation 'laterally from his family', namely their refusal to help him find his wife.[6] The judge disagreed, seeing no ground for sympathy, and the Home Office declined to intervene. The same year, a man killed Catherine Ballard, blaming her for influencing her daughter to break off her engagement with him. He struck her with a poker, then cut her throat after hearing she had said 'things against me'.[7] This time, there was no recommendation for mercy.

Of the 79 men hanged for killing women partners in this period, 51 were unmarried to their victims, most of whom were young women who paid the ultimate price for breaking off engagements or relationships with their killers. Twenty-four-year-old Margaret Morrison was shot dead in Liverpool by her former fiancé in 1900 after a four-year engagement. Enraged that she had ended the relationship after his first attempt to shoot her, he screamed at her mother, 'No other man will walk out with her. I will take her life'. The jury returned a murder verdict but recommended him to mercy. Thirty thousand signatures attached to a petition to reprieve his death sentence failed to save him from the gallows. They do however, testify to sharp differences of opinion about the extenuating circumstances attending intimate partner femicides.[8] When 19-year-old Edith Poole broke off her engagement, her former fiancé cut her throat 'in a fit of madness'. The jury convicted him of murder but strongly recommended him to mercy at his Old Bailey trial 'on account of the excited state of his mind, his previous good character and his youth'. It was to no avail.[9] Eighteen-year-old Sophia Lovell's former fiancé cut her throat when he saw her in a London street with another man after she broke off their engagement. He meant to kill her, and his motive was clear – 'If I don't have her no one else shall. I mean swinging for her'.[10] He did.

When Catherine Garritty broke off her engagement, he strangled her. Her devastated mother broke down in the dock during her testimony. Catherine, who was just 17, worked as a card-room operative, was 'bright, lively and healthy' and had left the house singing on the fatal day. Her killer denied 'the murder of a sweetheart', as newspapers headlined the case, until shortly before his execution, the jury's recommendation to mercy on account of his age and mercy petitions having failed to save him.[11] They were also to no avail for the 19-year-old former boyfriend of 16-year-old Clara Hannaford. He cut her throat when he saw her out with another man on a Plymouth street but claimed he did it 'on the spur of the moment'. It was not premeditated 'in any way'. Clara's killing, which caused a great stir in Plymouth, where a crowd of nearly 5000 people attended her funeral, became a great test case for mitigating passion. In court, her mother, who had been convicted of running a brothel, testified that she had objected to her daughter keeping company with the defendant because he would not work. Her daughter had 'more fear than fondness' for him. The defence tried to make the most of her criminal conviction, casting aspersions on how Clara had been 'brought up'. But to applause the prosecutor stated that 'no matter how immoral the surroundings might be, that did not justify murder'.[12]

Then as now, the most common motive for impassioned homicide was a woman's departure from a marriage or live-in relationship. In the early twentieth century, that was no excuse to kill. As most of the defendants were not married to their victims, they were deprived of the customary right of a husband to plead provocation by an unfaithful wife and were duly convicted of murder. When Amelia Wood moved in with the man who was to kill her in Gateshead she continued to work as a prostitute. This angered him. A few days before the murder they went to a police station, her to ask for protection, him to say he wanted her to stop her line of work. Police told him that as she was not his wife, she could do as she pleased. Could she? Not in his view. Her leaving him was the last straw: 'I killed her, I loved her and I'll swing for it'. He did, Amelia's 'loose behaviour' not extenuating the crime and his defence of a temporary derangement of mind not convincing the jury.[13]

Not that husbands' possessory rights over their wives automatically saved them from the gallows. What we might call their 'adultery light' killing scenarios – outbursts of rage at wives who spoke to another man or demonstrated otherwise suspicious conduct – were simply too far removed from the classic excusatory tale of finding a wife *in flagrante* for juries to find extenuating circumstances. The reality was that in almost every case of wife-killers executed in the early twentieth century, the woman had left to escape his violence. Sarah Pachett was one. After leaving her husband who had been convicted twice of assaulting her, she wrote to say she would not return unless he found her a home and gave up going to public houses. He denied strangling her in a field near Lincoln, but witnesses heard him say he had 'done a murder'; another that he would 'give himself up for manslaughter'. A large crowd outside the court at Lincoln Castle rushed for seats, two balconies packed with women watching on as the jury convicted him of murder after only 12 minutes of deliberation.[14]

When 22-year-old Eliza Marsh's husband appeared in court charged with her murder in Chesterfield, her father challenged his story that he had received 'great provocation' from an idle and intemperate wife. On the contrary, his daughter had often been seen with black eyes and neighbours used to call him to come and assist when her husband was ill-treating her. The jury was unimpressed with the defence argument that he had only used the razor in 'the heat of passion' after 'great provocation' such as her throwing things. It took just 20 minutes to find him guilty of murdering what one reporter called a 'perfectly faithful wife'.[15] When Charlotte Jones left her husband and took out a summons against him in Wolverhampton, he begged her to return. She refused, so he shot her. Rejecting his self-defence tale, the jury took just ten minutes to return a murder verdict.[16]

The only motive Margaret Bouldry's husband could supply for killing her was that after separating from him, she had written to him seeking support for their children. Angered by her letter, he went to her lodgings near Hythe, assaulted her landlord who tried to intervene and, 'like a wild beast', cut Margaret's throat. Calling it a case of cold-blooded murder, the prosecutor said that her 'simple letter' was in 'no way' provocative. Found guilty of murder, the jury recommended him to mercy on the ground that he acted 'in a moment of frenzy'. The judge agreed he was in a 'state of passion', one that might have excusatory force at the Home Office.[17] But he too hanged as did Elizabeth Dyson's killer, a married man with whom she had been having an affair. He offered various explanations for cutting her throat in Stafford in 1902. It was a suicide pact. She annoyed him. He was insane or at least not responsible for his actions because she had provoked him into 'a frenzy'. None prevailed.[18]

These were indeed frenzied killings, the sort conventionally characterised as 'hot-blooded'. The killers' rage was palpable, the victims' bodies mutilated by multiple stab wounds, kicks, throat cutting with axes and hatchets clear testimony to that. But when the killings were so far removed from the classic 'crime of passion' scenario, there was little lawyers could do to save enraged men from the gallows. Lucy Wilson's lover, a married man, said she had demanded he leave his wife and insulted him, so he killed her. His rage continued in the courtroom where he harangued the judge, even ordering him to take off the black cap when he passed the death sentence. This behaviour caused a 'sensation' in court, one reporter explaining that passion 'plays strange tricks with some people', producing in them 'an irresponsible condition'. That he had a violent temper and had become angry when Lucy swore at him, hearing 'a ringing in his ears like a storm', was hardly a viable defence. Having a 'bad temper' was simply no excuse, the jury returning a murder verdict without leaving the box.[19]

Three of the six men awaiting execution at Newgate in August 1900 were wife-killers. One of the victims was 32-year-old Catherine Irwin. She had left him and was supporting herself and her three children. Annoyed that she had started seeing another man, he stabbed her to death. After all, he was 'passionately fond of her'. The jury took just a few minutes to find him guilty of murder, though strongly recommending him to mercy.[20] Another in this batch of condemned wife-killers was a Jamaican who, acting on an obscure motive related to a family dispute, cut the throat of his 19-year-old wife, Pauline Lacey. The newspaper headline, 'A black man murders his white wife', surely reminded readers of *Othello*, he performing that role admirably at his trial, 'fervently' protesting his love for his wife, 'almost shrieking in his passionate appeal to the Bench and deeply moving those present in the crowded court'. The eyes of many were 'dim with tears'.[21]

Tellingly however, the romanticised notion of a 'transport of passion' favoured by defence lawyers in late eighteenth and nineteenth centuries barely featured in defence narratives now. Nor did 'heat of passion', the defence mounted for Mary Donovan's husband being a rare exception. He said he killed her while in a drunken 'heat of passion' bordering on insanity when she attacked him. Indicted for murder at the Old Bailey, he was found guilty of manslaughter and received a 12-year sentence.[22] By contrast, killing while in a so-called 'fit of passion', a concept that now made its way into defence narratives, did not have the same traction as 'heat of passion'. Nancy Price's common law husband claimed to have killed her in 'a fit of passion' when he saw her talking to another man near Chesterfield. When he interrupted the judge sentencing him to death to say 'it was all due' to seeing Mary with another man, the judge rebuked him, saying he was 'the last man' to complain of the victim's 'immorality'. Witness testimonies to his previous temper tantrums and threats to kill her cancelled out his as an extenuating passion.[23] Margaret Chisholm, a 20-year-old married woman, was killed by another boarder in a house in Seaham, 'Murdered for love' as one headline put it. He confessed to having strangled her 'in a fit of mad passion'. But that could never amount to an exculpatory defence, he having no proprietary rights over her. No matter that he had been driven to a desperate act by her 'handsome face' or that she was the only woman he had ever loved.[24]

Passion taking the form of insane 'sudden revulsions', 'explosive impulses' or violent tempers did not fare well in early twentieth-century courts either. Hannah Shea was living in a workhouse in Tredegar, Wales with her four surviving children when her partner, from whom she was separated, cut her throat when they met on a nearby street. His motive was obscure but was thought to be 'passion arising from drink and a violent temper' and suspicion she was seeing other men. His insanity plea, based on a claim he suffered from 'delirium tremens', failed. So did a petition for his reprieve, it being noted that his only delusion was that he could not sleep.[25] When Maud Luen rejected a man's advances in June 1903, he told her, 'Maud, you are the only girl I love', and cut her throat in Colchester. His lawyer offered a plea of insanity based on both his family history and his lack of motive for his 'sudden repulsion of feeling' towards Maud. The judge could not have been more scathing. Most murderers, he said, 'had some taint of insanity about them, usually brought about by drink', especially in the case of murderers. If a man were to be excused simply because his great grandmother had been in an asylum, 'where were they going to stop?' That would lead to a 'dangerous state of affairs'. The jury agreed, taking 13 minutes to return a murder verdict with a recommendation that an inquiry be made into his mental state.[26]

The judge was even more dismissive of the insanity defence presented for Jane Haywood's husband later that year. He killed her at a quarry in Leominster. He claimed he had a head injury that exacerbated his mental illness. A medical witness from the local asylum agreed he was 'mad at times' and not in full possession of his senses. His feebleness of mind associated with alcohol intoxication had led to 'a sudden and explosive impulse on receiving some trifling provocation', the victim being given to 'nagging'. The judge did not hold back, telling the jury not to trouble themselves with 'nice questions and distinctions raised by medical men'. They should use their common sense. After all, 'plenty of lunatics knew when they were committing sin' and they needed to be held accountable. The defendant was fully conscious of his actions. He was probably drunk but drunkenness was no excuse. The ferocity of his assault on his wife could not be pleaded in his exculpation, otherwise it would mean the greater the crime, the greater the chance of escaping with impunity. The jury agreed, taking little time in bringing in a verdict of murder.[27] Alice Foster's fiancé was depressed about being unemployed. When Alice accused him of being lazy, taking him to task for not getting work, he shot her dead in Northampton. A defence of temporary insanity was based on his family history, the absence of a motive and his 'fondness for the girl'. He had killed 'the person he appeared to have loved best in the world'. The jury returned a murder verdict without leaving the box.[28] A defence of 'impulsive insanity' presented for Jane Hirst's killer said to suffer from 'delirium tremens', also failed. After bludgeoning her to death with a hatchet at a house in Rotherham, he told police: 'It is murder I think'. As it turned out, he was right.[29]

Passions ignited by 'provocative' women rather than by impulsive insanity did not always mitigate murder either. Sophia Hepworth's killer said he had received 'great provocation' during a violent alcohol-fuelled struggle. She had wrongly accused him of infidelity. So he knifed her to death in their home in Gosport. According to the police report, the numerous stab wounds looked 'more like a murder committed with great passion rather than with deliberation'. Convicted of murder, he was strongly recommended to mercy because of the alleged provocation. The judge refused to support that application, and, despite a suggestion in the police report that Sophia 'probably did much to earn' her ill treatment, the Home Office declined to interfere. There had been little hope of a reprieve, one newspaper reporting that the circumstances were so 'revolting' that 'even the sentimentalists' who petitioned for one found 'but a scanty following'.[30] An 'impulse of rage' was said to have compelled 16-year-old Emily Tredea's former fiancé to choke her to death at her home near Penzance. The prosecution argued he had harboured thoughts of killing her from the moment she ended the relationship. Verdict: murder. The judge criticised the jury's mercy recommendation, saying it was a brutal murder and that the law should take its course. By contrast, the police report called it a borderline case where a reprieve might be granted as there was no premeditation such as the procuring of a weapon. Also, he had a good character. There was no reprieve, the Home Office seconding the judge's view that whatever they were called, 'impulses of rage', 'temper tantrums' or 'fits of passion', they were no excuse for murder.[31]

Lawyering up – framing excusable homicidal rage

Defending early twentieth-century wife-killers was an uphill task. So many had killed in front of witnesses or been overheard making threats to kill. One even gave himself up to police for 'murdering my wife', as Elizabeth Marsland's husband put it, after cutting her throat in Oldham in 1902. They had been married for four months, but she had left for a week, which 'exasperated' him. A quarrel secured her fate and, as it turned out, his, the jury rejecting his defence that he was not responsible at the time.[32] Swindon barmaid Esther Swinford was shot at the hotel where she worked by her former fiancé when she ended their relationship. He said he had no intention of harming her. It was an accident. He only meant to frighten her. He loved her. He could not explain why he had written 'the curse of my life' on her photo.[33] Clara Howell's killer had mistreated her for years according to their neighbours before he killed her at their Leeds home after a quarrel. Telling his fellow workmen he had 'done the tart in' and 'left her as dead as a mackerel' left little room for a viable defence. The jury took half an hour to return a murder verdict, the judge calling it 'the last of a long series of brutalities' inflicted on 'that unhappy woman'.[34] His appeal failed. Drunkenness was no excuse for murder. None of these killers had excusatory passions. They all hanged.

Quick verdicts with no recommendations to mercy were not uncommon for femicidal men who killed without reasonable cause. In 1906, 22-year-old Jane Gamble left a man because of his cruelty, refusing to return. He stabbed her in a Nottingham street three weeks later. The jury took 15 minutes to convict him of murder.[35] Another jury took five minutes to find Mary Ann Rees' killer guilty of murder. He had told police he had thrown her down a disused furnace in Merthyr Tydfil, Wales, when she threatened to report him for living off her earnings from prostitution.[36] The man who stabbed 19-year-old Dorothy Lawrence to death at her Welsh village home because she refused to kiss him, was a lost cause. When she left him six months earlier, he had threatened to kill her unless she returned, later confessing to have made up his mind to kill her then. The judge agreed with the murder verdict: it was 'one of the most cruel and atrocious stories ever told in a Court of Law'. The condemned man did not think so, declaring shortly before his execution that: 'Girls that get tired of a man after promising to marry him are better dead than alive'.[37] That was not the view taken in the early twentieth-century courts.

When all else failed, when garrulous femicidal men sealed their own fate by killing women in front of witnesses, immediately confessing to the police or spouting far-fetched contradictory stories that made defending them impossible, their only hope was a reprieve from the inevitable death sentence. Accordingly, defence lawyers followed up jury recommendations for mercy for condemned men by organising petitions for reprieves. Reprising the defendant's story of the victims' 'great provocation' was the tried-and-true reprieve strategy as illustrated in three 1901 cases. After his conviction for murder at his Old Bailey trial, Florence Irving's killer was strongly recommended to mercy on account of her 'great provocation'. She had left him for another man. Her own father, seeing her arm-in-arm with the other man, had told the defendant he should give her a black eye.[38] This killer won his reprieve. So did Barbara Price's husband, a man with a 'jealous disposition' who had made previous threats to kill her. He shot her when she returned to their London home after living with another man because she had started taunting him. The jury felt he had suffered 'great provocation' – ramped up to 'extreme provocation' by the Home Secretary who granted him a reprieve. After all, the man said he had been 'compelled' to do it, and the judge had agreed with the jury that he had been 'more or less goaded' to the crime.[39] In the third case, Ellen Kirk, the mother of six children, had been nursing a farmer's wife in Boston, Lincolnshire when her jealous husband cut her throat. He thought she was having an affair with the farmer. His defence argued he was not responsible for her death because he suffered from a delusion that she was unfaithful. Sentenced to death, he was reprieved when a further medical examination concluded that he was insane.[40]

Of course, a reprieve was not much of a win, some condemned men preferring execution to a life sentence.[41] Their lawyers, most of whom were appointed under the Poor Prisoner's Defence Act which gave briefs to those with under seven years' practice, had to learn fast how to frame murder as manslaughter. To that end they began calling for 'justifiable' manslaughter verdicts for crimes committed, if not during a 'transport of passion', hardly ever mentioned now, then at least while in an 'excited state' occasioned by a provocative wife. This could be difficult, the alleged provocations leading men to kill wives being so far removed from finding them in adultery. But lawyers were up for the challenge, their occasional success stories providing important indices of conflicting contemporary views of passion's mitigating force.

The 20-year sentence handed down to the man who in 1902 battered his wife, Elizabeth Crumpton, to death in Oldbury caused great consternation there. A petition, signed by over 600 workmen and 'all classes in the town' eager to testify to his excellent character, stated that he had acted 'under great provocation'. They hoped for 'the greatest possible mercy'. After all, she had sworn at him when he asked for his supper, annoyed him by asking for a separation order and hit him. Such provocation to a 'peaceable man', his counsel argued, would justify a manslaughter verdict. Not in the view of the judge. No provocation, by words, signs or gestures would warrant that. Furthermore, aside from that 'one exceptional case' – no one seeming to notice just how exceptional the finding a wife in adultery exception was – 'nothing but physical injury' was sufficient provocation. And even then, the injury must be such as to 'put a reasonable man out of his ordinary temper and make it not unnatural that in hot blood he should kill his assailant'. Then, in an about turn, he told the jury that if they believed Elizabeth's blows had carried her killer's temper 'beyond its usual balance', they would be 'justified' in returning a manslaughter verdict. They did. But as it was a borderline case, only 'a thin line' divided it from murder. He thought a 20-year sentence warranted.[42]

That sentence was much debated in the press. Some felt that it was 'straining justice to the breaking point' to place Elizabeth's killer on the same level as 'the ruffianly wife-beater'. She was a 'drunken, aggravating woman' who 'harried him with insults and blows beyond the limits of human endurance'. Surely a sentence of 10–15 years was more appropriate. Others, noting the evidence that the crime was premeditated, worried that a shorter sentence could lead to a 'dangerous doctrine', namely that:

> If a woman's intemperance and waspish tongue were sufficient to excuse her husband of murdering her, or even materially to reduce the gravity of his crime, we are afraid it would lead to a terrible increase in the number of domestic tragedies.[43]

As we shall see the all-important question of the 'sufficiency' of a woman's waspish tongue for reducing the gravity of femicide would lead, if not to an increase in 'domestic tragedies', then to a massive increase in manslaughter verdicts for wife-killers in the second half of the twentieth century. As for Elizabeth Crumpton's killer, disquiet over his sentence continued until 1907 when the Home Office reduced it to 12 years on receiving a memorial with 1000 signatures attached urging that a sentence of 20 years was far too long for a wife-killer acting under 'great provocation'.[44]

At law, provocation was only available as a defence to murder, but it was also raised in trials of men charged with manslaughter or attempted murder. Take the case of the man who went to strike his daughter, thinking she should be doing housework, but accidently killed his wife, Diana Summers. Charged with manslaughter, he was found guilty but was sentenced to just six months with hard labour, his lawyer arguing convincingly that a head injury rendered him more susceptible to an 'excited state' when he became violent.[45] Harriet Smyth's husband kicked her to death during a drunken altercation and was charged with her manslaughter. He was found guilty at his Old Bailey trial but recommended to mercy on the ground of her provocation. The judge was unsure how far to act on that recommendation. He felt it would be 'very mischievous to pass over lightly' the defendant's brutal attack. Had she died from 'simply being knocked down in a moment of temper produced by her aggravation', he could better have appreciated the jury's view.[46] He decided a four-year sentence was in order.

As with murder cases, sentences for men found guilty of lesser crimes depended on an assessment of the victim's triggering conduct and her relationship to him. Consider two cases heard at the Old Bailey in January 1902. In the first, a man was charged with the manslaughter of his wife Harriet Holmes. Her provocation? She had accused *him* of adultery which he denied. While the judge felt there was nothing to 'justify the fatal blow', the killer's 'ebullition of temper' caused by her false accusation was understandable. So he sentenced him to 14 days' imprisonment without hard labour.[47] In the second case, a man appeared charged with shooting with intent to murder. He had shot a married woman, Twickenham barmaid Annie Walklett, because she refused to receive a present from him. He was found guilty but strongly recommended to mercy. Interpreting the jury's recommendation to mean they believed the defendant had been 'actuated' by a mitigating 'mad infatuation' – after all, he was said to be 'exceedingly fond of her' – the judge sentenced him to four years imprisonment.[48]

Later that year, 21-year-old wife Ellen Barnaby's husband was charged with her murder in London. His defence argued self-defence or, alternatively, that he was mad and wholly irresponsible for the crime, both defences framed around his history of epileptic fits.[49] Recall from Chapter 2 Iago's claim that Othello fitted when confronted with 'evidence' of his wife's infidelity – 'My lord has fallen into an epilepsy/This is his second fit'.[50] Might epilepsy be raised in Othello's defence were he tried for murdering Desdemona today? It was in the Barnaby case, a Brixton prison medical officer testifying that the defendant's epileptic fits made him 'excitable'. The doctor had read a German medical report that epileptics could sometimes be 'liable to sexual passions' if their victims laughed at them. Of course, that was an extreme view – 'Continental views on the sexual question are much stronger than ours'. But certainly, if the defendant's wife laughed at him that could irritate him and if she frightened him, he might believe he was acting in self-defence. Buttressed by this expert evidence, the defence argued that the defendant was a temperate and hard-working man of good character who suffered from fits *and* from a quarrelsome and aggressive wife. The jury acquitted him of murder. While agreeing with the verdict, the judge felt the jury had taken a rather merciful view. There was nothing to 'justify' saying he had acted in self-defence. There had only been 'something of a scuffle' and perhaps some provocation from the wife such as throwing things at him that produced an 'angry impulse' leading him to stab her to death. On the other hand, he was 'an affectionate son, a good workman, steady and sober', albeit afflicted with epileptic fits tending to make him more excitable. Nevertheless, the public needed protection against the use of knives, the Swedish knife used in this case being 'a most deadly weapon'. If only these foreign knives had not been introduced into England. Even making every allowance for the victim's 'aggravating' behaviour – she had treated him unkindly – he had to take the crime seriously. A five-year prison sentence was in order.[51]

Raising the spectre of a delusional, fitting-prone Othello type was not a sure-fire defence. Epilepsy was raised again at the 1903 Old Bailey trial of the man who killed 18-year-old Fulham laundress, Brigid McQuaid, because she broke off their engagement. He was said to suffer from fits, possibly epilepsy, that could lead a man to 'absolutely lose control and consciousness'. Unconvinced, the jury returned a murder verdict, though strongly recommending him to mercy on account of his youth and previous good character – previous, that is, to killing Brigid. He won his reprieve.[52] From the killer's perspective of course, a manslaughter verdict was vastly preferable but difficult to obtain, the victim's provocation not usually being sufficient at law to warrant one. But this would change as their lawyers, still in the early stages of honing their craft, would continue to build a picture of the compelling figure of the unruly provocative woman who could depose a balanced mind in an otherwise peaceable man.

Hot-blooded passion rules OK

Tales of provocative women were not confined to femicide cases. They also cropped up in assault cases. Consider, for example three cases heard at the Old Bailey on the same day in June 1905. In the first, a man pleaded guilty to grievous bodily harm and was sentenced to three years' imprisonment. He had kicked his partner, Ada Horkley, in the mouth 'in an excess of passion during a sudden quarrel'. Calling it a brutal assault, the judge railed against the 'blot on our law' that the punishment inflicted on men who ill-treated their wives and women partners 'was often less than if they had committed some trifling felony'. Against those who thought it 'more serious to steal a sixpence or six pounds than it was to half kill a woman', he insisted it was past time to put a stop to this brutality. Yet compare the sentence he handed down in the very next case he presided over that day – that of a man charged with the manslaughter of his infant son. He had killed him accidently when throwing a boot at his wife. Notwithstanding evidence that he had a history of drunken violence against his wife, described in court as 'a frail woman', the jury found him guilty but 'under great provocation'. She had laughed at him and called him names. He escaped with a 12-month sentence with hard labour. In the third case, a man was indicted for wounding his wife, Charlotte Capon, with intent to murdering her. He claimed Charlotte, who had been living in the Lewisham workhouse since she separated from him, had 'misconducted herself' with his brother in 'a filthy manner'. He was found guilty and sentenced to five years' imprisonment, the judge taking account of medical testimony that his mind was 'not as strong and well-balanced' as others.[53]

Returning to completed femicide cases, how well did men's homicidal rage at allegedly dissolute women hold up as an excuse for murder in the first decade of the new century? If verdicts and sentences for manslaughter are any guide, opinion was still in flux. Consider two cases decided in 1907. In March a man was charged with murdering his wife, Elizabeth Newsholme, in Bradford. She had left him and was living with another man. She did return, but continued her relationship with the other man, prompting her husband to kill her. He said she had 'driven' him to it as 'she's bothered with another man for years'. So he had his revenge and would swing for it. Not if his counsel could help it. Here was a man so 'goaded' by her extra-marital relationship that he was 'driven out of his self-control', striking her while in 'a fit of frenzy'. It was a jealous or 'mad state of mind'. The jury returned a manslaughter verdict but the 20-year sentence suggests that the judge, who said there was no evidence of legally acceptable provocation, took a sterner view.[54] Judge and jury were more in sync in the case of the man charged with murdering his 18-year-old 'girl wife', Maria Jones, in Bermondsey in 1907. They had married a few months earlier because she was pregnant. The marriage was troubled from the start. Witnesses had heard Maria's mother, who put them up at her house, calling him a 'lazy bastard'. He said they were both always 'jawing' him, 'chipping' him about being out of work. Also, Maria wanted to leave him. So she had 'brought it on herself'. Praising the jury's 'merciful' verdict clearing him of murder – in which the prosecutor appeared to have concurred – the judge sentenced him to ten years for manslaughter.[55] An even more merciful view of a wife-killer was taken in another Old Bailey 'nagging' case. Sarah Leaning was said to have a 'nasty temper'. Charged with her manslaughter in 1908, her husband said she had abused him and threatened him with scissors. When she 'started nagging' he had threatened to 'knock her b...head off' but that was only to stop her quarrelling. Found guilty 'but under severe provocation', he was given a three-year sentence.[56]

Jane Cross' husband thrashed her to death while in a drunken rage in their home near Blackpool in 1909 after they returned from drinking at several public houses. They had been married for 25 years with nine living children, five of whom were at home when he killed her. He was said to be a good husband and father who had received 'some provocation'. While her funeral was attended by a large crowd, there was so much sympathy for his plight that a public meeting was called to petition for a reduction of the charge against him and to raise funds for his defence. More than 3000 signatures were gathered for what the *Manchester Courier* called a 'Wife Killer Petition Movement'. At his trial, he testified that Jane was very quarrelsome. He admitted beating her but was surprised to find her dead in the morning. Directing the jury to clear him of a murder verdict, the judge described it as a 'very bad case of manslaughter', 'nearly a case of murder'. Jane's killer had let himself 'get into a great passion', albeit one with some excusatory force for a man burdened with a wife who was addicted to alcohol. Sentence: 14 years.[57]

In sum, defence lawyers' valiant efforts to frame men's homicidal rage at women as excusatory met with mixed fortunes in the courts. The aptly named 'domestic discount' – that widely shared 'inclination to spare femicidal killers from the gallows' and to resist treating wife-killing as homicide of the first rank – worked for some but not others.[58] For the most part, early twenty-first century juries registered wife-killing as murder, only occasionally finding killers of 'provocative' wives guilty of no more than manslaughter. The question of the appropriate verdict for them was not confined to the courtroom. Take the case of the man who appeared at the Old Bailey in 1902 charged with the murder of his wife, Emily Dickson. Her 'extreme provocation' founded his successful manslaughter plea. As the defence told the story, this 'steady hardworking man' had quarrelled with Emily over her relationship with their lodger. He begged her to give him up but she refused. So, he almost decapitated her while in 'a fit of despair'. The judge was satisfied he committed the crime under 'the extremist' provocation and would gladly have 'let him go with no other punishment than that he had already suffered'. But in the interests of public order and to vindicate the law, he sentenced him to six months imprisonment.[59] Newspaper headlines ranged from the neutral 'Manslaughter of a Wife in London' to the suggestive 'Wife and Lodger' and the openly sympathetic: 'A Wife's Infidelity. Distressing Tragedy', 'A Husband's Despair' and 'Outrage by a Wronged Husband'.[60]

At least that was the view taken in the English press. By contrast, the *Edinburgh Evening News* headline, 'Six Months for Killing his Wife', could be read as Scottish cynicism about the lenient English sentence for Emily's killer.[61] But there were also signs of English disquiet over short sentences handed down to impassioned wife-killers. The one for Emily Dickson's husband was regarded as risibly short by two *Times* correspondents. One recalled the 1895 case of a man who, goaded by a wife 'whose temper and morals made his life miserable' and whose conduct drove him 'almost to madness', had stabbed her 'in a moment of ungovernable passion'. Petitions signed by 30,000 people led to a commutation of his death sentence and rightly so in this correspondent's view. Compare his disdain for the sentence for manslaughter for Emily Dickson's killer. This was a sad story of 'domestic unhappiness' caused by the wife's 'unfaithfulness' and general conduct. Her 'perfidy' had so exasperated her husband that he cut her throat 'in a fit of fury'. But did he deserve sympathy? Not in the view of this *Times* correspondent. Scandalously, the judge had passed a sentence of only six months without hard labour and had 'almost apologised for having to punish him at all'. Yet this killer had a history of threatening his wife, whereas the 'entirely unpremeditated' impassioned femicide committed in 1895 had led to a death sentence. The second *Times* correspondent, a lawyer, agreed that the judge in the Dickson case had got it wrong. In his view, it was in the interest of public order to pass a sentence that would emphasise 'the principle' that in no case except when acting in self-defence was a man justified in 'avenging himself by taking away the life of a fellow creature'. A six-month prison term hardly did that. It would be 'terrible' if 'the idea got abroad' that a man who cut the throat of a drunken or adulterous wife in the course of a quarrel, even under circumstances of 'almost extreme provocation', might get an 'astonishing' sentence of only a few months.[62]

Five years later, another *Times* correspondent criticised a reprieve he thought undeserved for a man who killed another man after a failed extortion attempt. In his view, it was a cold-blooded murder and deserved the death penalty unlike hot-blooded ones committed by poor wretches who after 'a long course of nagging and quarrelling' kills someone (read: their wives) whose death they quickly repent. He felt that these men whose offences are 'far less to be reprobated' than premediated murder, should be reprieved.[63] Within and without the criminal courts then, the hot versus cold-blooded distinction still ruled OK. But it was difficult to uphold, so many men having slaughtered women in circumstances clearly indicating premeditation, they having previously made threats to kill and openly planned revenge on 'their' women.

Victims' voices

To dwell as I have on early twentieth-century excusatory trial narratives about impassioned men being propelled to commit femicide is to risk losing sight of the victims. They haunt the killers' accounts only as slaughtered bodies. It is surely past time to hear from the women who survived men's fatal attacks and, where possible, to reclaim something of the lives of those who didn't. Some are more present in the records than others, though none as eloquent as London charwoman, Hannah Abbott, whom we met in Chapter 3, making the singular claim in an early nineteenth-century criminal court that her life mattered as much as that of the husband who cut her throat. Nevertheless, we can catch glimpses of the lived experience of early twentieth-century femicide victims before they were slaughtered. Countering the defence narratives of drunken, dissolute women whose 'indifferent habits' drove men to kill them that are retold in offender-focused legal histories are the stories of desperate women living in dire poverty who tried to survive with or escape from violent men. Reading the cases from their perspective throws an entirely different light on the circumstances leading to 'hot-blooded' femicide.

As I suggested in Chapter 3, scouring the records for evidence of the lived experience of the victims provides a counterpoint to the dominant historical narrative of much put-upon men disposing of an impossibly provocative woman. In that narrative, retold over and over in the courts and in defendant-centric histories, the victims disappear, only to be replaced by stereotypes of intolerable harridans. Even their names were frequently omitted from the law reports, sending the victim-orientated historian on a search of for local newspapers that might identify them and record the courtroom testimonials to their lives. Left untold are the details of the horrific violence inflicted on them, the multiple stab wounds, throat cuttings, near decapitations and strangulations.

With one exception, these women saw their slaughter as unwarranted and therefore unquestionably murder, none more poignantly than Brigid McQuaid, the young Fulham laundress we met earlier. 'I am being murdered', she cried, as her former partner cut her throat when she returned his engagement ring.[64] Amongst others we have encountered so far and whose killers were executed, 32-year-old Catherine Irwin made a dying statement documenting how she had supported herself and her three children while living separately from her estranged husband. He had made her feel 'awfully frightened'. She was on her way to work in London when he stabbed her for refusing to talk to him.[65] Twenty-two-year-old Eliza Marsh, whose father testified in court about how he had tried to protect her from her violent husband, had applied for a separation order on the ground of his persistent cruelty. It was not granted because of insufficient collaboration and his 'excellent conduct'. Eliza had told her sister he terrified her. He had threatened to 'do a John Silk on her', referring to a man who had killed his mother the previous year.[66] So many victims applied for separation orders. Three months before she was killed in Hull in 1908, Gertrude Siddle, also 22 years old, obtained one because of her husband's drinking and ill treatment. *The Times* report that 'it was supposed that jealousy was at the bottom of the crime' was belied by Gertrude's defiant response when he threatened to kill her if she had another man – 'I am not frightened of you. There is no other man'. Her friends vouched that there was no cause for his jealousy, the police report attributing his rage to his impending imprisonment for non-payment of the arrears owed to Gertrude.[67]

So many women were killed or injured in similar circumstances, including four women who were attacked in 1900, two fatally. These cases were reported under the headline: 'Four London Tragedies Through Jealously'. They were 19-year-old fur sewer Sarah Willett who had ended her engagement when she discovered her fiancé had been in prison and was unemployed. She told him: 'all I want is an honest hard-working fellow, not one who robs others'. So he shot her. He hanged, the execution reported under the headline: 'Lover's cold-blooded murder expiated'.[68] The second 'tragedy' was that of 21-year-old Ada Burrett who affixed her mark to her dying statement. There she recorded a quarrel with her husband who refused to work. She had told him: 'if you don't go to work, I will leave you'. In retaliation he had stabbed her 'all over with a knife'. She stated further how she had paid the rent and bought food from her earnings as a prostitute while he lived off her earnings. Her 'immoral earnings' notwithstanding, public sympathy was with her. He was hooted by a large crowd, many of them women, on his arrival at court. The judge might have thought it 'a shocking thing' to see women in court in a murder case, directing them to leave the courtroom, but Ada's story won the day, her killer found guilty of murder after 15 minutes' deliberation.[69]

The other two 'London tragedies' were those of women who survived being attacked by men who subsequently committed suicide. Forty-four-year-old dressmaker Louisa Abbott had left her husband to live with their lodger.

It was an unhappy relationship, her daughter saying it was 'a common thing' for him to threaten to murder her mother if she returned to her husband.[70] But Louisa did and within two weeks of her leaving, he telegrammed her saying he could not live without her and demanded a meeting. Louisa said it would be their last. It was. He threw her under a train and then killed himself. The fourth tragedy, 18-year-old Susan Annie Westland was a nurse who had moved in with a man but refused to stay unless they married. He locked her in a room but she escaped. When he found her, she refused to return, telling him he was 'a brute and a fool'. She found his jealousy unbearable and feared it would 'be my death' but she survived the shooting and after recovering in a Paddington hospital, gave evidence at the coroner's court about his possessiveness and threats to kill her.[71]

Theirs were not the only tragic stories that year, many other women paying the ultimate price for leaving violent men. Isabella Bowes, described as a respectable, hard-working woman who picked up coal on the beach at Seaham harbour for a living, had left her husband because of his violence and taken out a separation order. When he demanded that she return, she replied: 'No, I want nothing more to do with you'.[72] So he beat her to death but said it was an accident. There were no calls for a reprieve from his death sentence. When Elizabeth Shufflebotham's husband was convicted of assaulting her, she obtained a separation order requiring him to move out of their Staffordshire home. On learning she had given birth to their child, he moved back in with her. When he was arrested for yet another assault, she went to live with her mother. That was where he killed her. The jury took ten minutes to return a guilty verdict.[73] The following year, Louisa Claydon's husband beat and stabbed her to death. While her murder was described as a 'terrible domestic tragedy', there was no 'domestic discount' for him or two other wife-killers sentenced to death in July 1901.[74]

While Louisa did not survive the murderous attack, she was one of the few victims not subjected to post-mortem maligning in the court, even becoming something of a cause célèbre for other women. A contemporary commentator found the case to be 'of intense sociological interest' inasmuch as it was an 'almost motiveless' crime committed by a typically habitually drunk and periodically unemployed Northampton tradesman. From his report we learn that Louisa, who took in washing to support the family, had obtained a separation because of his violence; that he had been summoned for non-payment of instalments due on a maintenance order and had gone to prison for it. Despite this, she reluctantly let him return to their home. But his continual drinking led to a fatal quarrel in which Louisa allegedly called him a 'dirty dog', saying 'she would rather have a serpent sleeping by her side than him'. At his trial she was described as 'a spirited, active, little woman' who had shown great determination in obtaining the separation order and taking him to court for the arrears. Her funeral was attended by a 'tremendous crowd' consisting mainly of women and girls.[75]

In May 1901, Martha Holmes' husband cut her throat and that of their 20-year-old daughter Hannah. On trial at the Leeds Assizes for Martha's murder, he claimed she had been unfaithful and that Hannah was not his daughter. An argument had led to a fight. Despite medical evidence that his injuries were likely to have been self-inflicted and hers inflicted from behind, his counsel argued self-defence, telling the jury they would be 'justified' in finding him guilty of the lesser crime of manslaughter. They did, preferring his story to that told by witnesses that he was 'a man of violent temper'. Evidence was presented that he had been violent to Martha, that she had left him twice and taken out a summons against him because of his violence. Her own voice is very faint, but if we listen carefully, we can hear it indirectly through her eldest son's testimony. He told the court that on the fatal night, his father had flown into a rage because he had no tobacco. His mother, a 'quiet sober woman', had had many arguments with her husband, especially over his wishing to 'carry on' with Hannah.[76] Yet the killer's tale prevailed over the story told by witnesses of a mother of five children, the youngest four years old, who was married to a violent man who had made sexual overtures to her eldest daughter.

Later that year, 28-year-old Welsh barmaid Eliza Bowen tried to end her involvement with a man she had briefly 'walked out with'. So, he cut her throat, saying 'I did it for love and I'll die like an Englishman', adding for good measure: 'If I can't have her, the others shan't'. A police report called it 'another instance of the old and sad story' of 'an illicit intrigue between two parties' wherein the woman 'changes her situation, finds the old relations irksome, repels the man, a rival appears on the scene – drink, jealousy, murder'. Eliza did indeed try to repel her intoxicated killer, but there was no rival and so no cause for jealousy. However much her killer tried to dress up her murder as an impassioned crime for which he would gladly swing, the story that emerged at his trial was one of premeditated murder by a possessive man. We strain to hear her voice in this 'love tragedy', discovering it only in her letter rejecting his persistent overtures. She found them 'very objectionable' and no longer wished to see him. This act of resistance turned out to be her death warrant. Enraged at receiving her letter, he walked for miles to the Shropshire inn where she worked and knifed her to death. The case received widespread coverage, one Irish newspaper reporting it under the pointed headline: 'Another English Tragedy'.[77]

There were many more such tragedies to come, most involving the killing of women who had obtained separation and maintenance orders which served to further inflame a man's anger. Some of the victims had left for another man. But more often than not, they returned to their parents or a friend's home for support and protection. Ellen Barnaby, the young wife killed by the man who escaped a murder conviction on the ground that his epilepsy made him prone to 'sexual passions', told a neighbour she wanted to get police protection because he was 'going to do something' to her. She sought shelter at her father's house. Still demanding she return home, her husband cut her throat in a street.[78] Emily Coates' partner killed her in a Shadwell street in 1902. She had frequently complained of his violence, their landlady testifying to seeing him pushing her down the stairs as she cried: 'someone go for the police, he will murder me'. Emily took out a warrant against him for assault before leaving to live with a friend. Enraged at receiving the summons, he went to her new London lodgings where she refused to speak to him. He stabbed her when she was on her way to work the next day. Against his story that she was a 'false woman', her friends described her as a hard-working and obliging woman who had financially supported her killer.[79]

Twenty-six-year-old Mary Starr left home in 1903. She did as much as she could to protect herself and their child. She wrote to her husband asking for support, consulted a solicitor for advice on how to get a maintenance order as well as custody and food for the child and, suffering from malnutrition herself, went to live with her mother in Blackpool. She was stabbed to death with a bread knife in her mother's kitchen the day after taking out a summons against him for maintenance.[80] Forty-two-year-old Annie Yarnold was also stabbed to death by her husband at her home in Worcester in October 1905. At face value, this was an open and shut case for manslaughter, she having drawn on his pension when she lived with another man while her husband was away at the Boer War. But in her lengthy dying deposition, she got to tell her side of the story, one that was to prove fatal for the defence. She had returned to her husband but he started 'knocking' her about again so she went back to the other man. Her unemployed husband had been 'a horrible brute' and made her keep him by prostitution. Sixteen years of unhappy marriage ended when he 'went at me with great revenge'.[81]

Esther Bedford was unusual amongst the victims inasmuch as she sought to exonerate her killer, just as the dying Desdemona had Othello. 'Who has done this deed', Emilia asked Desdemona. 'Nobody. I myself' she replied.[82] Esther denied she had been attacked when the police were called in. Witnesses to his increasing violence were astounded: 'don't tell stories Esther, you know it's Mack that has done it'. Are they 'taking him away', she cried?[83] Her denials continued in her dying deposition where, describing herself as a single woman, she said she had left a violent man in Manchester to live in Oldham with the defendant. He had promised to marry her. He had beaten her but on the rare occasion when he struck and kicked her it had 'always been my fault'. His scalding her with boiling water was an accident. Her devotion to 'the brute who slowly slew her' was reported as extraordinary and difficult to understand – she was like a faithful hound to its master. The *Dundee Evening Post*'s report, headlined 'Revolting Story from Manchester. Kicked. Scalded and Jumped On', might have evinced Scottish bias in the face of yet another 'English tragedy'. But its sub-title, 'A woman's amazing devotion', summed up the widespread amazement at Esther's 'most remarkable' unflinching devotion which 'no brutality seemed capable of destroying'. The defence suggestion that he had hit her to break her intemperate habits fell on deaf ears, her portrayal in court as a drunken, 'immoral' woman notwithstanding.[84] No attempt was made for a reprieve.

Straight from the Othello playbook – who did this? 'Nobody. I myself' – Esther Bedford's disclaimers render her an outlier, most victims of early twentieth intimate partner femicide making every effort to save their own lives. They took out separation orders from violent men, served them with maintenance orders to support their children and fled with their children to what they hoped was the relative safety of their parents' homes, only to be slaughtered either there or on their way to work. There were others, too numerous to be named, desperately trying to escape. All-male juries and judges usually had little trouble condemning their slaughter as unjustifiable. Then as now exiting from a violent relationship was seen as a dangerous time for a woman, hundreds of femicide cases harsh testimony to that.

Holding fast to the 'unwritten law'

In her dying deposition written in 1900 after her husband's lethal assault, Annie Thomson disputed his claim that she had provoked him by raking up another man's name. It was not through any 'aggravation' on her part that he threw a lit paraffin lamp at her. He was the one 'always raking up the other man's name'. She never said she would 'rather have him'. Her voice was not heard at her husband's trial where the judge took an extraordinary step that, as he acknowledged, 'might seem to be straining the law in favour' of the defendant. It certainly did. He told the jury that Lord Blackburn's decision in the famous *Rothwell* case, discussed in Chapter 3, that some provocative words might potentially found a defence to murder had 'great weight'. It suggested that words of the kind attributed to Annie Thompson – that she 'preferred another man' – might constitute mitigating provocation. Taking the hint, the jury took just 20 minutes to return a manslaughter verdict.[85]

This certainly was an unusual position for a judge to take, the judiciary at this time seldom straining the law in defendants' favour. In the coming years, it would be for defence lawyers, not judges, to invoke Blackburn's opinion. Judges continued to hold fast to the received Othello-inflected adultery rule: ocular proof of adultery was required if a man was to escape a conviction for murder. Accordingly, *Rothwell* did not turn out to be the lively warrant for wife-killing that defence lawyers had hoped for.[86] With no cases coming before the courts in the always accepted 'exceptional' case of a man actually finding his wife *in flagrante*, defence lawyers had to settle for beefing up other forms of troublesome wifely behaviour. Offensive words played their part but the outcome was by no means assured. The man who killed 18-year-old weaver Alice Beetham on a Blackburn street was hanged in 1912, his excuse that she was going to 'throw him over' not mitigating the crime. While hundreds of her fellow mill workers attended her funeral, over 60,000 signatures were attached to a mercy petition for him, a man 'genuinely in love' with the victim. Alice's rejection had momentarily 'robbed him of his self-control, the final rebuff leaving him 'morally and mentally powerless'.[87] The Home Office was unmoved. Other femicidal men were more fortunate that year, especially if the victim's bad words were accompanied by her bad behaviour. For example, Jane Kay's husband was charged with murder when he kicked her to death at their London lodgings. But when the jury heard how she had called him names, had 'intemperate habits' and, on the fatal night, quarrelled and 'rushed' at him, it found him guilty of manslaughter – 'but under great provocation' – and strongly recommended him to mercy. Concurring, the judge said Jane had undoubtedly provoked him 'during the greater part of his life' and sentenced him to six months without hard labour.[88]

Two wife-killing cases heard at the Old Bailey in 1912 which resulted in reprieves for condemned murderers provide more insights into evolving views of the excusatory force of wifely provocation. Agnes Philpot's husband strangled her at their Wimbledon home during a quarrel over payment for a Christmas tree. He claimed she had reproached him about his infidelity and hit him, causing him to snap and lose control as if he were 'holding a very strong galvanic battery' that he could not let go. Found guilty of murder, he was strongly recommended to mercy. On appeal, his defence argued that the jury's hesitations during their deliberation proved it was 'not really murder'. The Court of Appeal disagreed, leaving it to the Home Office to decide his fate.[89] He was reprieved as was Annie Fitzgibbon's husband. He had stabbed her to death on a London street. On arrest, he explained that 'she would nag, nag, nag' but at the trial he changed his story, saying he cut her by accident as he ate his dinner. As the Court of Appeal observed, that made it difficult for his counsel to 'make too much of the suggested nagging'.[90] Lilian Mason's husband was also reprieved after being convicted of her murder at the Manchester Assizes. They had agreed to separate but she still nagged him, driving him to cut her throat while in 'a mad temper'. Several witnesses testified to her 'nagging characteristics'. Convicted of murder, he was strongly recommended to mercy on account of her provocation and appealed. The Court of Appeal agreed with the trial judge that a 'mad temper' would never reduce the crime to manslaughter. Nor would mere words. However, if the victim spat at him while saying offensive words that might be 'sufficient provocation', just not in this case. That was the law. A petition with 7000 signatures helped secure his reprieve.[91]

What was to count as sufficient provocation to reduce intimate partner femicide to manslaughter was to expand exponentially after mid-twentieth-century reforms to the law of murder, saving hundreds of wife-killers from convictions for murder. But not yet. Judges put their foot down in a series of appeal cases decided in 1913 where defence counsel tried to extend Lord Blackburn's suggestion in *Rothwell* doctrine that words could count as provocation. The first was the case of *Palmer* where, once again, the court laid it down that it was 'well established by law' that a husband killing a wife found in adultery was guilty of manslaughter, not murder. Certainly, *Rothwell* opened up the possibility of treating a wife's sudden confession of adultery as 'equivalent to a discovery of the act itself'. But while it was a grave offence against the husband for the wife to commit adultery, there was no such offence when the woman was a fiancée or co-habiting with a man. Even if 21-year-old Ada James, the victim in the *Palmer* case, had relations with other men, there was no authority that would reduce the crime to manslaughter. Indeed, it was 'quite impossible to treat words' suggesting she had 'immoral relations' with other men as being sufficient to justify a manslaughter verdict.[92] Nor was throwing her engagement ring at his face. So Ada's killer hanged.

In the second case a man who killed his brother believing he had committed adultery with his wife was convicted of murder. He also lost his appeal, the court explaining again that mere suspicion of a wife's adultery was not sufficient. The question, once again, was whether the victim's words would amount to such a provocation as would 'in an ordinary man, not in a man of violent or passionate disposition' provoke him in such a way as to justify him striking her. And once again it was ruled that while *Rothwell* was authority for the view that a wife's confession of adultery was sufficient provocation, that was an 'extreme' case and had not been extended. In the case at hand, the victim had not said anything to put the appellant 'in a passion' and made no confession of adultery.[93]

In the third 1913 case, the defence argued that shooting a woman 'who was practically his wife' who was found drunk in a house of ill-repute was provocation justifying a man killing her. The judge disagreed. Even if 28-year-old Elizabeth Hearne was a dissolute drunk and a nag who hurled taunts at him, life had to be protected, even hers. No doubt he shot her 'in a moment of passion'. But that amounted to murder 'unless there is evidence otherwise'. Indeed:

> I have to tell you that no provocation by words, no provocation by gesture, can amount to such a provocation as will reduce the crime of killing to manslaughter. A man is not entitled because somebody provokes him by insulting words or provoking words, or because a woman nags him, or does something he objects to her doing, a man is not entitled to draw a revolver and shoot her.

While this emphatic statement on the law of provocation would not stand the test of time, the jury in this case took just fifteen minutes to return a murder verdict with no recommendation to mercy. An appeal failed, the court citing *Palmer* to affirm that while it was the 'gravest possible offence' against a husband if his wife commits adultery, there was no such offence against a common law wife. Common law husbands had no 'right to control' a woman as a husband has to control his wife. Accordingly, only a husband could legally complain if his wife visited a house of ill fame if indeed that was where the defendant in this case found her. Furthermore, there was no evidence that Elizabeth was having 'or even intended to have connection with another man'.[94]

This strict view of mitigating provocation was reinforced when Ada Ellor's husband bashed her to death in Hyde in 1921. Ada had left him twice on account of his violence. Shortly before he killed her, she took out a separation order and a summons against him because of his persistent cruelty. On the day of the murder, he begged her to return. He claimed she refused, telling him to 'put his head under a train' and boasting she was 'going to enjoy herself that night'. Delivering the unanimous judgment dismissing his appeal against his conviction for murder, the Chief Justice insisted that words were insufficient to deprive a man of self-control. No authority supported the defence proposition that a manslaughter conviction was possible if a wife said the words attributed to Ada Ellor. It was not the law of England that a wife telling her husband that she was about to commit adultery would amount to provocation so as to reduce murder to manslaughter. Indeed, the authorities supported the 'contrary view'. Certainly, it was the 'unwritten law' that if a man discovered his wife in the act of adultery that would be manslaughter because that was regarded in law as 'equivalent to a blow struck at the husband'. *Rothwell* had extended that principle to meet the case of a wife's sudden confession of 'past adultery'. But that was a 'special exception' to the general rule that words were insufficient to justify a manslaughter conviction. Furthermore, the appellant never said he killed Ada because he thought she was about to commit adultery. In fact, he admitted killing her for refusing to return to him.[95] There were limits even to a husband's rights over his wife and Ada's killer hanged.

In 1943, a French-Canadian soldier shot 30-year-old cinema attendant, Annette Pepper, with a machine gun when she told him she was in love with another man. He killed her in her Sussex home where she lived with her eight-year-old daughter. The other man, who was at the house at the time, was shot but escaped out the back door. At the first trial, the jury disagreed. The defence had argued for a manslaughter verdict for a young man who, 'swept by circumstances into the eddy of tremendous passion', found himself 'engulfed by the crime'. It probably confused the jury about the gravity of the provocation to hear the prosecutor calling it a cold-blooded murder but then describing the victim as 'a bad character' who was 'deceitful towards her lovers', unfaithful to her husband and seemed to have 'led a thoroughly disreputable life'.[96] Damningly too, the fact that her husband was a prisoner of war at the time was endlessly repeated in the huge press coverage of the case as if to suggest that deceiving a man while he was imprisoned made her conduct all the more reprehensible. But at the killer's re-trial, the judge refused to leave provocation to the jury. They did not live in a country where 'a man can say to a woman, not even his wife, a woman whom he had known for a couple of months: "You look at another man and I will kill you"', and then when she does, he kills her. What would 'become of this country' if ever 'such a matter should ever be argued before you?' The defendant telling the victim that he would kill her if she 'fell or made love to another man' and that 'if he had reason to be jealous' he would shoot her, was 'murder in this country'. The judge did not know what it was like in French Canada but in England it was murder.[97] The jury agreed after just 20 minutes deliberation.

The appellate judges were scathing about the appeal. There was not a 'scintilla of evidence' of provocation that could have been left to the jury. Just because she had left him for a sergeant? Because he was jealous? A man might 'conjure up a motive or reasons sufficient for himself to cause him to kill', but that did not provide evidence of provocation. Moreover, 'the mode of resentment' had to bear some relation to the alleged provocation. A Bren gun firing bullets in quick succession is one thing, but 'a woman showing preference for a particular lover is another'.[98] In mid-twentieth-century England, jealous men who killed women not their wives who preferred other men had no moral warrant for murder in the eyes of the law. Nor indeed could husbands unless, of course, they found their wives *in flagrante* with another man. For that – although left unsaid – was still the highest invasion of property.

The second jury strongly recommended Annette's killer to mercy and then followed that up with a petition for a reprieve on the ground that he suffered from 'jealous insanity'. To them it seems the killing had the hallmarks of a mitigating impassioned crime. Certainly, that's how the condemned man saw it. In a letter written to his wife shortly before his execution, he explained that 'frankly', the love he had for Annette was 'not a true love. It was only passion'. He assured her that it took a 'very passionate' woman for him 'to have completely lost' his head and killed her. He had suffered terribly since. To his mother he wrote that he did not commit the crime voluntarily. He had lost control. No doubt she had read newspapers reporting that the judge said he had killed the woman 'in cold blood'. That was 'ridiculous and false'. He had the backing of the prison chaplain who pleaded to the Home Secretary for a soldier in a foreign land who, 'longing for his own people', had been accosted in a public house by a woman 'who evidently had little sense of moral values'. No wonder it 'upset his mental and moral balance'. His crime was committed in 'a moment of mental aberration when he was suffering the pangs of jealousy'. Moreover, he and his wife had adopted a child in Canada, a 'wonderful act of Christian charity' that could not change suddenly into 'hatred without reason'. It must have been his changed environment, an explanation attracting a curt hand-written rebuttal expressing the official view: 'The crime was due to sexual jealousy'. That was no ground for a reprieve.[99]

Holmes – 'Othello's crime was murder and nothing else'

The refusal of trial and appellate court judges to indulge men who killed allegedly adulterous wives reached its apogee in the famous case of *Holmes*, high point of judicial resistance to expanding the 'sexual infidelity' defence script beyond ocular proof of adultery.[100] Thirty-year-old Peggy Holmes, the mother of six children, was killed at her home in Walesby, Nottinghamshire in November 1945. Her husband, a returned soldier, had started a relationship with another woman. He hatched a plan to dispose of Peggy by accusing her of confessing to infidelity so that he could kill her and plead provocation. Sending a telegram to his new woman saying: 'See you Sunday or Monday for sure. All fixed' sounded more like premeditation. As the trial judge explained the law, even if Peggy said she had been unfaithful that was not sufficient provocation to reduce murder to manslaughter. In fact, there was no evidence to show she had been other than 'a good wife and mother' but quite a bit to suggest it was 'a very cold blooded murder'.[101] The jury took just 25 minutes to return a murder verdict. The Court of Criminal Appeal dismissed the appeal but the question of the mitigating effect of women's words was too momentous to be left there. So, Peggy's killer appealed to the House of Lords.

The judgment handed down in April 1946 dismissing the appeal warrants a close analysis. Not only did it recognise the inherently sexed operation of the provocation defence; it also acknowledged the need to balance respect for human frailty (read: his) with a consideration of the sanctity of human life (read: even hers). The Crown had argued that it would be most 'unfortunate' if returned soldiers were to believe that on a wife's confession of adultery 'there is something like a licence to kill'. No 'special quality' attached to confessions of adultery – words, 'whether an insult or an admission of adultery, never constituted provocation'.[102] The appellant countered with a prediction, accurate as it turned out, that in future 'there will certainly be ordinary reasonable men in this country who will hear confessions of adultery from their wives, and some of them will be so deprived of their self-control that they will kill them'. If the Crown's argument was accepted, these men would be 'bound to be convicted of murder'. For while the death penalty might deter a killing planned 'in cold blood', it would not 'a man in a state of frenzy'.[103]

Delivering the unanimous judgment of five law lords dismissing the appeal, Lord Simon outlined the law as it had been applied for centuries. A confession of adultery, 'grievous as it is, cannot in itself justify the view that a reasonable man (or woman) would be so provoked as to do what this man did'. The 'actual finding' of a spouse in the act of adultery had always been treated as a 'very special exception' to the general rule about sufficient provocation because there could not be a greater provocation. But it had been 'rightly laid down' that the exception should not be extended. Seeing the adultery – 'ocular proof' such as Othello had demanded – was essential. Without it, Lord Simon famously declared, the crime was murder: 'Even if Iago's insinuations against Desdemona had been true, Othello's crime was murder and nothing else'.[104]

The case was a media sensation, newspapers headlines breaking the news that the Court of Criminal Appeal had decided that 'Infidelity is No Excuse for Murder'. That was surely not 'too widely known'.[105] The House of Lords' judgment, published in July 1946, was also summed up in headlines: '"Mere

Words" No Excuse for Murder'; 'Mere Words Insufficient Provocation'; '"Mere Words" Cannot Justify Murder'; 'Holmes Guilty of "Othello" Murder'; 'Othello Reminder in Murder Appeal Judgment' and 'Othello is Quoted by Law Lords Against Jealousy-Murderer'.[106] Lord Simon's final observations went unnoticed. Deploying impeccable gender-neutrality terminology, he announced that England had left behind 'the age when the wife's subjection to her husband was regarded by the law as the basis of the marital relation'. Now parliament had conferred on the aggrieved wife the same right as her husband to divorce for 'unfaithfulness alone'. It followed that no one, on hearing an admission of adultery, could kill their spouse and then claim that such provocation reduced the crime to 'mere manslaughter'. Opinions on such matters might differ and 'must to some extent be controlled by the evolution of society'. Back in the day – and here sex-specificity takes over his description of the typical provoked assailant – if a man's nose was pulled and he killed the aggressor, it was only manslaughter. That accorded with the 'natural feelings of a past time', the 'injury done to a man's honour' by minor assaults being assessed differently then. But these days, 'words of a vile character' might deprive a reasonable man of his customary self-control '*even more*' than physical violence. Nevertheless, the power of self-control exercised by the 'ordinary person' is affected by 'contemporary conditions and attitudes', and as 'society advances, it ought to call for a higher measure of self-control in *all* cases'.[107]

The Home Office declining to reprieve Holmes, he was duly hanged. But his counsel need not have worried so that many more men would hang for killing women if confessions of infidelity were not to count as sufficient provocation. He was one of the last femicidal men executed in England and Wales.[108] From then on, very few men who committed intimate partner femicide would be convicted of murder. The floodgates to successful manslaughter pleas were about to be opened for 'provoked' wife-killers, alas too late for him. The *Holmes* case marked the end of an era in which judges steadfastly tightened the law in relation to the mitigating force of a wife's alleged adultery, endlessly repeating the mantra that it was essential to find her in the act or, at the very least, hear her confess it. They had also refused to extend law's compassion to unmarried men who killed their partners. Paradoxically however, the very act of drawing of a line between the rights of married and unmarried men had the effect of buttressing the received notion that disposing of an 'unfaithful' wife was 'mere' manslaughter. Equally, referencing wife-killing as frenzied crimes committed in the heat of passion – whether or not such defences succeeded – reinforced the early modern distinction between hot and cold-blooded killing that was the very marker of mitigating passion, one reinforced in yet another provoked wife-killing case decided a few months after *Holmes*.

In December 1946, a man was charged with the murder of his 23-year-old wife, Doris Din, in Birmingham. She wanted to leave him for a wealthier man so he cut her throat, almost decapitating her, before she could get a separation order. Responding to the defence calling Doris as unfaithful and a 'bad lot', the prosecutor declared that 'immoral people still have a right to live'. Following Lord Simon's dictum, he also pointed out that her husband could have opted for divorce instead of homicide. That argument was no match for the defence narrative transforming the 'jealous Indian' defendant into a tragic hero who loved his wife but 'she did not want him', a man of excellent character who had struggled to keep his marriage from breaking up in the face of 'long and intense provocation'. Moreover, it was of no moment that the defendant was an Indian migrant. It 'made no difference that he was of a different colour' for 'the figure of justice is blindfold, and she can't see the colour of a man's skin'. The judge agreed: English law was 'the same for every man and woman whatever their colour, and it is the same wherever British justice is found'.[109] On the other hand, the court could not but see the defendant's colour, his lawyer comparing him to Othello, no less. Under the headline, '"Othello" Killer Loved His White Wife', one newspaper report cited his address to the jury that, tellingly, misquoted *Othello*: 'This man of colour, like another man of colour in literature, was almost damned by a fair wife'. In *Othello*, Cassio is not damned 'by' a fair wife but '*in* a fair wife'.[110]

Certainly, damned 'by' a fair wife sounded worse, something an all-male jury could perhaps readily identify with. But either way, damned 'by' or 'in' a fair wife, the jury took just 20 minutes to clear him of murder. Concurring with the verdict, the judge sentenced him to five years for manslaughter. After all, this was not simply a case of 'mere words'. There was no disputing the evidence that Doris wanted to leave her marriage, distressing her lovelorn husband. To English eyes, this was a classic crime of passion, the kind ordinarily committed by an over-emotional foreigner weighed down by a wayward wife, one erased in the records as surely as Desdemona effaced herself. Who did this, Emilia asked her. Nobody, I myself.

.....

The history of the legal response to impassioned homicide in the first half of the twentieth century is the history of passion contained. The passion defence had not fared well in the courts. Many wife-killers hanged. And while the Home Office occasionally reprieved wife-killers, much to the relief of campaigners against capital punishment, the fact remains that they had been convicted of murder. Like Othello, they were found guilty of that crime and nothing else. This, at least, was post-mortem vindication of sorts for the women named in this chapter and for others too many to include. Lord Simon was mistaken however, in thinking that the availability of divorce courts would obviate the need to kill an adulterous spouse. Divorce was no solution for a man determined to exercise his property rights over a separating wife by taking the law into his own hands. As we shall see in Chapter 5, mid-century reforms overhauling the law of murder would allow passion – the un-mastered passions of men infuriated by 'their' women – to continue along a devastating homicidal path for the next 50 years.

Chapter 5

Homicidal rage in 'modern times' – Passion unleashed

IAGO *What an eye she has! Me thinks it sounds a parley to provocation*

Othello 2.3. 21–22

OTHELLO *All my fond love thus do I blow to heaven:*
'Tis gone!
Arise black vengeance, from the hollow hell,
Yield up, O love, thy crown and hearted throne
To tyrannous hate!

Othello 3.3.448–452

Introduction

The history of impassioned homicide in the second half of the twentieth century is the history of passion unleashed. The pivotal enabling event was the passing of the Homicide Act 1957. Though reviled as an unsatisfactory compromise between those wishing to abolish capital punishment outright and those wanting to retain hanging for some homicides, the Act revolutionised the law of murder. The story of how it came about and of its unhappy reception in the courts is conventionally told from the defence-orientated, pro-abolitionist perspective of historians preoccupied with charting the decades-long fight to end hanging. This chapter takes a different approach. While recognising that the passing of the Act was an important step towards ending the killing field of state-mandated executions, it also highlights how it gave the green light to another much larger killing field. Impassioned hot-blooded killing, indicatively wife-slaughter, would now become a barely punishable form of homicide, barely even a crime. Short prison sentences, even non-custodial sentences for manslaughter would become the norm for impassioned men who finally 'snapped' after intolerable provocations from an always already loquacious woman taunting a man about his sexual inadequacy.

Chapter 5 continues my commitment to bringing the victims of domestic femicide and their advocates into the conversation about passion as excuse

DOI: 10.4324/9781003301974-6

for murder. My main agenda, however, is to explore the impact of the mid-century law reforms on the conceptualisation of impassioned homicide. As we shall see, the wife-killer in the dock was to undergo an important transformation in the second half of the twentieth century. No longer a justifiably angry man of honour, nor even a partially excusably ill-tempered man provoked by an 'unfaithful' wife, he is now a man driven to distraction by all manner of provocations. Alternatively, his criminal responsibility will be said to be diminished by a mental disorder that, for the most part, will be attributed to that same provocative wife. As for his crime, tellingly that is rarely referred to as a 'crime of passion' which, in English eyes, remained a foreign and especially French predilection. The unleashing of homicidal passion that followed the enactment of the new law would be called, more prosaically, manslaughter.

The Homicide Act 1957 – femicidal rage unleashed

Conventional legal histories invariably tell the story of the Act as an unhappy compromise between abolitionists, those advocating the abolition of capital punishment, and their opponents, the 'retentionists'. In the post-war decade, abolitionists pursuing their decades-old goal of ending hanging secured a partial victory, the Act limiting the circumstances in which murderers could be executed and requiring mandatory life imprisonment in all other cases. Their opponents in the conservative government retained the death penalty for those they considered particularly susceptible to deterrence. But hanging was effectively abolished for everything other than killing a police or prison officer, murder committed in the furtherance of theft, killing by shooting or causing an explosion, while resisting arrest or killing more than once.[1] Accordingly, intimate partner femicide was now classified as non-capital murder so long as the victim was not shot or blown up and she was not the killer's first victim. This meant, as one legal scholar noted, that 'nearly all killings of passion and depression' were now excluded from the death penalty. However, that is not what has caught historians' attention. For them the passing of the Act marked 'a critical moment in criminal justice history', one that accelerated the decline in the use of the death penalty.[2]

The Act's significance did not however, lie solely in its reduction of the scope of capital murder. Just as crucially for defendants in murder trials, especially wife-killers, the Act adopted the Royal Commission on Capital Punishment's proposal that provocative words could reduce murder to manslaughter. Section 3 provided that the question of whether the provocation was enough to make a reasonable man do what the accused did must be left to the jury. In determining that question, the jury should take into account everything done and said and the effect it would have on a reasonable man. Furthermore, judges could no longer prevent a provocation defence from going to the jury as long as there was some evidence, however slight, of provocation. Nor could they dictate the characteristics of the reasonable man to a jury. The ambit of the provocation defence was thus expanded by eliminating its common law restrictions such as those laid down in the famous *Holmes* case discussed in Chapter 4. The Act also introduced a diminished responsibility defence. Section 2 provided that anyone suffering from an abnormality of mind arising from 'a condition of arrested or retarded development of mind or any inherent causes' or 'induced by disease or injury' was entitled to a diminished responsibility defence.[3] The availability of these two defences would be of far more consequence for femicidal men than the new restrictions on capital murder. Over the next five decades, they would save hundreds from murder convictions, ensuring instead that they received risibly short sentences for manslaughter.

Contemporary legal commentators saw the new legal status quo otherwise. In their view, the new defences did not go far enough to exonerate murderers. They were happy enough with the extension of the provocation defence which they felt would 'eradicate at one blow the blots on the law' created by Lord Simon in the *Holmes* case. Recall that he ruled against words being sufficient provocation and specifying that under no circumstances would a confession of adultery be adequate. *Holmes*, the culmination of a movement that since the nineteenth century allowed judges to decide the question of provocation as a matter of law, was now overturned. The Act restored the provocation defence to its proper place as a question of fact to be determined by the jury. The commentators felt that the *Holmes* restrictions on provocation had been necessary to limit the plea after the war when returning ex-servicemen were confronted with confessions of adultery by their unfaithful wives. But now thankfully, the Act had dispensed with these 'artificial and illogical' restrictions.[4] Nevertheless, many felt the Act did not go far enough. Some complained that the diminished responsibility defence, though helpful in adding a 'supplementary doctrine of extenuating circumstances that may justify a lesser punishment', was too qualified. It was too restricted to defendants with a proven abnormal mind.[5] But it was the retention of provocation's objective or 'reasonable man' test in order to keep provocation pleas in check by insisting there had to be such provocation as would upset a reasonable man, your 'average stolid Englishman', that was especially irksome. It was regrettable that this test had been preserved. After all, as one commentator put it, 'we are all uncomfortably aware of our own propensities to behave unreasonably' and the only justification of defences to murder that 'makes sense' is that the provoked and mentally abnormal are 'like us'.[6]

The expansion of provocation to include the victim's words was said to have widespread approval inasmuch as 'the public' was reportedly 'uneasy' that homicides committed under severe provocation by words' were categorised as murder. Citing the Mass Observation surveys of the 1950s, one study found that 'the public' differentiated between murders, showing particular empathy for crimes of passion.[7] Historians exploring the shifting emotional economy of mid-century Britain have offered an explanation for such sympathies, suggesting that by then, British emotional culture had begun to 'mutate from one that valued self-control to one that valorised self-expression'.[8] There was, it is argued, a significant shift in British social values from a culture of self-discipline to a culture of self-expression. Overlooked in this account is the fact that while uncontrolled emotions might have 'transgressed a conception of British (or more accurately, white Anglo-Saxon) national identity that was rooted in self-restraint', British wife-killers had been transgressing that conception for centuries.[9] Their acting out of homicidal rage at women in anything but British self-restraint did not affect contemporary positive assessments of the Act either. Impassioned homicide was barely mentioned in all the excitement over the new law, the radical expansion of the circumstances qualifying it for law's mitigation implicitly dismissed as not germane to the main question of the day, namely capital punishment.

The impact that a reform proposal distinguishing capital from non-capital murder would have on the conduct of murder trials, and of the wife-killer's trial in particular, had not been lost on leading retentionist, Winston Churchill. During the parliamentary debates over reforming the law of murder a decade earlier, he had protested against just such a proposal. It was to remove from the death penalty the 'more frequent types of murder' such as 'wounding, stabbing, strangling, drowning' committed 'for all the most wicked motives, jealousy, greed, revenge'. Tellingly, he framed his objections to 'the folly of trying to categorise murderous brutality' with reference to wife-killers. He pointed out that if the proposal was accepted it would mean a man may 'deliberately kill his wife with a chopper' without being sentenced to death. Moreover,

> if you decide to kill your wife because after cold, calculated and deliberate consideration you come to the conclusion that you will live more agreeably alone or with another woman ... you have a variety of methods at your disposal, without risking your life even if found guilty. You can strangle her or hold her head in the gas oven until she expires.

This occasioning much mirth in the house, Churchill continued:

> You can stab her. You can cut her throat or dash her brains out ... you can set her on fire, push her off the station platform in front of an oncoming train ... you can drown her in the bath.

But whatever you do, you must not have any assistance, otherwise you risk the death penalty.[10] How amusing it all was to his fellow parliamentarians. Yet despite making light of the proposal to limit capital punishment to certain kinds of homicides, Churchill correctly diagnosed intimate partner femicide as calculated, cold-blooded murder. His prediction that any bid to rank homicides in terms of seriousness would locate intimate partner femicide as the least offensive would also turn out to be accurate.

Nine years later, the passing of the Act would leave it to juries to determine whether a reasonable Englishman would do as the defendant did in a murder case. They could take into account everything done and said, thereby opening the floodgates to impassioned provocation pleas. Now '*any* infidelity' could amount to provocation. 'Passion' – the passion of men aroused by taunting, departing women in scenarios far removed from discovering her *in flagrante delicto* – could follow an unabashedly subjectivising path, becoming embedded in what is colloquially referred to in Britain as 'the nagging and shagging defence'. Henceforth mere suspicion of a wife's 'infidelity' – say, her departure from an unhappy and often violent relationship – would not bar a successful provocation plea. All her killer need allege was that she had taunted him about something, usually some aspect of his sexual inadequacy. Alternatively, they could claim that her conduct, whatever it was, so unhinged him as to found a diminished responsibility defence. Whether modern-day Othellos were guilty of murder was for juries, not judges, to determine, taking into account everything twentieth-century Desdemonas did to bring about their own slaughter.

Impassioned wife-killing – a 'savage sort of devotion'

The impact of the mid-century law reforms on the narration of impassioned homicide can be registered most clearly by comparing how lawyers framed provocation pleas for femicidal men in cases decided before and immediately after it was enacted. At mid-century, the legal understanding of mitigating provocation received its classical expression in the 1949 case of *Duffy* where the judge declared it to be an act or series of acts done by the victim to the accused. These acts would cause in any reasonable person, and actually causes in the accused, a sudden and temporary loss of self-control, rendering the accused so subject to passion as to make him or her not master of his or her mind.[11]

The impeccably gender-neutral 'his or her' formatting of persons 'subject to passion' who fail to master their emotions was occasioned by the fact that the defendant here was a woman. Killing her husband after a long history of domestic violence as he was sleeping did not endear her to the judge. He could not see how a sleeping man could render a woman so transported by passion that she would resort to homicide. Hers simply did not fit the bill of an extenuating impassioned crime, and she was convicted of murder. It is however, the judge's summary to the jury that is most remarkable. You are not, he told them, concerned with blame here:

> the blame attaching to the dead man. You are not standing in judgment on him. He has not been heard in this court. He cannot now ever be heard. He has no defender here to argue for him. It does not matter how cruel he was, how much or how little he was to blame, except in so far as it resulted in the final act of the appellant. What matters is whether this girl had the

time to say: 'Whatever I have suffered, whatever I have endured, I know that Thou shalt not kill'.[12]

Not concerned with blaming the victim? In the far more common wife killing cases, the victim is always blamed, always judged for her failings, a blame-game that increased exponentially after mid-century. Rarely did judges notice that these victims had no defenders in their corner. Nor, on the other hand, are there any records of juries being asked to determine whether the femicidal man had time to reflect before his 'final act' on the biblical injunction not to kill. At the same time, it should be acknowledged that prior to 1957, time to reflect barred a provocation defence even for them.

The cases of two femicidal men condemned to hang in 1950 are especially illuminating. The first demonstrates continuing judicial scepticism about the deployment of medical evidence to mitigate murder. The man who killed 17-year-old school girl Christine Cuddon had no apparent motive save for her parents' disapproval of their relationship and his own wish to die. Unconvinced by his insanity defence, the jury convicted him of murder. The appellate judges were also unsympathetic. Rejecting his appeal, they said they were 'only too familiar' with this type of case where men resolve that no one else should possess 'their' women. As for the medical testimony that the defendant 'knew he was killing the girl, but he did not realise the seriousness of it', the court was emphatic: it was for the jury and 'not for medical men of whatever eminence' to determine the matter. Whether he suffered from a sudden impulse, from schizophrenia 'or from whatever doctors may call it', the jury in this case had found he was responsible.[13] He hanged. In the second case, Elsie Clare's husband was scheduled to die on the same day. He was reprieved, the usual domestic discount for wife-killers kicking in during the Home Office deliberations. The jury had strongly recommended him to mercy, feeling he had been 'driven to it through passion and loss of control'. Elsie, he said, had told him he was not the father of their recently born child, an infidelity-inflected taunt that would feature strongly in subsequent provocation defence narratives.[14]

Nora Cobon, shot in the back by her husband at their Cheshire home the following year, was destined to become a prototype of the provocative wife 'asking for it'. As the defence told the story, her constant nagging had caused her husband to momentarily lose his head. Problems started when Nora demanded he be sterilised if he wanted to resume sexual relations. His sympathetic doctor, who had tried to talk him out of taking 'such a terrible step', said he was a 'kind man and a most attentive husband' – evidently too attentive in Nora's view, she not coping with two children from his first marriage and another three with him. The prosecutor told the jury that whatever sympathy they might have for man with a nagging wife, he was not entitled to shoot her. The defence conceded that a man should not shoot even an 'incessantly nagging wife'. But the jury could not 'brush aside' the 'excessive nagging' in this case. A 36-year-old man undergoing, at his demanding wife's insistence, an operation which 'cuts him away from his manhood' showed the extent to which he was prepared to submit to her will for the sake of harmony in the home. Instructing them not to let their verdict be influenced by sentiment, the judge asked the jury to consider whether shooting a woman who had 'given him hell for ten years', was more likely to have been accidental or intentional. Certainly, Nora had broken her word about resuming relations after the operation and was 'as cold as ever afterwards'. But that had occurred two years ago and so could not have caused a sudden loss of self-control. The jury convicted him of murder. Dismissing his appeal, the Chief Justice said he had no doubt 'the dead woman was a bad wife' who had made his life a misery. But it was still murder. Not in everyone's view. Outside the court, people read damning newspaper reports. One titled, 'She forced her husband to take a terrible step', included a photograph of the victim captioned, 'She nagged her husband'. Another captioned her photograph 'woman with uncontrollable temper'. A petition with 10,000 signatures attached ensured his reprieve, reported under the celebratory headline: 'kind and gentle killer reprieved'.[15]

Four wife killers were hanged in 1952 after committing homicides that within five years would be registered as barely manslaughter. Twenty-seven-year-old Eileen Harris' husband lost his temper and killed her. They had often quarrelled. Eileen used to do 'silly things' such as going to the cinema without him just to annoy him. Convicting him of murder, the jury strongly recommended him to mercy. It was to no avail. The second condemned man stabbed his wife, 17-year-old Jean Cull, to death with a bayonet at her father's London home after receiving a letter saying she wished to leave him. He said 'she asked for it' by 'two-timing' him. The third man shot his 29-year-old wife, Eunice Simon, and a man she was talking to, the shooting making it a capital crime. Surprisingly it was the prosecutor, not the defence, who called it a 'crime of passion', albeit not a mitigating one. Anticipating the diminished responsibility defence that would be introduced in 1957, the defendant's counsel argued he had mental abnormalities that made it difficult to control himself. There were not enough abnormalities to convince the jury to clear him of murder at his Birmingham trial. Twenty-seven-year-old Kathleen Norcliffe's husband stabbed her in the back. His insanity defence failed despite him having no discernible motive. Asked if he had anything to say before he was sentenced to death, his only comment was that nobody seemed puzzled as to why he did it.[16] That was a question that would not go begging in subsequent wife-killing cases. In fact, the question of why husbands killed their wives was to become the central issue, one intensely focused on what she did to upset him.

These were some of the last wife-killers who got anywhere near the gallows. By the time Nora Cobon's killer was released on licence in 1958, very few femicidal men would be convicted of murder. But Gladys Nuttall's husband was. The prosecutor in this 1955 case called it 'a plain case of a man murdering his wife under the influence of anger and jealousy'. Gladys had left him, telling her mother she would rather drown herself than go back to him. The defence claimed he was devoted to her but conceded it was 'a savage sort of devotion', all too savage in the view of the jury. It returned a murder verdict. He then lost his appeal, the court referencing the *Holmes* case to declare that there was 'really no question' of provocation reducing the crime to manslaughter. Moreover, it was 'about time that husbands and people learnt that mere unfaithfulness by a wife' did not excuse murder, especially if she had separated from her husband. Bluntly, if a man wanted to 'get rid of his wife' he should divorce her. It was no excuse to say she was unfaithful and then kill her as her 'mere unfaithfulness' was insufficient provocation. She had to be caught in the act. Then she rightly reaped the consequences of a man's savage devotion.[17]

That had been the consistent judicial view for centuries. But by the mid-1950s, judges were fighting a losing battle. Public opinion was now firmly with killers like Gladys Nuttall's husband who was reprieved following a mercy petition signed by 3000 sympathisers. Not that the Court of Appeal was immune to being swayed by stories of intolerably provocative wives. Take the case of a man sentenced in 1956 to five years' imprisonment for wounding 31-year-old model Myrtle Healey with intent to murder. The court hearing his appeal against his sentence pronounced that it had 'pointed out again and again that because a man thinks his wife is unfaithful to him that is not an excuse for attacking her'. Nevertheless, in a judgment that proved to be a harbinger of things to come, it granted him leave to appeal on the ground of a 'combination' of mitigating circumstances. The appellate judges agreed with counsel that the defendant had a mental illness that caused him to lose control and attack his 'unfaithful treacherous' wife in the face of her 'gross infidelity'.[18]

By giving the imprimatur to the defence strategy of combining her provocation with his mental impairment, this judgment signalled a relaxation of judicial attitudes towards impassioned crimes. Three years later, the court heard a man's appeal against his conviction for the attempted murder of his wife, Jessie Loughlin, in Wyke. He told police he was 'in love with her' but suspected she was having an affair. Recovered from her injuries after three weeks in hospital, Jessie denied it. The jury convicted him but evidently did not find her testimony that convincing. They recommended leniency as he had been subjected to 'great provocation'. The judge handed down a three-year sentence. The Court of Appeal was even more lenient, quashing the conviction for attempted murder and substituting a sentence of 18 months for the lesser offence of causing actual bodily harm. It did so notwithstanding what it described as a 'worrying feature of the case' – namely, that the evidence against him was 'so strong'.[19] This particular worrying feature would soon stop being one, disappearing under a tidal wave of compassion for men who disposed of women while in a homicidal rage ignited by the slightest 'provocation'.

Taunting words, diminishing minds

DESDEMONA	*Am I that name, Iago?*
IAGO	*What name, fair lady?*
DESDEMONA	*Such as she said my lord did say I was.*
EMILIA	*He called her whore...*

Othello 4.2.119–122

With the passing of The Homicide Act 1957, the English understanding of a mitigating impassioned homicide was to expand exponentially. Only one of the 30 men executed in England and Wales once it came into force had been in a relationship with the woman he killed. She was Alice Buxton murdered in a Kent village in 1961 by a man with whom she had an affair. But hers was a non-capital murder. Her killer had bludgeoned her to death with the rifle he shot her husband with. *That* was the capital murder for which he hanged.[20] Henceforth, murder convictions for femicidal men would become exceptions proving the rule that killing a provocative wife was barely punishable manslaughter, all thanks to the availability of the expanded provocation defence and the newly minted and equally capacious diminished responsibility defence. Where the wife's provocative conduct might be thought too slight even for the expanded provocation defence, diminished responsibility could step in to accommodate all kinds of easily enraged men. In fact, diminished responsibility would turn out to be especially serviceable to defence strategists. It enabled them to bypass the reasonable man standard embedded in the provocation defence, replacing him with a mentally 'abnormal' one, a man suffering from depression caused by relationship breakdown. From the 1960s, these defences invariably resulted in manslaughter convictions and sentences of five years or less as the victim's abusive words moved to centre stage in the defence narrative. What she allegedly did and especially what he claimed she said to upset him mattered, his words about hers condemning her as surely as Iago's did Desdemona.

What words provoked the man who killed his third wife, Lisbeth Ashworth, in 1960? He told the court at the Berkshire Assizes that Lisbeth, a widow with two children of her own, wanted him to have his children with his previous wives adopted. This caused him, a 'devoted father', to strangle her. Something just 'snapped'. She had promised she would be a good mother to them. His conviction for manslaughter was reported under the headline, 'He Killed Wife Who Said "Give Away the Children"', accompanied by a photograph of an unrelated woman happily holding a baby. The judge thought it 'a more than usually distressing case' – distressing, that is, to the killer and his sympathisers. While wanting to extend mercy as far as he could, he felt unable to shut his heart to the fact that 'an inoffensive woman was done to death'. He sentenced him to four years.[21]

Inoffensive women were hard to come by. Welshwoman Marguerite Howard was not one of them. Her husband strangled her to death in 1961 after she subjected him to a verbal barrage that, according to his defence, was 'liable to reduce any man to breaking point'. The jury agreed, convicting him of manslaughter by provocation. The judge agreed with the verdict. Marguerite had used 'the most vulgar language' to torment him, brutally rejecting his 'overture of friendliness'. While the 'interests of justice demanded' a custodial sentence, he assured the defendant it would be 'a very short one'. Moreover, he hoped he would 'face the future with courage'.[22] Less verbally abusive but still provocative, 20-year-old Marlene Whiting, the mother of a two-year old daughter, had left her husband and went to live with her brother where she became attached to another man. Her husband persuaded her to return but when he found a letter indicating she was planning to leave again for the other man, he killed her. The prosecutor at his Bristol trial called it 'cold-blooded murder'. He had 'decided quite cold-bloodedly to murder' her 'rather than let her go'. The defence argued provocation, namely, her goodbye letter, prompting the judge to lay down the law: had he had killed her there and then when he discovered the letter, 'one might almost have a classic example of a killing in hot blood as a consequence of provocative conduct by the wife'. Almost but not quite – he had delayed killing her until the following day. Unbothered by the delay, the jury cleared him of murder. Marlene's slaughter was hot-blooded enough for them.[23]

In 1963, 21-year-old Christine Holford's husband shot her dead at their Brighton home in what became the closest thing to a 'crime of passion' that the English could muster. It featured an unfaithful young wife and an older man who took to the press shortly after being cleared of her murder to pen a loving ode to her. It was also an exemplary case of a defence based on the expanded conception of provocation by infidelity combined with diminished responsibility. Counsel informed the jury that they would hear from 'eminent medical gentlemen' who would explain the 'imposed forces' on 'a boy's mind'. These were the 'experiences sexual which were left behind 2000 years ago in the classic Greek dramas and tragedies, but which apparently still exist in this county of yours in Sussex'. The prosecutor called it 'a clear case of capital murder' by shooting. It had been preceded by a vicious attack which had hospitalised Christine and which she cited in her goodbye letter as a reason for leaving him. Jealousy was no defence. As for the killer's mental state, the prosecution's psychiatrist testified that he did not suffer from 'pathological depression' but rather from 'a normal depression' because his wife wanted to leave him. This testimony rather surprised the judge who intervened to inquire what the doctor thought of the fact that according to the defendant's evidence, Christine had run off to France and gone 'completely off the rails' with another man. She had taunted her husband about his 'lack of sexual powers' and demanded he prove otherwise, prompting him to consult his doctor when he failed the challenge. What, the judge wanted to know, would be the 'cumulative effect of all these happenings on the mind?' The psychiatrist was adamant: they would certainly be upsetting, but they would not produce 'a pathological process'. Astonished, the judge insisted: 'you cannot picture anything much more shattering, can you?'[24]

Writing the script that would be followed in many femicide cases to follow, counsel presented the defendant as suffering from an abnormality of mind that substantially reduced his responsibility. It also left him vulnerable to the victim's numerous provocations – her affairs, her letter saying she was leaving him and most damningly, her telling him the child was not his. That was the last straw, worse even than demanding he show her what a man he was. That demand had conjured up an image of her with the other man which left him 'numb'. It was in this state of 'numbness' – the 'numbness that hits a man' who is exposed to all these 'forces' – that he shot Christine six times. As if this wasn't enough to win him sympathy, the defence quoted Shakespeare's sonnet 61 to bring home 'to the full' the killer's tragic love for a wife who loved him less than he did her:

> thy love, though much, is not so great.
> It is my love that keeps mine eye awake,
> Mine own true love that doth my rest defeat,
> To play the watchman ever for thy sake.
> For thee watch I whilst thou dost wake elsewhere,
> From me far off, with others all too near.

English culture providing no higher authority than Shakespeare, counsel had hit upon the perfect literary warrant for murder committed by a man devastated by a wife waking with another elsewhere. Though today we might read sonnet 61 as a stalker's manifesto, the judge was moved by the defence story. His summing up was a masterpiece of double-negatived disavowal that law's much-lauded concession to 'human emotions' was actually a concession to men's proprietary fury. Directing the jury not to 'let your hearts rule your heads', he told them to put 'out of your minds any feelings of mere sympathy you may have' for this 'poor father'. Do not think that because you feel sorry for him you should take 'a lenient course'. Not that the law says you should not consider 'the frailties of human emotion'. Indeed, these had 'their place in our law'. And furthermore, English law now left it open to juries to return verdicts of manslaughter by provocation, by diminished responsibility or even on the ground of both 'principles'. In the case of Christine's killer, it would be 'quite logical' for them to do so on whatever ground they thought fit.[25]

Logical or not, this kind of circular reasoning had effectively transformed the provocation defence's reasonable man into a man of limited mental capacity, one suffering from 'an abnormality of mind' caused by an unfaithful wife. Pressing hard for a manslaughter verdict, the judge reminded the jury that three of the four medical witnesses said the defendant was suffering from diminished responsibility and that Christine had sorely provoked him. If the jury thought the defendant shot his wife 'in a moment of passion' while smarting under 'intense provocation', they were entitled to return a manslaughter verdict. After all, her provocation was 'very great', especially her abusive taunting. Juries were no longer hindered as they had been in 'the old days' when provocation was legally limited to provocative actions. This was thanks to that new law – the Homicide Act 1957 – which now allowed them to take account of provocative words as well. Could anything be more 'shattering' to a man than his wife telling him he was not the father of their child? The jury didn't think anything could and duly returned a verdict of manslaughter. This outcome was well received. The judge said the jury had 'perfectly rightly' acquitted him of capital murder. There was applause and clapping from the public gallery and the *Sunday Mirror* pronounced it the only possible verdict in a 'sordid and sorry case of a husband who discovered his wife was a slut'.[26]

Henceforth, defence narratives would follow this 'nagging and shagging' script usually to the letter. It would begin with a woman's rowdy departure from a marriage. She would say hurtful things deriding his sexual capacity, compared him adversely to the new man and, the trump card, tell him their child was not his. A winning narrative, it would assure her killer of a short prison term or even a non-custodial sentence for manslaughter. Aided and abetted by expansive conceptions of provocation and diminished responsibility that could be deployed in tandem if necessary, the script worked over and over again to excuse the disposal of wives now invariably represented in the courtroom discourse as taunting sluts. As for Christine Holford, the prototypical taunting slut, her condemnation in the criminal court and the press was remarkable for standing the test of time. When her killer died in 2006, by which time the movement to stop men getting away with murdering women was well under way, the *Daily Mail* recalled the Holford case as 'one of the most sensational murder trials of the sixties'. Under the headline 'Taunted to death', it portrayed Christine as 'an archetypal small town good-time girl' with a 'potent sex appeal' and a 'disturbing quality of heartlessness about her' that distressed the local boys. And tellingly, it is her words rather than her actions that still invite the harshest criticism – calling her husband a 'little boy', telling a patron at his bar that he was 'no good at it', that he was 'damaged goods'. Christine was simply far too garrulous for her own good such that four decades after her death, hers was still perceived as a classic case of having 'asked for it'. Even her daughter, whose 'disputed paternity innocently triggered the tragedy' agreed with that assessment. Well tutored in the matter of where sympathy should lie in a wife-killing case, she was quoted as saying that her father loved her mother 'very much', so much in fact that 'he never got over her death and what he had done'.[27]

Noise, worry, distress

Excellent Wretch! Perdition catch my soul
But I do love thee! And when I love thee not
Chaos is come again

Othello 3.3.90–93

Defence lawyers would re-enact the victim-blaming script in hundreds of intimate partner killings over the five decades following Christine Holford's death. Just a few will suffice to illustrate how far mitigating passion would stretch after the mid-century reforms to the law of murder. By now the impassioned killer in the dock had been transformed into a sorely provoked man or a mentally diminished one. Or he could be both. For example, a man's eight-year sentence for the manslaughter of his wife Vilma McPherson in their Essex home was reduced to four years at his 1963 trial. While the jury's verdict was on the ground of diminished responsibility, the Court of Appeal said it could equally have found manslaughter due to provocation. Vilma had left him, asked for a divorce and apparently made unfavourable comparisons between him and her new lover. No wonder the court was satisfied that 'justice would be done by halving the sentence'. That would be justice for a man described by his counsel as 'a paragon of all the husbandly virtues'. He had been in love with his wife and was now 'in love with her memory'.[28] Two years later, 18-year-old model Susan Meech was stabbed 49 times by her ex-husband when she met him to discuss child custody arrangements. Love letters from another man – motive for murder – were read out in court. It was said she had compared him unfavourably to other men. The judge found that unsurprising given how he had 'goaded and probed her in an extremely disagreeable way'. Little wonder she preferred the company of other men. The jury was more sympathetic to the killer, returning a manslaughter verdict after accepting the defence case that the killer was 'so mentally abnormal that he was unable to control his temper and viciousness' when stressed.[29]

For all the changes the Homicide Act 1957 made to law's understanding of adequate provocation, the age-old distinction between hot-blooded manslaughter and cold-blooded murder remained intact. Witness the 1964 trial of a man charged with murdering a man who had been associating with his wife. Under cross-examination, he agreed he had killed the man in cold blood. He then confused the matter by saying 'but not to the extent that I went to'. Re-examined by his lawyer, he corrected his testimony to say he was 'really mad' by the time he killed him. In fact, his blood was 'boiling'. The jury convicted him of murder, though strongly recommending him to mercy. Tellingly, his equivocal testimony as to whether or not he committed cold-blooded murder earned him the judge's praise: 'you could easily have built up a picture which would have brought you within the ambit of the law relating to provocation'. Building up that picture was precisely the strategy deployed in the far more frequent wife-killing cases.[30]

While judges appeared to approve of the Act's widening of defences to murder, its distinction between capital and non-capital murder was another matter entirely. During a House of Lords debate on capital punishment in July 1965, leading abolitionist Lady Wootton slammed the Act as a 'disastrous failure' that had produced 'not justice but anomalies'. Chief Justice Lord Parker agreed. It had indeed resulted in 'complete absurdities' and he was certain the Queen's Bench judges agreed with him 'almost to a man'. Unlike Lady Wootton, however, Lord Parker was a reluctant abolitionist. He believed the death penalty to be a deterrent for some crimes though not for 'sexual crimes' or those resulting from 'grave emotional disturbance'. Furthermore, life sentences should be restricted to the 'real thug, the really dangerous man' who should be imprisoned for 20–30 years. By contrast, he felt the 'emotionally disturbed man' was unlikely to commit another murder. Eight to ten years was the 'right sentence' for him, Lord Parker not having considered that women may regard impassioned wife-killers as the real thugs, the really dangerous men.[31]

Take the case, decided during the House of Lords debate, of a married man, a police officer, who faced a charge of capital murder for shooting his mistress, 24-year-old Veronica Baker. Upset at finding she had a photograph of another man, he went to her parents' London home, shot her dead and wounded her parents. His defence was that he became 'consumed by an insane jealousy coupled with an urge to kill her'. As he said himself, he was 'very much in love' with her and, surely, insane jealousy was 'usual with a passionate love affair'. In fact, the jealousy associated with passionate love affairs had not traditionally been seen as 'insane' but rather as an understandable reaction to loss. Now however, calling it insane brought it within the ambit of a diminished responsibility defence. A psychiatrist testified that the killer had been in the grip of powerful emotions which seriously influenced his judgment. His intense jealousy and his inability to get Veronica out of his mind derailing his sense of responsibility. Challenging that view, the Crown's medical witness denied that the 'building up of a misconceived feeling of jealousy' constituted temporary insanity. Convicted of murder he was sentenced to death and his appeal dismissed. A reprieve was not needed however, as the bill to abolish capital punishment was about to obtain parliamentary assent. Several newspapers gave Veronica's father the last word. His daughter had wanted to get police protection because of his violence but was too frightened to report him. As for her killer, he 'wasn't satisfied with killing' his daughter. He had 'blackened her name by calling her a slut'.[32] Slut-shaming femicide victims was fast becoming standard operating procedure.

Manslaughter convictions for provoked and mentally diminished femicidal men proceeded apace in tandem with defence narratives trashing victims' reputations. The cases were not prosecuted vigorously. In November 1965, the same month that the Murder (Abolition of Death Penalty) Act 1965 came into effect, Emma Fletcher was beaten to death by her partner. He explained to police that his first wife was 'a good'un for 30 years and then this bitch drives me to this. I am well rid of her'. Unknown to him, she had not divorced her first husband and so was not his lawful wife. A conviction for manslaughter and a short sentence were inevitable after the prosecutor described him as a 'hard working man of good character' who killed Emma because he could 'no longer bear his married life with her. She was 'a bad wife', in fact a bigamous one, and 'one is left with the ironical possibility that, had he known' she was still married to another man, 'he might never have killed her'. Had he known, it seems to be implied, he would have had no need to kill her.[33] The prosecutor at the murder trial of Sheila Goldsworthy's husband the following year acknowledged that her friendliness with another man had caused him 'worry and distress'. But did that excuse stabbing her to death? The jury thought so, accepting he suffered from depression.[34]

Occasionally a judge expressed reservations about the avalanche of manslaughter convictions handed down to femicidal men. In 1966, 25-year-old Carol Meech was killed because she was leaving her partner for another man. Worse, she had teased him on the way out. There was a struggle leading him to go berserk with a poker and a knife because he wanted her to stay. The jury cleared him of murder but the judge clearly had reservations. This was the sixth man to have appeared before him in recent weeks charged with, but cleared of, murder. This prompted the judge to lament that while he honoured the jury's verdict, it was 'terribly disquieting' that although provocation reduced murder to manslaughter, 'a life has been lost'. It 'must be realised that although there is provocation, killing is still a crime'.[35] He was not the only disquieted judge. In May 1967, a man appeared at the Central Criminal Court charged with the murder of his second wife, 17-year-old Marion Dillingham, the mother of his sixth child. This was his second murder charge for wife-killing, he having battered his first wife to death in a jealous rage three years earlier. Convicted of manslaughter by diminished responsibility at his first trial, he was given a conditional discharge, the judge declaring that 'society would best be served by allowing him to look after his children'. He said he strangled his second wife because she wanted to send two of his five children with his first wife to a Dr Bernardo home. Once again, he was found guilty of manslaughter on the ground of diminished responsibility. This time however, his first manslaughter conviction helped focus the judge's mind on 'the risks that the public may face'. He found it especially worrying that the jury had accepted his defence when none of the medical testimony supported it. So he handed down a life sentence, the defence lawyer's plea in mitigation that this double wife killer had made up his mind never to marry again not holding any sway.[36]

The benefits of combining defences were on show again at the trial of the man who killed his 44-year-old partner, Mary Gerrard, and her 17-year-old daughter, Liverpool shop assistant Ann Best in 1966. He was cleared of both murders, Mary's on the ground of provocation and Ann's on the ground of diminished responsibility. As the judge explained the second verdict, 'the effect of the first killing, coming on top of everything thing else', had 'affected his mind so that he behaved irresponsibly'. Besides, witnesses testified that he was a kind, 'mild man' and a police officer testified that he had found no evidence of violence. Presumably he meant aside from that of the slaughtered bodies, Mary having been beaten to death with a hammer and Ann asphyxiated. But there was plenty of evidence of Mary's 'provocation'. The previous year she had sent a letter to her killer when he was in prison saying she wanted to end their relationship. After his release, they were still living together until Mary asked him to leave in protest at the way he disciplined her daughter.[37] It seems that was enough to secure him a manslaughter verdict, no sniff of 'infidelity' required. No question of infidelity arose either at the trial of Irene Hartt's husband, charged the following year with murdering her at their Berkshire home. The case centred on Irene's 'noise', he saying he put his hands on her throat to 'shake some sense in her' and 'stop her noise'. Collaborating his evidence, their daughter testified that her demanding and domineering mother had put her husband down as a 'working-class beast'. The judge told the jury that if he strangled her 'on purpose' it was murder, but if it was 'simply to stop her arguing', the 'proper' verdict was manslaughter. Opting for manslaughter, they pleaded for a lenient sentence. Handing down the standard three-year prison term – the most lenient sentence he felt he could – the judge nevertheless felt he should remind the killer that 'the fact remains that your wife is dead'.[38] That was not a fact that weighed heavily on judges or juries in wife-killing cases after 1957.

Wife-killing in 'modern times'

This then is how impassioned femicide was being framed in the courts after the mid-twentieth century reforms unleashed men's passions. The expanded provocation defence had become precisely what one contemporary legal observer feared it might – 'merely an attempt to make appear as a *crime passioné* what was in reality nothing but cold-blooded murder'.[39] There were however, some limits to what angry men could do to their wives. For instance, they could not kidnap them. In 1972, a man appealed against his conviction for kidnapping his wife, Maria Reid. She had left him, presumably to escape his violence, a stabbing attack having hospitalised her three years earlier. She was living at her aunt's house where he threatened her again with a knife, forcing her to return. Found guilty, he appealed his conviction but dismissing his appeal, the court said a husband carrying his wife away against her will could be charged with kidnapping. The traditional idea of a husband's rights upheld in 'ancient cases' that he could legally confine his wife to prevent her from eloping had been 'swept away' in the late nineteenth century. Indeed, 'even in order to enforce conjugal rights a husband could not keep his wife in confinement'. True, a husband could not be charged with raping his wife because marriage implied consent. But the court found it 'impossible to stretch that doctrine' to say that she has also consented to be taken away by force or threats. The criminal law protected her from that. The notion that a husband could treat his wife, whether separated or not, with 'any kind of hostile force' was 'obsolete'.[40] At least, it was obsolete as far as kidnapping went. In marked contrast, a femicidal husband could still kill his wife and be partially excused for doing so, the domestic discount entitlement proving much more difficult to dislodge.

There were though some limitations on what defence counsel could argue for femicidal defendants, especially when it came to introducing medical testimony. Take the case of the man charged in 1973 with the murder of his partner, Wendy Butterfield. He was deeply in love with Wendy. He thought she was pregnant by him. But one day, while sitting in a car with him, she told him that she had slept with other men while he was in prison and that the child was not his. So he hit her with a hammer which he happened to have with him. He was convicted of murder. The issue on appeal was that the trial judge had ruled inadmissible a psychiatric report that he was likely to be easily provoked despite being 'a placid rather quiet and passive person' who was sensitive to the feelings of others. He was regarded by his family as 'not in any way aggressive'. This submission rather surprised counsel for the Crown who knew the appellant had been convicted of assault with intent to rob the previous year. Pressing on, the defence produced a psychiatric report that while there was no evidence of mental illness, the defendant's relationship with his victim was such as to 'make him particularly vulnerable to be overwhelmed by anger'. Indeed, given his personality, it was no surprise that he responded to her alleged confession of infidelity with 'an explosive release of blind rage'. The appellate judges were scathing about the report. What 'in plain English' was the psychiatrist saying? That the killer had 'a deep emotional relationship' with his victim? That this was likely to have 'caused an explosive release of rage' when she confessed to 'wantonness'? That he behaved like someone in profound grief after killing her? No psychiatrist was needed to tell the court that:

> We all know both men and women who are deeply in love can, and sometimes do, have outbursts of blind rage when discovering unexpected wantonness on the part of their loved ones; the wife taken in adultery is the classical example of the application of the defence of 'provocation' and when death or serious injury results, profound grief usually follows.

Juries did not need psychiatrists to tell them how 'ordinary folk' react to 'the stresses and strains of life'.[41]

Not that appellate judges were opposed to expert evidence or to the idea that provocative words could reduce murder to manslaughter. And they were still very much wedded to the view that 'unexpected wantonness' can provoke men and women equally to kill, notwithstanding their bird's eye view of the overwhelming evidence presented in the courts that it is almost exclusively men's blind rage that is unleashed in response to such a disclosure. Their own 'classic example' of provocation reveals as much. But they did want to prevent experts wandering into the terrain of what 'ordinary folk' know about the effect of confessions of adultery. Some were also unhappy about the way defence counsel sought to argue diminished responsibility. Take the case of the man who in 1979 pleaded guilty to the manslaughter of his wife, 40-year-old Gillian Vinagre, the mother of his five children. After stabbing her 34 times, he explained to police that she 'was going to leave me and I couldn't bear it'. Given a life sentence, he appealed. The Court of Appeal found the case troubling. He was 'undoubtedly guilty of homicide of some kind', but what, exactly? After all, his was 'a story of conduct of a common kind':

> Jealous husbands do kill their wives. Sometimes there might be good reasons why they should be jealous. In other cases, they may not have any reasons at all for being jealous. On some occasions the reasons are flimsy. It is a kind of conduct against which wives should be protected by the law. Before 1957, there would have been no question about it, this man would have been found guilty of murder. He could not have had any defence.[42]

But courts now needed to consider whether there was any evidence of diminished responsibility. A medical report suggested the defendant was suffering from 'Othello Syndrome' – defined as 'morbid jealousy for which there was no cause'. It seemed to the appellate judges that 'if justice was to be done', this submission would require them to determine whether Gillian had been unfaithful. If so, it was a 'straightforward case of a jealous husband'. If not, the 'Othello Syndrome' could be 'called in aid'. That concept did not appeal to them. Besides, the law makers had never intended that diminished responsibility pleas be accepted on 'flimsy grounds'. There had to be clear evidence of mental imbalance. There was none in this case. However, there was 'clear evidence of a killing by a jealous husband which, until modern times, no one would have thought was anything but murder'.[43]

Opening the floodgates

Murder, cold-blooded murder, was what the prosecutor called the killing of 26-year-old Monika Telling in Devon in 1983. Dubbed 'the headless corpse' case, it raised once again what the judge called 'a variation on a not unknown theme' – a man kills his wife who taunts him about her affairs and belittles his sexual prowess. Asked why he killed her, he said there were '101 reasons' – she 'kept pushing me. I just snapped in the end. She was horrible in many ways'. Urging the jury not to deliver the accused 'one final rejection' by finding him guilty of murder, the defence insisted a manslaughter verdict would be 'a true one, not one of sympathy'. Supporting that view, three psychiatrics testified that the killer's mental disorder was 'a deeply rooted failure to adapt to life as he matured and to people around him and to control his emotions and impulses'. He was not 'a cool, cold-blooded' man but rather one 'of mixed and barely controlled emotions'. The victim's taunts on 'any normal man' would be 'profoundly humiliating and hurtful', distressing and 'deeply upsetting'. But he was not a normal man. He was very immature and lacking confidence, generally and sexually. The judge told the jury to 'put aside your emotions and dispassionately consider the evidence'. They returned a manslaughter verdict. Monika's father was furious at the way the defence had portrayed her: she was 'certainly not a saint, but she was nothing like she was painted'. To 'put my daughter on trial like that was absolutely disgusting'.[44]

Two cases resulting in non-custodial sentences reported on the same day in October 1984 show the provocative wife narrative reaching a pinnacle of its excusatory force. Both killers pleaded guilty to manslaughter by diminished responsibility. As the pleas were accepted by prosecutors, no jury was required to test the evidence; a man's uncorroborated story of distress caused by a departed or exiting woman sufficed. In the first case, a man shot his former wife, Pauline Fenton, and her new husband because he couldn't live without her and couldn't believe she had left him. The prosecutor, not the defence, described him as a 'thoroughly decent man', who had unrealistic hopes that his former wife would return to him. Deciding that neither justice nor the public would be advanced 'one jot' by leaving him in prison, the judge at the Bristol Crown Court handed down a sentence of three years' probation. The second case, summed up in the headline: 'Taunted man kills wife', was that of Mildred Wilkes' killer. The judge at Shrewsbury Crown Court concluded that he had suffered from diminished responsibility and there was substantial provocation. Mildred, who had been having an affair with a younger man, had 'insulted, abused, lied, threatened and goaded' her husband for months. Moreover, his neighbours begged that he be freed so that he could 'return among us'. Sentence: two years' probation. 'Two wife-killers walk free' rang the *Daily Mail* headline.[45]

Did that headline suggest disquiet with the sentences? There was certainly outrage two months later when a man who killed his three daughters, aged between three and six years, was cleared of murder at Oxford Crown Court. He strangled them in order to cause the maximum possible distress to his estranged wife, Sue Lambert. She had moved to a 'battered wives' hostel', but he wanted her back. Then he discovered she was having an affair. The prosecutor called it 'a simple straightforward case of murder', but cases featuring provocative wives were anything but. Hearing that he had been a loving father until he started thinking about his unfaithful wife with her new partner and that he had an abnormality of mind brought on by his wife's infidelity, the jury returned a manslaughter verdict. Senior police slammed the six-year sentence. So did Women's Aid, incensed that Sue's evidence was never heard and that the case gave men 'licence to kill or attempt to kill women and children'. A 'bit shocked' at the lenient sentence, one journalist wondered whether sympathy was being wasted on such men. He hoped it wasn't 'becoming a habit'.[46]

Alas it was already a well-ingrained habit, juries accepting mitigating provocation in numerous wife-killing cases throughout the second half of the century. To take just a few cases decided in one busy year, let us start in January 1985 when the Court of Appeal considered a man's appeal against a five-year sentence for the manslaughter of his wife, Christine Mellentin. The court acknowledged that his story that she had provoked him by disparaging his sexual ability and boasted about her encounters with other men could not be corroborated. Yet there was 'no reason' to suspect it was not true. Never mind that the killer had been imprisoned for a dishonesty offence. Such was the assumed truth of the goading-wife story retold over and over again. Reducing his sentence to four years, the judge agreed with the view implied in, and emboldened by, the Homicide Act 1957 that 'to taunt a man about his lack of sexual inclination or prowess does involve striking at his character and personality at its most vulnerable'.[47]

Vulnerable men upset by a woman's conduct continued to reap the benefit of the 'domestic discount' for wife killers. Two months later Margaret Hogg's husband received a three-year sentence for her manslaughter. Criticising the sentence as 'derisory', the Law and Order Society expressed amazement that this 'cold, calculating villain' could be free after only 32 months. It was 'quite incredible'. Actually, for anyone paying attention, such short sentences had become standard. What *is* noteworthy is that this killer's provocation narrative passed scrutiny a decade after he had killed Margaret and dumped her body in a lake. The discovery of her body prompted him to recall her provocative conduct. It was not just how she behaved 'at the eleventh hour' when she apparently 'attacked him like a tiger' during an argument over her lover. There was also 'unfaithful and bad behaviour' over many years to consider – conduct that marked her, in the defence account, as a 'piece of erring humanity'. The jury agreed, taking only an hour to acquit him of murder.[48]

Juries continued to clear femicidal men of murder on a regular basis, no one seeming to notice that something might be amiss. In April 1985, a man was jailed for life at the Old Bailey for murdering his common law wife, Doreen Wilcocks, whom he stabbed and battered to death in a 'jealous frenzy'. He was a double wife-killer, having hacked his first wife, Dorothy Lewis, to death with a cleaver in 1969 during an argument about their nine-year-old epileptic daughter disturbing his sleep. Back then, his plea of guilty to manslaughter by provocation was accepted at the Bedford Assizes and he was sentenced to two and a half years' imprisonment.[49] The two killings were described as 'carbon copies' of each other, but that did not alert the courts to the risks associated with handing down short sentences to other wife-killers. They were soon back to business as usual. In October a man convicted of manslaughter by diminished responsibility was sentenced to three years' probation for killing Sheila Wilson, his wife of five weeks. He said she had teased him. Agreeing with the jury that there was only one verdict – manslaughter – the judge felt it would be 'useless' sending him to prison as he had led 'a blameless life and a very worthwhile one'. Besides, there was not 'the slightest risk' in setting him free.[50]

The prosecutor at the December 1985 trial of Christabel Boyce's husband argued her killing was a 'cool and deliberate murder'. Marriages might break down, but 'an ordinary person does not resort to butting his wife with tremendous force then strangling her when she is defenceless'. The jury disagreed. An ordinary person did just that. The defence argument that provocation was at 'the heart of the case' was utterly convincing. Christabel had subjected her husband to 'a non-stop form of humiliation and degradation which drained every bit of self-respect from a grown man'. He used to 'sneak home, terrified', finally snapping after months of nagging, humiliation, sexual taunts, mental torture and threats to leave with the children. Christobel had screamed abuse and accusations – would it not have 'worn down any person?' The jury agreed it would, ignoring the prosecutor's warning that it is 'easy to make allegations' about the victim in court when she was not there to dispute them. But the judge was unimpressed with a killer who had 'cooked up a story' that he had acted in self-defence and pretended he had no idea where his wife's body was. The evidence showed clearly that he had disposed of her body parts around London. Noting that the usual sentence for manslaughter by provocation was between three and seven years, he sentenced him to six years.[51]

It is only fitting that we conclude this brief overview of the late twentieth-century cases by noting that women were not the only victims. It is a measure of just how expansive the notion of 'provoked' killing had come since the mid-century law reforms that in October 1985, the same month that Christobel Boyce's husband won over his jury, a man succeeded in his appeal against his conviction for murdering a 'provocative' newborn baby.[52] Its incessant crying had deprived him of sleep. The issue before the Court of Appeal was that the judge had refused to allow the provocation defence to be left to the jury on the ground that it was natural for newborn babies to cry and be 'burdensome'. He thought child killers should not be able to escape justice by claiming provocation. Quashing the murder conviction and life sentence and substituting a five-year sentence for manslaughter, the appellate judges said that the jury's common sense would ensure that killing a crying child would only be considered the response of a reasonable man where the facts 'fully justified it'. After all, the Homicide Act 1957 had stipulated that the question of what provocation would make an ordinary and responsible person lose self-control should be left to the jury. The court was not swayed by the Crown's argument that provocation defences should be limited to cases where there is 'some element of wrongfulness' triggering the fatal assault. Nor was it convinced that public policy required that a baby's cries, even if persistent, should not found a plea of provocation because otherwise the floodgates would be open to provocation pleas in all battered baby cases.[53] That the floodgates to provocation pleas were already well and truly opened for men who killed nagging, shagging wives was yet to register in the courts.

Law's logic in 'domestic' cases – querying the weight of authority

When, in the late twentieth century, the Court of Appeal finally started to query homicidal anger's excusatory force, it was not femicide cases but rather what it referred to as 'domestic attempted murder' cases that attracted its attention. It comes as no surprise to learn that all these cases concerned attacks on women by husbands and male partners. All were appeals against lengthy sentences and in all but one, the appeals were successful. But what is especially noteworthy about these cases is that the appellate judges made it clear that they felt constrained, indeed obligated by 'authority' or precedent to do so, much to their growing consternation. The foundational case of *Townsend* was an appeal in 1979 against a 15-year sentence for attempted murder. Janice Townsend had left her husband, so he shot her causing severe injuries from which it was thought she might not recover. In the court's view, the 'real question' to be decided was whether, 'bearing in mind the domestic nature' of the offence as contrasted with an armed robbery causing the same kind of injuries, it was possible to take a 'more merciful view' than the trial judge had. The court decided that it was and that 'justice would be done' if the sentence was reduced to ten years.[54]

Townsend was the first of three revealing Court of Appeal decisions in cases of attempted murders 'arising out of domestic conflict'. The court discussed these cases in the 1986 case of *Green*, an appeal by a man against his 12-year sentence for the attempted murder and rape of his estranged wife. The second case, *Haines*, was the only one where the court dismissed the appeal, refusing to reduce the 12-year prison sentence for a man who had broken into his former partner's flat and discharged a gun into her face. Mystified as to how the victim had survived, the court upheld that sentence as 'condign'.[55] The third case, *Donnelly*, concerned a man who had behaved 'in an extremely jealous manner' over a long period, accusing his wife of infidelity, threatening her and hitting her with a hammer. The *Green* court thought him 'lucky' to get his sentence reduced from nine to seven years. But for the 'authorities' – that is, their own recent decisions – the appellate judges would have been 'content' to dismiss all the appeals, Green's included. However, while they were in no mind to vary his sentence for rape, they felt bound or 'obliged', as they put it, to reduce his sentence for attempted murder from 12 to 10 years. Effectively, they were saying this decision had been forced on them by their own precedents. A sense of being oppressed by 'authorities', albeit their own, pervades the judgment – authorities providing a still lively warrant for them, most wretched, to perform the like, as Titus Andronicus put it to support his killing of his daughter. But whereas Titus had enlisted precedent to justify femicide, these late twentieth-century judges felt entrapped by authorities that, paradoxically, warranted longer sentences for attempted femicides than for completed ones.

Unsure how to deal with this illogicality, the court continued to reduce sentences for domestic attempted murder. Dorothy Drinkald's ex-husband attacked her with an axe and a knife when she met him after an access visit with their child. The judge called his jealousy 'obsessive and unjustified' but on appeal, his eight-year sentence was reduced to six on the ground that had he killed her, it would have been a case of manslaughter by diminished responsibility rather than murder. The court heard that he was 'fond of his wife and wanted to resume living with her'. The probation officer's report noted that he was suffering from such 'intense grief' that he was suicidal. He had become obsessed with her rejection and, unable to accept his loss, had a breakdown. He would need 'substantial' help to cope with these 'tragic events in his life'. The court agreed. Given his remorse and 'medical background' – two psychiatrists said he suffered from 'acute depression' – eight years was too long, notwithstanding the 'savagery of the attack'.[56]

While Tina Whitehouse's life had been 'totally ruined' after suffering brain damage when her partner tried to strangle her, his 15-year sentence was reduced to 12 years. Once again, the court noted that the authorities, which now included the *Green* case, clearly indicated that 15 years was 'outside the bracket for an attempted murder of this type'; namely, the 'domestic' type.[57] Men continued to commit this 'type' of attempted murder and to appeal their sentences. One, who had set his wife alight when she initiated divorce proceedings, had his 14-year sentence reduced to 12 years' imprisonment, the court 'feeling constrained to follow authority' that indicated that a lesser sentence was appropriate.[58] Another man who attempted to murder his wife also by setting her alight had his 12-year sentence reduced to 10. While all three appellate judges thought there was nothing wrong with the original sentence, they felt bound 'in the light of the authorities' to reduce it.[59]

In 1995, a man appealed against his sentence for the rape and attempted murder of a woman he did not know. This gave the court an opportunity to review sentencing practices in the domestic attempted murder cases that had so troubled them. Once again, the Court relived its sense of obligation, stating that 'the weight of authority' had 'compelled' it to reduce sentences in domestic cases. A distinction has to be drawn, it said, between cases in which there was a pre-existing relationship between the victim and her assailant and those in which there was no such relationship. Whether that was 'a logical distinction' was not for the court to say. But the authorities clearly showed that in cases where 'such a relationship exists or has existed a somewhat lesser tariff is imposed', thus extending the domestic discount to men who attempted to murder current or former wives.[60] Not for this court the bold statement it had made in 1980 in a grievous bodily harm case that 'assaults on wives are to be regarded as very serious matters and not to be lightly brushed aside as due to emotional upsets or jealousy or anything else'. Back then, some appellate judges were of the view that wives were

> the most vulnerable people when it comes to violent husbands, and there is *no reason* why a man should not be punished in the same way for assaulting his wife as he would be for assaulting any other person.[61]

No reason? How could they have forgotten the long history of men being punished differently for assaulting wives? Having come so close to registering that something was awry with handing down longer sentences for 'domestic attempted murder' than for murder, the appellate judges resiled from drawing the obvious conclusion – the authorities they felt so compelled to follow cried out for a major overhaul. Recognising how far removed late twentieth century femicidal men's 'emotional upsets' were from the justifiable rage at finding a wife in adultery endorsed in *Mawgridge*, the foundational 'domestic discount' case, would have to wait.

Emilia critics

EMILIA — Good gentlemen, let me have leave to speak
O murderous coxcomb, what should such a fool
Do with so good a wife?

IAGO — 'Swounds, hold your peace.

EMILIA — 'Twill out, twill out … I peace?
No, I will speak as liberal as the north.
Let heaven and men and devils, let them all,
All cry shame against me, yet I'll speak.

Othello 5.2.193 and 217–221

While the Court of Appeal pondered over the logic of distinguishing domestic from non-domestic attempted murder, lower court judges continued to hand down short sentences for femicidal men in cases that were already attracting critical attention outside the courtroom. Signs of a growing disquiet became increasingly apparent as feminist scholars and activists joined the families of slaughtered women in expressing outrage at manslaughter verdicts and short sentences handed down to wife-killers. They did not hold back. By the early 1980s, the marriage licence was being condemned as a 'licence to kill' women and the freeing of wife-killers on probation as tantamount to the decriminalisation of violence against women, including 'wife-slaughter'.[62] As a result, the press started to take more interest in the 'licence to kill' cases. In 1990, 30-year-old Valerie Middleton was killed by a man on weekend leave from prison. He was six months into a two-year sentence for having attacked her in 1988. Five years earlier he had received a four-year sentence for the manslaughter of Julie Stead. This time his story of his victim's alleged taunts about her affairs did not wash and he received a life sentence, though Valerie's family was outraged that the judge did not set a minimum term.[63] A few weeks later, the *Times* reported that 'husbands or lovers kill half of women murder victims'. It highlighted the 'uproar' at a 'merciful' verdict in a case where a jury took ten minutes to return a verdict of manslaughter by provocation for the man who killed his former lover, 22-year-old Kay Kerbey. She had allegedly said she was pregnant to him and called his wife a 'blond slag'. The verdict was greeted with 'screams of abuse' from friends and relatives who, unimpressed with the judge's assurance that verdicts were always upsetting because they were either 'too much or too little', called it 'a joke'.[64]

Another case receiving headlines was that of the man given a two-year suspended prison sentence in 1991 after kicking to death O'Linda Marion Kennedy, his partner of 25 years. He said she had provoked him with a torrent of obscenities. Declaring that O'Linda would have 'tried the patience of a saint', the judge ordered a 12-month supervision order to help her killer 'overcome his feelings of remorse'. The sentence outraged Sarah Thornton who was serving a life sentence for murdering her violent husband. Her appeal for a reduction of her conviction for murder to one of manslaughter by provocation had been rejected in the same week that O'Linda's killer received his suspended sentence. Sarah started a hunger strike in protest, while campaigners for her release decried how 'provocation' defences succeeded for men subjected to verbal barrages but not for women reacting to violent men. Demanding that the law be 'more balanced', the protestors ensured that the discrepant outcomes in the two cases received massive media coverage, including a BBC programme.[65]

In the meantime, femicidal men were still getting away with murder. After killing Yvonne Raglan in 1993, her husband told police he knew it wasn't murder because he 'loved that woman'. His lawyer explained that he was 'unable to cope with the fact she had fallen out of love with him'.[66] He admitted manslaughter on the grounds of diminished responsibility and received a five-year sentence at Plymouth Crown Court. Sandra Greech's husband 'walked free', as the press put it, after receiving a suspended sentence for her manslaughter at Manchester Crown Court. The judge calling it an 'exceptional case'. Sandra, he said, had taunted him about his sexual prowess and threatened him with a knife. So he stabbed her 23 times. 'You have not only been a man of good character', the judge told him, 'but you are a good man also'. Victims' rights groups begged to differ. Slamming the sentence, they protested that there was nothing exceptional about the case. Furthermore, it was 'now almost acceptable for domestic violence to be followed by murder and a suspended sentence'.[67] In a twist on the standard provocation script, the man who killed his wife, Diane Hunt, in 1994 after she discovered he had been unfaithful also received a suspended sentence. The Stafford Crown Court judge said he had been 'outrageously provoked', even though it was his infidelity which had 'brought about that provocation'. She had been arguing with him but he had merely been trying to restrain her from getting out of the car when she died. The prosecution said he 'deliberately strangled' her. Her family pleaded for mercy for her 'kind and caring husband' who 'still remains part of our family'. They couldn't live with him 'suffering in prison'. She 'sacrificed her life', rather than he taking it. At least that was the way her sister saw it.[68]

'Leniency for wife killers' and 'Men who kill their wives escape jail' ran *Times* headlines to a report about a Channel 4 documentary on domestic killings in 1995. Research for the programme exposed 'an underlying belief that it is less wicked to kill your wife than a stranger'. Nearly half of 'domestic killings by men' resulted in manslaughter convictions compared to a third of non-domestic killings. Moreover, wife-killers got shorter sentences of five years or less.[69] Interestingly, diminished responsibility, not provocation, was singled out as 'the key to the special leniency given to male domestic killers'. Many suffered from depression attributed to the victims' behaviour, such as a wife initiating divorce proceedings. No such leniency was afforded non-domestic killers relying on this defence who had suffered from long-term illness such as schizophrenia. The six-year sentence for manslaughter handed down in December 1996 to Josephine Wilson's husband of 30 years for her manslaughter was a case in point. Described as a 'pathologically jealous' businessman, he stabbed her at least 50 times 'in a frenzy' after she left for another man.[70] Two years later, another wealthy businessman was jailed for three years for killing his wife of 34 years, Jillian McKeon. He said he 'snapped' when she told him details of her affair.[71]

By the late twentieth century, short sentences handed down to femicidal men were coming under sustained pressure from 'Emilia critics' in many Anglophone jurisdictions. Feminist scholars and activists spoke out for victims and against excuses for femicide, especially that 'small vice', as Emilia called it in *Othello*, of infidelity. Though not framed as such, the critics were effectively mounting a challenge to the very concept of *crime passionnel*. Their main focus was the operation of the provocation defence, exposing how it worked as a profoundly sexed excuse for men who killed 'their' women. In England and Wales, as in other jurisdictions, the defence inscribes the victim – the wife or partner who 'flaunts' infidelity, or who is alleged to have done so, or who nags, or leaves her man – as a provocateur, even a 'seductress' who, as Susan Edwards put it, 'provokes her own demise'.[72] In another searching investigation of provocation cases, Hilary Allen revealed how law had failed miserably in its grandstanding efforts to endow itself with a genderless ordinary or reasonable person standard. As she highlights, the criminal law's betrayal of the notion of a neutral legal person is nowhere more evident than in its fiction of a gender-neutral provocation defence. For inasmuch as sexed differences are taken as 'a fundamental a priori of legal reasoning', law could not even allow itself to conceive of gender-neutral provocation. Such provocation was simply 'unthinkable'. And where exactly was law's betrayal of a putatively unsexed objectivity laid bare? Why, in the provocation defence's inscription of a woman killed by her impassioned man as a provocateur 'asking for it'. Allen declared herself 'perfectly happy' with Lord Simon's pronouncement in the famous *Holmes* case that a confession of adultery could not justify the view that a 'reasonable man (or woman)' could be so provoked as to kill the adulterer. But by the late twentieth century, the intended neutrality of this standard had collapsed.[73] As for how the Homicide Act 1957 had opened up the floodgates to men's provocation tales, it had, as yet another critic put it, 'facilitated the regression of men's matrimonial evolution'. Most regrettably, it had validated the belief that their proprietary rights over women warranted homicide if their wives transgressed the patriarchal order in any way.[74]

.....

While the post mortem slander of slaughtered women would continue untrammelled in the courts until the end of the century, the traditional presumption of a domestic discount for impassioned wife-killers was fast losing its currency outside the courts. Dismissed so cavalierly in the courts for decades as nothing more than blameworthy provocateurs, femicide's victims were about to come into their own as fully human subjects who, for the most part, had lived with or tried to leave violent or otherwise unsatisfactory men and paid the ultimate price for it. In the view of many Emilia critics, the time had come to abolish the provocation defence. It not only defamed victims; it was encouraged and exaggerated, 'a view of human behaviour which is sexist, homophobic and racist'. It was past time to 'move beyond provocation as an organising concept in excusing or mitigating homicide'.[75] It was way past time.

Chapter 6

'Red mist' rage unmasked

> *O murderous coxcomb, what should such a fool*
> *Do with so good a wife?*
>
> *Othello* 5.2.231–232

Introduction

On 30 December 2001, Madelaine Humes' husband stabbed her to death in front of their four children, the eldest a 14-year-old girl covered in blood as she rang 999 while trying to revive her mother. He said he was 'in a red mist' at the time and had 'lost it totally' – 'It's like they say, you can see a red mist, I was bellowing like a bull'. Maddie was going to leave him for another man for whom she had 'big style' feelings. Or so he said. A jury did not hear the case, the prosecution having accepted the killer's plea that Maddie had provoked him. He received a seven-year sentence for manslaughter.[1] Three months later another man killed his partner, Nicole Lewis. She had left him, taking the children to a women's refuge. The court noted he had found this 'difficult to accept'. It was also alleged that she had provoked him by saying that she had the children, but he only had their photographs. In retaliation, he had 'just boiled over' while in a 'red haze' and choked her to death, saying 'Do me a favour and die'. Acquitted of murder, he was sentenced to four years for manslaughter.[2] These cases were the last straw for Solicitor General Harriet Harman and her parliamentary allies who had tired of seeing femicidal men get away with murder by claiming 'provocation'. The stage was now set for a confrontation between law reformers bent on curtailing the deployment of provocation defences in intimate partner femicide cases and a judiciary that was, for the most part, content with the legal status quo. It would be a hell of a fight.

Building on a critical undercurrent that can be traced back to Shakespeare's querying of moral warrants for femicide in *Titus Andronicus* and *Othello*, the law reformers staged a feminist revolt against the manslaughter verdicts and lenient sentences handed down to femidical men. This chapter tells the story of the reform movement, the opposition to it, the implementation of the reforms and their impact in the courts. It highlights the inflamed rhetoric of the reformers'

DOI: 10.4324/9781003301974-7

parliamentary and judicial critics who, still blinded to the realities of impassioned homicide, staunchly championed provocation by infidelity as a historically mandated defence to murder. In doing so, they were in effect staging a last ditch stand in defence of the notion of a mitigating 'crime of passion'. Their near hysteria over the move to abolish the provocation defence and their efforts to uphold 'red mist' rage as an ungendered, time-honoured right to homicidal fury could not conceal what was actually at stake. The reformers had in their sights men's proprietary rights over 'their' women as enshrined in that foundational provocation case of *Mawgridge*, authority for the proposition that jealousy is the rage of a man and adultery is the highest invasion of property. Ushering in revolutionary changes to the English law of murder, the reforms would be nothing less than a stunning counter-hegemonic challenge to the received English version of impassioned homicide.

'Red mist rage' on trial – querying warranted excuses for murder

The criminal justice system's response to Maddie Humes' death outraged her family. Decrying the seven-year sentence for manslaughter handed down to her killer at Sheffield Crown Court in July 2002, her brother spoke out against the prosecution's decision to accept his provocation plea. The family was determined to do 'everything in our power to reverse that decision', including campaigning for a change in the law to prevent prosecutors accepting manslaughter pleas in such cases. Maddie's case was 'a cause of great concern to victims of domestic violence throughout the country' inasmuch as the provocation defence allowed killers to 'literally get away with murder'. They were bitterly disappointed that 'such a vicious killing has attracted so lenient a custodian sentence'.[3] Maddie's sisters agreed. If she had survived, her killer would have got a longer sentence for attempted murder or grievous bodily harm. What 'kind of signal' was it for him to get less for killing her? Throughout, he was seen as the victim while Maddie 'wasn't heard at all'. The provocation defence was a 'charter for domestic violence' and the family was bent on changing the law 'for Maddie's sake'.[4] They petitioned the Solicitor General, the Attorney General and the Director of Public Prosecutions to intervene, thereby setting in motion an appeal on the ground of undue leniency. In the government's view, a seven-year sentence did not reflect 'the sanctity of life to which a civilised society should have regard'. As society expected a higher degree of self-control where a relationship had broken down, the sentence should be increased to ten years.[5]

Would the Court of Appeal agree? Would it decide that the sentences handed down to Maddie Humes' and Nicole Wilkinson's killers and to another man sentenced to three and a half years for the manslaughter of his partner were too lenient? The court began by noting that it was established that the 'normal range' of sentences in domestic manslaughter cases where, as it euphemistically put it, 'one party to a relationship' had a defence of provocation arising from 'the faithless conduct or disenchantment of the other', was between five and seven years. The sentence could rise to seven or eight years in a case where a man killed his wife because she wished to end the marriage, as long as she did not 'boast about' having an affair or 'disparage' her husband and had not been found *in flagrante delicto*. But there were cases where sentences of much less than five years had been 'deemed appropriate' and some where a non-custodial disposal had been considered 'efficient'. Nor did the court think it was illogical that sentences for attempted murder were often higher than those given for manslaughter by provocation. After all, the English law of murder held that certain assumptions had to be made in the provoked killer's favour, namely that he had lost his self-control; that he had had been caused to do so by the victim and that his loss of control was reasonable. This was so even allowing for the fact that people are expected to exercise 'reasonable control over their emotions, and that as society advances it ought to call for a higher level of self-control'. In fact, in the judges' view, the present level of sentencing in provocation cases was 'if anything, higher than it ought to be'.[6] Accordingly, in a unanimous decision, the court declined to interfere with the sentences, much to the despair of the victims' families. Nicole Lewis' mother was 'appalled and disgusted' by the court's refusal to increase the four-year sentence handed down to the man who strangled her daughter. Justice 'still hasn't been done for Nicky'.[7]

Try as the appellate judges might to formulate sentencing policy in scrupulously gender-neutral terms, the harsh reality of impassioned 'red mist' homicide kept breaking through. For a start, the 'existing authorities' providing them with 'sufficient guidance' in matters of sentencing were all cases in which men had been convicted of manslaughter after killing 'provocative' departing women. What they called 'disenchantment' arising from 'faithless conduct' was almost exclusively one way. This did not pass by government ministers who, it was reported, were 'secretly' reviewing the provocation defence with a view to inaugurating a 'shake up of so-called "crimes of passion"'. Options included abolishing the defence altogether – said to be Solicitor General Harman's preference – or excluding sexual infidelity as an excuse for murder. In any event, they felt it was imperative to change a law which from a victim-orientated perspective was way past its user date. '"Crime of passion" is no defence' rang the headline reporting the government's plans. The Court of Appeal had had its say about sentences for wife-killers and been found wanting. Next up: a Law Commission inquiry into defences to murder.[8]

Querying sexual infidelity as a legally recognisable excuse for homicidal fury made some sense to the Law Commissioners charged with reviewing the operation of partial defences to murder in England and Wales. But not enough to recommend excluding it as an excuse for murder. Instead, they recommended that the defence of provocation be retained, proclaiming it to have a 'moral basis'. Fascinatingly, this 'moral basis' turned out to be the early modern notion of having a 'legitimate ground to feel seriously wronged' by the deceased. If defendants killed in response to grossly provocative words or conduct that gave them a justified sense of being severely wronged, the moral blameworthiness of the homicide was significantly lessened. Accordingly, the Commissioners advocated that provocation's excusatory premise based on loss of control should be abandoned, allowing it to operate instead as a justificatory defence. The focus should be on whether the defendant had some 'moral right on his side in relation to the victim rather than simply being an example of human frailty in giving way to overwhelming anger'.[9] Herewith an astonishing revival of the Aristotelian man of honour retaliating in justifiable rage to slights on his personhood whom we encountered in Chapter 1. Would this man's 'moral right' apply to killing an unfaithful wife today? The initial impression given in the Commission's report was that it would not apply to those cases, the Commissioners agreeing with Lord Hoffmann, who famously declared that male possessiveness and jealousy 'should not today be an acceptable reason for loss of self-control leading to homicide'.[10] Moreover, more than 50 years ago in *Holmes*, Lord Simon said that 'Othello would be guilty of murder, even if Iago's insinuations had been true, and we think this should be so'.[11] However, there was an important caveat: it would lessen the gravity of the crime if a husband killed his wife when, on discovering she was having an affair, confronted her and then she taunted him about his sexual inadequacy. Such taunts constituted provocation sufficiently grave to provide a defendant with a 'warranted excuse' for retaliatory violence.[12]

How remarkable that in the very same instance that the Commissioners endorsed the view that Othello was guilty of murder, they embraced the notion of a 'warranted excuse' for femicide that Shakespeare had shaken it to its classical foundations in *Titus Andronicus* and queried in relation to wife-killing in *Othello*. They drew instead on law academic Virginia Nourse's much-cited analysis of the operation of provocation defences in intimate partner homicide cases in the United States. Addressing the 'lurking normative questions' left unaddressed by those defending passion as a mitigating factor, she had wondered why some losses of self-control, say 'infidelity-inspired rage', counted as provocation, while others, notably 'till-inspired greed' did not. Her research into late twentieth-century American cases revealed what is always revealed in analyses of intimate partner femicide cases in Anglophone jurisdictions – that men are the beneficiaries of expanding provocation defences, that 'infidelity' might encompass a fiancée dancing with another, a girlfriend dating someone else or a woman pursuing a new relationship after divorce and that a majority of men's provocation claims are not actually based on infidelity but rather on a woman's attempt to exit the relationship. Nevertheless, Nourse rejected the abolitionist option advocated by provocation's most ardent critics. Refusing to give up on law's 'compassion for sincere emotion', she insisted that abolition was unnecessary inasmuch as her proposal for a 'warranted excuse' would bar most provocation claims in intimate exit and infidelity homicides because such behaviours, 'though upsetting to men, are protected by law'.[13]

Recall from Chapter 1 the journey that Horder took us on in *Provocation and Responsibility*. Tracing the origins of the provocation defence as far back as medieval juries' reluctance to convict impassioned men of murder, he tracked its progress all the way through to the early 1990s. Recall too my spoiler alert that he concludes his book by debunking the whole notion of a 'moral warrant' for murder and arguing for the abolition of the provocation defence on the ground that there is 'no moral justification' for individuals taking retributive action.[14] Significantly, it was the statistics demonstrating the sexed asymmetry of killers and killed in domestic homicides – 103 men compared to only 26 women were convicted of killing a partner or former partner in 1989 – and what he perceived to be the disturbing operation of provocation defences in intimate partner femicide cases that led Horder to this conclusion. Angry retaliation had 'insufficient ethical status to warrant reducing murder to manslaughter'. Refusing the 'excusatory distinction' between revenge killing and killing in anger, he insisted there was 'nothing morally understandable' about an angry exaction of vengeance to warrant 'the exceptional mitigation of provoked killings from murder to manslaughter'.[15] There was nothing to warrant it, nothing at all.

Yet remarkably, when Horder came to sit on and lead the Law Commission inquiry into the law of murder in 2006, he joined the other Commissioners in unanimously endorsing the Commission's earlier recommendation that the provocation defence be retained even for some forms of sexual infidelity femicides. Even more surprisingly, he came to champion the notion of a 'moral warrant' or 'warranted excuse' for murder, reinstating it in the very same intimate partner femicide cases that had once so troubled him. But not only did the Commissioners jettison the close analyses of the highly problematic operation of provocation defences in these cases that Horder and others have conducted; they recommended that provocation be retained on the basis of a consideration of fanciful hypothetical cases. The most striking was that of an imaginary Asian woman who, on finding two white men attempting to rape her 15-year-old daughter, gets a knife and, as the men shout racist abuse and run away, she chases them and kills one. No such case has ever come before the English courts. But that's how far the Commissioners felt they needed to go to justify retaining provocation to cover 'any case' where there was 'gross provocation'. And that could include grossly provocative words that may have caused a defendant to have 'a justifiable sense of having been seriously wronged'. Gross provocation could also cover any case where the defendant had acted in response to fear of serious violence', say, women who killed abusive men after a long history of violence.[16]

Perhaps the Commissioners were distracted by the reference asking them to pay particular attention to homicides committed in the context of 'domestic violence' rather than in a broader domestic context. In any event, they paid insufficient, indeed no discernible, attention to the cases that had led to the establishment of the reference on partial defences to murder. To repeat the point that, it seems, can never be too laboured: the precipitating events leading to the review, the triggers, if you will, for the establishment of the early twentieth-century inquiries into the law of murder were not the infrequent 'domestic violence' cases, the so-called 'slow burn' cases usually associated with women who killed after a long history of assault and battery from their partners.[17] They were the 'red mist' rage intimate partner femicides that have been documented in this book and that had once led Horder to advocate the abolition of the provocation defence. There can surely be no stronger testimony to the resilience of the fiction of the notion of a mitigating 'provoked' killing than that of eminent scholar Jeremy Horder resiling from his earlier abolitionist position. That's how potent the notion of provoked killing as a lesser form of homicide is. It can trip up the very best of legal scholars, even one who wrote a book-length critique of its justifying and excusatory foundations.

Recall how in the *Humes* case the Court of Appeal refused to increase the seven-year sentence handed down to the man who killed his wife, Maddie, because she had been unfaithful and that she wanted to leave her marriage. In the eyes of the Law Commissioners, such behaviour constituted 'legitimate grounds' for feeling seriously wronged. An unfaithful woman's 'verbose' departure provided a 'warranted excuse' for murder. With Horder's arguments in *Provocation and Responsibility* against precisely this viewpoint overlooked by the very same Commission on which he sat, it is clear that law reformers bent on curtailing provocation defences in wife-killing cases had a major fight on their hands. It is equally clear that with a legal analyst of the highest calibre now arguing for retaining provocation even in certain femicide cases, we need to look elsewhere for the necessary *gravitas* to contest this age-old 'moral warrant' for murder. Once again, we need look no further than Shakespeare's demolition of the 'mighty warrant' for femicide in *Titus Andronicus* or his querying in *Othello* of the unnameable 'cause' of a femicidal man's homicidal fury. Othello could not bring himself to name that cause, but we can. It is the impropriety of a man losing control of his property in his wife when she strays or, just as damningly, if she is imagined to have done so. The cause morphs imperceptibly into a warrant for femicide, a fixed belief that as the Law Commissioners demonstrated, is difficult if not impossible to dislodge.[18]

The furore over ending the 'heat of passion' defence

While many in the legal fraternity held fast to the belief that adultery or, at least, adultery exacerbated by taunting constituted a moral warrant for murder, men continued to escape with murder convictions for killing 'provocative' wives in scenarios far removed from that of finding her *in flagrante*. In January 2002, a month after Maddie Humes was killed, a man was cleared of murdering his wife, Jillian Parnham. He had hit her more than 70 times with an iron bar after she allegedly taunted him about her affair with a 'real man'. He received a six-year sentence for manslaughter.[19] The next year another man appealed successfully against his murder conviction for killing his wife, Linda Rowland, on the ground that fresh psychiatric evidence linked his depression to her 'provocation'. That included her drinking problem; her working at a social club he disliked; her sexual withdrawal; her making him feel jealous and taunting him about the bend in his penis caused by scar tissue from a medical condition. On the fatal night, she continued to taunt him about his bent penis, causing him to lose his temper and knife her to death. His lawyer argued that in determining the degree of self-control expected of a man in this situation, account should be taken of the effect of personality characteristics that had lowered his threshold for impulsive behaviour. He suffered from anxiety and depression that had been exacerbated by his stressful marriage. Here was a man too weak to stand up to his wife and too weak to leave her. Three appeal judges quashed his murder conviction and sentence of life imprisonment, substituting a verdict of manslaughter by reason of provocation and a sentence of seven years' imprisonment.[20] Or consider the case of the man who killed his former partner, Sarah Spurgeon, in a frenzied knife attack after seeing a photograph of her new boyfriend. He could not bear to think of her with another man. He admitted murder and was sentenced to life in December 2006. On appeal, his minimum sentence of 14 years was reduced to 13 years, the court reasoning that if the 'actual trigger' to his 'readiness to kill' was his discovery of his former partner's 'latest relationship', this could amount to 'an element of provocation' that could mitigate the sentence.[21]

Occasionally courts did place limits on what *her* behaviour permitted *him* to do in response. It did not, for example, warrant a man setting alight a departing wife and burning the house down to conceal her body. That's what Amanda Birks' former husband did to her in 2009. Buying an 'infidelity kit' to detect from his wife's underwear whether she was having an affair, the late modern equivalence of 'ocular proof', was certainly a novel response to her telling him their marriage was over. But he admitted murder and was given a life sentence.[22] The Court of Appeal found nothing in his 'infidelity' story to mitigate his 19-year minimum sentence. But by now anyway, the reformers had had enough. They declined to follow the Law Commission's recommendations for reforming the structure of the law of murder but retaining provocation. Opting instead to abolish the defence, they replaced it with a 'new' defence of loss of control which, if successful, would have the same effect as successful provocation pleas, reducing murder to manslaughter.

The new defence, set out in the Coroners and Justice Act 2009, consisted of three elements. First there must be a loss of self-control. Second, the loss of control must have a qualifying trigger. Third, a person of the defendant's sex and age, with a normal degree of tolerance and self-restraint and in the circumstances of the defendant might have reacted in the same or in a similar way to the defendant. The triggers for loss of control are that it was attributable to the defendant's fear of serious violence or to a thing done or said which constitutes circumstances of an extremely grave character and caused a defendant to have a justifiable sense of being seriously wronged. Most controversially, sexual infidelity was now expressly excluded as a trigger for loss of self-control, omitted from the list of things done or said that constitute 'extremely grave circumstances or that caused a defendant to have a justifiable sense of being seriously wronged'.[23]

The culmination of a reform campaign led by Harriet Harman, now Minister for Women and Equalities, the new law addressed long-standing concerns raised by women's rights groups about the operation of partial defences to murder in femicide cases. As she explained, for centuries, the law had 'allowed men to escape a murder charge in domestic homicide cases by blaming the victim'. It followed that ending the provocation defence in cases of 'infidelity' would be 'an important law change and will end the culture of excuses'.[24] But it would be a hard-fought battle. Many criticised the clause excluding sexual infidelity as a trigger for losing control as 'uncompromising' and poorly drafted. Speaking in his capacity as a Law Commissioner, erstwhile abolitionist Jeremy Horder thought the proposed reform 'fraught with difficulty' and worried about 'being "absolutist" in this area'. He found the wording 'bizarre' and questioned in what circumstances 'a thing "said" in itself' could be said to constitute sexual infidelity. How strange that he had forgotten that what femicidal men *said* about their allegedly unfaithful wives had been at the heart of provocation defences for centuries. At any rate, he suggested 'binning' the clause or, at the very least, 'rewording' it to say that in so far as a defendant was 'motivated by sexual jealousy or envy, these motivations are to be disregarded'.[25] In his view, 'tweaking or reshaping the law a little', especially with a reform of such fundamental importance and that had been so 'controversial within the legal community and beyond', was very concerning.[26]

Contentious it certainly was, many legal commentators condemning the whole idea of ripping up the time-honoured cultural script that killing on the ground of known or suspected sexual infidelity merits law's compassion. Some felt it had the potential for 'grave injustice'. After all, 'unfaithfulness by a supposedly committed sexual partner is liable to cause deep shock and hurt, and for some of them, quite likely to provoke explosive anger'. It was 'outrageous' that a 'person' who loses self-control and kills must now be convicted of murder.[27] But nowhere did the exclusion of sexual infidelity as a trigger for loss of control cause more consternation than in the upper echelons of the judiciary, several law lords publicly expressing their continuing support for this long-standing excuse for murder. Lord Chief Justice Lord Phillips confessed to feeling 'uneasy' about a reform that 'so diminishes' the significance of sexual infidelity as to exclude it from 'even the possibility of amounting to provocation'. No ministerial statement had persuaded him it was necessary for reforms to 'go that far'. Indeed, no change was needed because, in his view, the current law did not let men 'off lightly' – it required provocation to be conduct that would cause a reasonable man to act as the defendant acted. Furthermore, if juries were declining to hold that infidelity meets that test, he could not understand why it should be suggested that they are 'stretching the law to its limits'.[28] This was Harman's extraordinary riposte:

> This defence is *our own* version of honour killings, and we are going to outlaw it. We have had the discussion, we have had the debate and we have decided and are not going to bow to judicial protests ... I am determined that women should understand that we won't brook any excuses for domestic violence ... It is a terrible thing to lose a sister or a daughter, but to then have her killer blame her and say he is the victim of her infidelity is totally unacceptable. The relatives say 'he got away with murder' and they're right.[29]

Outlaw *our own* version of honour killing? What an astonishing statement of intent, one pointedly rejecting the conventional practice of racialising wife-killers as foreigner others. Such a singling out of 'our' English law's concession to wife-killers recalls Shakespeare's querying of excuses for femicide in 'civilised' societies such as the Romans claimed theirs to be. As for the howl of disavowals that greets any bid to challenge received ideas about where and by whom murders are committed, we need look no further than *Macbeth*. 'What, in our house?' Lady Macbeth asked disingenuously when informed that Duncan had been killed, she being fully aware and indeed actively involved in the plot to kill him there. 'Too cruel anywhere', Banquo responded.[30] But for Shakespeare, as for Harman and the law reformers, it was specifically 'our house' and its tradition of adultery as excuse for femicide that was the crux of the problem. For their part, in disavowing any problems with the operation of English law's provocation defence in wife-killing cases, the reformers' opponents had their Lady Macbeth moment – 'What, in our house?'

The dispute over the move to abolish provocation by infidelity continued in the parliamentary deliberations on the reform bill. Shrillest objections were raised in the House of Lords where emotions ran very high over the idea of depriving men of the ancient right to plead provocation after killing an unfaithful wife. Objections were once again couched in scrupulously gender-neutral terms. Lord Neill of Bladen, the retired judge we met in the Introduction was, as we saw there, most eloquent on the subject, objecting to turning 'French-style *crime passionnel*' into something that stiff upper-lipped Englishmen could no longer commit. Lord Lloyd of Berwick agreed: 'Why should we exclude infidelity from a jury's consideration?' Was Parliament 'really to say that sexual infidelity can never give rise to a justifiable sense of being seriously wronged? Surely not'.[31] In response, Attorney General Baroness Scotland reiterated the government's position that an 'important policy shift' was essential. It was no longer 'adequate to treat violence as a justified response to anger' and the government wished to 'raise the bar in relation to the partial defence in order to reflect this'. The provocation defence was 'too generous to those who kill in anger' and this, she said, was a 'deliberate and carefully considered shift in policy'. It was unacceptable today for 'a defendant who has killed an unfaithful partner to seek to blame the victim for what occurred'.[32] Lord Thomas of Gresford, a deputy high court judge was unconvinced. What, he asked, was meant by 'sexual infidelity'? Did it mean 'only between married partners', or did it mean 'between a man and a woman, or a man and a man'? Looking 'back in history', he recalled that adultery was described as one of the four categories of adequate provocation in the foundational case of *Mawgridge*. Lord Thomas did not 'want to go back to those days'; he did not want to 'go back to provocation'. But if the law was to be based on loss of self-control, 'how can we exclude the deepest feeling and passions, the breach of trust and breach of faithfulness, from our considerations?'[33]

Such was their opposition to the reform proposals that, in October 2009, the House of Lords voted against the motion to exclude sexual infidelity as a trigger for loss of control by 99 votes to 84, Lord Henley condemning the proposed reform as 'gesture politics'. Lord Lloyd of Berwick, called it 'truly objectionable'. It is 'little short of astonishing that Parliament should be asked to tell a jury whether sexual infidelity is enough to cause a man or woman to lose their self-control'. Lord Thomas of Gresford was still complaining that banning sexual infidelity as an excuse for murder was 'illogical' and 'outstandingly obnoxious'. Lord Neill was there too, talking about opera and novels featuring sexual infidelity. Nothing could convince them of the government's view that as Lord Bach put it: 'passions may run very high' over sexual infidelity, but it was no longer acceptable to resort to retaliatory violence if a partner was suspected of being unfaithful or even being found *in flagrante*.[34]

The following month, the lower house decided by 299 votes to 145 to overturn the peers' vote against the troublesome sexual infidelity exclusion clause but not before further objections were raised there. Junior Justice Minister Claire Ward tried to reassure the worriers. While it was unacceptable today 'for a man to be able to say that he killed his wife as a result of sexual infidelity', if 'other factors came into play, the courts would, of course, have an opportunity to consider them'. It was only sexual infidelity 'in itself' that was excluded. But some still thought the proposal unjust, a product of the reformers' desire to be 'politically correct'. As Tory justice spokesperson Dominic Grieve saw it, the government had decided that the defence should be jettisoned for the sake of 'political correctness' in the form of 'a declaratory statement that sexual infidelity can never justify violent behaviour'. For her part, Conservative MP Ann Widdecombe was completely flummoxed by the proposed reform: What, she asked, was 'unique about sexual infidelity that it must be removed from the almost endless list of circumstances in which somebody might be provoked?'[35] It made no sense to her at all, she not having registered hundreds of years of English history in which infidelity had been the most persistently raised excuse for wife-killing. But let us give Lord Thomas of Gresham the last judicial word on the matter, he declaring in the House of Lords that the reformers' claim that the provocation defence institutionalises a 'culture of excuses' was 'just nonsensical rhetoric in an area of law of great sensitivity'.[36]

Theirs was not the only opposition. *The Times* reported the reform bid under the headline 'An unjust, feminist view of murder'. A 'trio of feminists' – Harman, Solicitor General Vera Baird and Justice Minister Maria Eagle – were bent, this commentator lamented, on ensuring that a man who kills an unfaithful wife will be convicted of murder 'straight up'. How outrageous:

> No excuses about provocation or loss of control, thank you very much. As Ms Baird put it: 'The days of sexual jealousy as a defence are over'. So much for poor Othello's account of himself as 'one not easily jealous, but, being wrought, perplex'd in the extreme'. The Moor would get short shrift from Ms Baird.

Indeed, he would if such 'politically motivated' proposals producing such an 'unjust, feminist view of murder' were put into effect.[37]

Judicial defiance – provocation by infidelity's last stand

The law lords may have lost the fight to retain sexual infidelity as an excuse for murder but they were not done yet. The Court of Appeal, presided over by a new Chief Justice, Lord Judge, was to become the last bulwark defending infidelity as excuse for impassioned homicide. Not that all senior judges were on the same page. Appeals heard at the time against sentences considered unduly lenient in cases where men attacked women, sometimes fatally, reveal divergent judicial views. Consider, for example, the Attorney General's successful appeal in 2009 against a sentence of two and a half years for grievous bodily harm for a man who, suspecting his wife of infidelity, had branded her with an iron. Delivering the judgment, Lady Justice Hallett observed that:

> if there is anyone in or outside the criminal justice system who still believes that infidelity can justify or mitigate violence of this kind, they are mistaken. Whatever the hurt or anger that a betrayed partner feels, they must understand that they should not resort to violence. If they do, they do so not only at the peril of their victim but at their own peril.[38]

She increased his sentence to five years. Compare that to the Attorney General's unsuccessful appeal in 2010 against a six-year sentence for a man convicted of grievous bodily harm against a woman who had left him and started another relationship. He said she had also sexually taunted him. Delivering the judgment, Lord Judge noted that Justice Hallett's observation in the previous case about infidelity not mitigating violence had to be 'closely examined'. Certainly, there was 'no justification for violence arising from infidelity. Unlawful violence is unlawful violence'. However, her observations in relation to mitigation were 'clearly confined to the kind of systematic torture' such as branding a victim as had occurred in that case. In the context of such 'cold-blooded violence', infidelity would not provide mitigation. But that did not mean that infidelity can never mitigate violence. That would contradict 'the reality of human behaviour' and the approach taken by the courts 'for generations' to 'the possible impact that infidelity may have on men and women who are normally peaceful and calm'. Justice Hallett would not have 'departed from such well-established principles without doing so expressly and unequivocally'.[39] In Lord Judge's view, those historically mandated principles ensured that infidelity still had mitigating force, at least in cases where there is no systematic torture.

How though did the Court of Appeal respond to the law abolishing provocation and expressly excluding infidelity as a trigger for loss of control in the new loss of control defence? An appeal in June 2011 by the Attorney General against a man's five-year sentence for the manslaughter of his 'nagging' partner, Sylvia Rowley-Bailey, gave appellate judges their first opportunity to comment on the reforms. Noting that the reforms 'appeared to create a higher and certainly different threshold than the common law', Lord Judge acknowledged 'a greater focus on the death of the victim equally fell to be considered'. A greater focus on her death meant a longer sentence for this killer despite his having 'seen red' when Sylvia goaded him about his ageing mother. It was increased to seven and a half years.[40]

The same month, the court heard another appeal on the ground of undue leniency against a man's sentence for murder of life imprisonment with a minimum specified term of 15 years. He had entered the home of his former partner, twenty-one-year-old Casey Brittle, in the middle of the night. Then he killed her in a prolonged beating witnessed by their two-year-old daughter while shouting: 'Have you slept with him?' with reference to an affair she had after their relationship had ended. While increasing his minimum sentence to 20 years, the court took pains to point out how sexual infidelity as mitigating excuse for murder might still survive the reformers attempt to outlaw it. The sexual infidelity exclusion clause in the new legislation was concerned, it said, with the substantive criminal offence of murder, not with determining the minimum sentence for murder. Accordingly, provocation, even if not amounting to a defence, could still provide relevant mitigation to murder. That accorded 'with common sense'. It also reflected the sentencing principle which allows for mitigation when 'the same material' – stories of 'unfaithful' women who leave men – arises in attempted murder or grievous bodily harm cases. While the court found 'no provocation of any kind' to mitigate Sylvia's killing, it made it clear that 'sexual infidelity' as mitigating excuse for murder would survive at the sentencing level, notwithstanding the reformers' efforts to rein it in as an excuse for murder.[41]

A few months later the Court of Appeal went even further in reclaiming infidelity as an understandable trigger for eruptions of red mist homicidal rage. Conjoined appeals by three men against their convictions for murder handed down in three more wife-killing cases gave the court its first opportunity to test the new law expressly excluding sexual infidelity as a trigger for loss of control in the new loss of control defence. In the notorious *Clinton* case, the court lost no time in resurrecting a man's jealous rage at a wife's alleged sexual infidelity as a defence for homicidal fury after its seeming legislative demise, a momentous decision reported under the arresting headline: 'Crimes of passion defence restored in murder cases'.[42]

The decision was hardly a surprise. All along, the law lords had signalled their opposition to the reform banning sexual infidelity as excuse for murder. And for all their efforts to frame their objections in scrupulously gender-neutral terms, it was entirely predictable that the first time the new loss of control defence came before the Court of Appeal it would be in the latest round of femicide cases. The three appellants had killed women who had either left or wanted to leave them. While dismissing two of the appeals where the control defence had been put to and rejected by the jury, the court allowed the third appeal, that of the man who killed his wife, Dawn Clinton. Here it was held that the trial judge had 'misdirected herself about the possible relevance' of Dawn's infidelity' when she refused to put his loss of control defence to the jury.[43] In the court's view, 'infidelity' taking the form of a wife's departure from a marriage may properly be taken into consideration for the purposes of that partial defence when such behaviour was, as the presiding judge, Lord Judge, put it, 'integral to the facts as a whole'.[44]

What *were* the facts 'as a whole' in the case? Dawn had left him. He was desperate to get her back, but she had started a new relationship. He retaliated by destroying her car, her 'most treasured possession', as a preamble to confronting her with evidence of her sexual infidelity when she returned to the family home to see the children. On the prosecution's account, he had planned to kill her before she arrived. During the confrontation he beat her and strangled her to death before taking photos of her near naked body which he sent to the man with whom she was having a relationship. On the appellant's account, he had 'tortured himself' about sexual images she and the new partner had posted on the internet, images he found when he accessed her Facebook page. Confronted with this evidence, his wife had, he said, boasted in 'very graphic' detail about sex acts she had enjoyed with different men every night of the week and taunted him about his threat to commit suicide.[45] Did she? We shall never know but why, anyway, should such 'evidence' be ruled admissible, let alone mitigate murder? After all, the new law had expressly excluded anything 'done or said' related to sexual infidelity as a trigger for loss of control. Undeterred, the appellant's counsel followed the standard script highlighting these 'extremely grave' circumstances as pivotal to the all-important 'context' of the killing, circumstances that in the view of the

Court of Appeal may have grounded a loss of control defence and so should have been put to the jury.

Unsurprisingly, the court's brazen attempt to circumvent the new law attracted criticism, none more cogent than that describing it as 'completely wrong'. Not least it had overlooked 'the fundamental policy issues' that had led Parliament to enact a narrowed defence of loss of control. These critics do not stop there. Each step of the judgment was 'dangerously flawed' and setting 'a hazardous precedent'.[46] They contrasted Lord Judge's sympathetic approach to the infidelity that had, as the critics put it, so '*tortured*' the killer with his failure to clock his admission that he had bullied his wife in the past. They also rejected the judge's conclusion that infidelity is only to be excluded when it stands alone as a trigger for loss of control. That assertion was illogical, 'patently wrong' and based on a misreading of the statute which had the clear aim of reducing the defence of loss of control to 'almost nothing'. More it was 'contrary to justice'. It was inconceivable how sexual autonomy taking the form of a legal act of consensual adult sex could count as provocation excusing an illegal act such as murder in a modern democracy.[47]

Clinton is indeed precisely the kind of troubling case that had precipitated the law reform movement. This point bears emphasising. How quickly it had been forgotten that the movement was informed by decades of trenchant feminist criticism of the operation of the provocation defence in intimate partner femicide cases. Forgotten too was how it had been ignited by outrage over the Court of Appeal's refusal to interfere with the lenient sentences handed down in 2002 to Maddie Humes and Nicole Wilkinson's killers. So here we have two sets of 'infidelity'-inspired killings, all femicides, book ending a decade of reform effort to ban this excuse for homicidal fury. They put into stark relief not only the endlessly rediscovered yet constantly denied sexed asymmetry of sexual infidelity homicide but also the difficulties faced by anyone challenging the notion that impassioned femicide is not murder.[48]

To grasp the full import of this dilemma, it pays to look closely at how the *Clinton* court went about reclaiming 'infidelity'-inspired rage as mitigating excuse for murder in the face of legislation expressly designed to prohibit it. Two revealing disclaimers bear close scrutiny. First, Lord Judge declared that while the 'loss of control' might be 'evocative' of the old provocation defence, the new statutory defence was 'self-contained'. Accordingly, its common law heritage – the entire body of manslaughter by provocation case law containing hundreds of years of precedent for convicting infidelity killers of manslaughter – was 'irrelevant'.[49] Second, he opined 'that no one (male or female) owns or possesses his or her spouse or partner'. Relationship breakdown is 'always fraught with tension and difficulty, with the possibility of misunderstanding and the potential for apparently irrational fury'. After all, 'experience over many generations' has shown that sexual infidelity has the potential to 'produce a completely unpredictable and sometimes violent response'. Importantly, this 'may have nothing to do with any notional "rights" that the one may believe that he or she has over the other, and often stems from a sense of betrayal and heartbreak, and crushed dreams'.[50]

Lord Judge's impeccably gender-neutral language is belied by the very case law he sweeps aside. The most cursory glance at the cases he brackets as 'irrelevant' reveals that it is in fact men's rage, and very rarely women's, which is narrated there. Moreover, when outbursts of homicidal rage against women occur so frequently and so persistently over hundreds of years, wife-killing by rights-obsessed men has to rate as entirely predictable. Contrary to Lord Judge's view of the irrelevance of any notional rights, the pleas of femicidal men for compassion is indeed founded on possessory right, that very sex-specific right enshrined in the foundational provocation case of *Mawgridge* that we have encountered again and again: the right to kill an adulterous wife, adultery being 'the highest invasion of property'.[51]

A man learning of his former partner's latest relationship, that's the kind of 'infidelity' that the Court of Appeal decided should continue to mitigate murder in the post-reform era. The *Clinton* decision was a desperate rearguard action to ensure that a femicidal man's manslaughter plea would still be countenanced in an English criminal court no matter how strained and implausible his account of her 'infidelity'. That such accounts had been unmasked in case after case as code for a woman's decision to leave a relationship was simply ignored. Not that the court wished to allow for a free-for-all slaughter of women who left men. Some femicides were beyond the pale even for Lord Judge. Some were still murder. Just a few months later, the court heard an appeal from a man given a whole life sentence for murdering a woman who had left him.[52] Christine Chambers had left her partner, described as a 'violent, domineering man' and applied for a non-molestation order against him on the basis of several allegations of 'significant violence'. He breached the order on numerous occasions. On the fatal night, he entered the house where she was living with her two daughters, carrying a bag containing an axe, petrol, a knife and pliers and a double-barreled shotgun. While the older daughter managed to escape, her mother was subjected to what the court described as 'a series of degrading and humiliating assaults' in which she was ordered to 'hug and kiss him and say that she loved him' before being subjected to 'an attack of horrifying violence'. After shooting their two-year-old daughter in the head, he shot himself but survived. He was convicted of two counts of murder and given a whole life term, the trial judge concluding that he had killed Christine and their daughter 'simply because' he, like hundreds of men before him, was unable to accept that she could 'no longer bear to be with him and wanted to start a new life'.[53]

The Court of Appeal, Lord Judge presiding, unanimously rejected his appeal against this whole life term, agreeing with the trial judge that there was not a shred of mitigation. For the appellant it had been argued that his objective of killing his family and then himself was 'not unique', he having 'temporarily lost any sense of rational and decent behaviour or hope' as so many wife-killers have. Being so common, it seemed to be implied, this was not a case that fell within the exceptionally serious category. The court disagreed. This killer had not 'simply exploded into violence as a result of the stresses and strains of the breakdown of his relationship' as so many other men appearing before English courts had. His was a planned, revenge killing carried out with the intention of making his former partner's death 'the most terrifying and agonising ordeal that he could envisage'. He had 'in cold blood' quite deliberately, 'executed' their daughter as she screamed with fear at witnessing what he had done to her mother.[54] While Lord Judge could find some provocative 'infidelity' on Dawn Clinton's part when he looked at 'the whole context' of her departure from her husband, there was nothing to pin on Christine Chambers. No domestic discount applied here. Appeal dismissed: 'life' meant life for this domestic executioner.

Was it the planning of the attacks or the shooting of the child that set the court so resolutely against him? Either way, it is notable that it was the murder of the child and not that of Christine that was labelled 'cold-blooded', though both were seen as revenge killings and neither as the kind that resulted from an exculpatory momentary explosion of rage over relationship breakdown. Still, upholding his life sentence while substituting minimum sentences for other appellants who had received whole life sentences for raping or killing women unknown to them, and whose appeals were heard at the same time, was certainly a novel move. Ordinarily murderous attacks on women by strangers trump domestic ones in the seriousness stakes. But here the hot *versus* cold-blooded distinction that had served murderous men for centuries broke down. Was the Court of Appeal finally coming to see that given the lengths some men go in pursuit of former women partners, stalking them, hacking their Facebook pages, invading their homes, 'domestic' homicide was perhaps just as murderous as the killings of strangers? Perhaps, but what was yet to be fully grasped is that it is immaterial from the victim's perspective or that of her advocates how she is killed. Whether she is slaughtered in a supposed spur-of-the-moment rage before she could get away from a violent man or when he inveigles her to return or breaches a protection order, it is all the same homicidal rage, the rage of a man dispossessed of 'his' woman.

Post-reform cases – still getting away with murder?

The killing statistic, that two women are killed in the UK each week on average by male partners and former partners has remained fairly constant over the last three decades and is now getting a great deal of mainstream media coverage.[55] This is thanks in no small part to a new wave of anti-violence campaigners deploying innovative strategies in the blogosphere to keep lethal violence against women and children on the public agenda in Britain. None has been more influential than 'Counting Dead Women' campaigner Karen Ingala Smith. Her tireless work retrieving the names of women killed by men from media reports, the violent deaths of women at the hands of their husbands and intimate partners has been instrumental in ensuring that these cases did not disappear in media stories lamenting persistently ungendered 'tragic deaths of a couple'.[56] Smith's lists of 'women killed by men' formed the basis of a study I conducted of nearly 400 intimate partner femicides committed in England and Wales over a five-year period commencing in January 2012. What did the study reveal about the impact of the reforms to partial defences to murder? Is the legislation working as intended to stop men getting away with murdering women?[57]

The main findings can be summarised as follows. First, 78 femicidal offenders did not face trial, they having committed suicide after killing partners or died in prison before their court appearance. As with those who did face trial, the most common trigger for femicide-suicide was relationship breakdown. There were also a few latter-day Othellos who suspected that their partners had been unfaithful, including one said to have suffered from 'Othello Syndrome', a condition giving him paranoid delusions about his wife of 30 years. A newspaper report explained that the syndrome was 'named after Shakespeare's tragic hero who kills his wife Desdemona after becoming consumed with jealousy', adding that it affects men more than women but was 'relatively rare in both'.[58] Becoming consumed with jealousy to the point of erupting in homicidal fury is indeed far more common in men and not at all a rarity. As far as the records show, 'Othello Syndrome' has never been submitted as a defence for a woman who killed an intimate partner and intimate partner murder-suicides are still perpetrated exclusively by men.

Second, 75 per cent of the 317 defendants who did appear in court charged with murder either pleaded guilty to that offence or were found guilty of murder by a jury. That was a far higher number than in pre-reform cases where, as we have seen, pleading provocation or diminished responsibility almost always guaranteed a manslaughter verdict. Three received a whole life sentence, including two who had killed previous partners. The rest were given life sentences with minimum terms ranging from 11 to 38 years. What became immediately clear from the guilty pleas of the 90 men admitting murder was not only that allegations of sexual infidelity are losing their excusatory force. Furthermore, what were once dismissed as mitigating 'red mist' crimes of passion are now being more readily exposed as departure cases where the victim was estranged from a partner, in the process of leaving him or seeking a divorce. Moreover, of the 36 defendants running the new loss of control defence, only nine did so successfully. The rest were found guilty of murder, including one who claimed his wife had '100 secret lovers' during their 15 years of marriage, a claim reminiscent of Othello's even more outlandish charge that Desdemona had 'a 1000 times' committed the 'act of shame' with Cassio in a much shorter time span. This latter-day Othello began with the stock 'loss of control' excusatory tale. But neither that nor his claim that she had threatened to stop him seeing their children and bankrupt him if he did not agree to her terms for divorce was enough to found a defence in the post-reform era. So once the trial started, he changed his plea to murder.[59]

With provocation by sexual infidelity now off the table as a defence, some defendants opted for a diminished responsibility defence, almost all without success.[60] Of 75 diminished responsibility cases identified in my study, prosecutors accepted 41 pleas of guilty to manslaughter, almost all from men suffering from psychosis, dementia or delusional disorders.[61] If the manslaughter plea was rejected the case proceeded to court where medical evidence is called by the defence to show that the defendant suffered from a recognised medical condition or failing that from depression or 'separation bereavement' caused by relationship breakdown. While the reformed diminished responsibility defence had appeared to give more scope to the importance of expert psychiatric evidence in determining criminal responsibility, juries have taken their role as the ultimate arbiter of these cases seriously. Post-reform juries have proved to be unimpressed with wife-killers running this defence, rejecting 30 of the 34 pleas and convicting these defendants of murder. Minimum sentences ranged from 20 to 28 years, far higher than in the pre-reform cases.

What though of exit cases complicated by a man learning of his wife's affair around the same time as he hears she is leaving him? Prior to the reforms tightening up partial defences to murder, this was the kind of killing scenario that had led to successful provocation defences resulting in convictions for manslaughter. Sentences had ranged between four and seven years. Not now. My analysis of the cases showed that the reforms are achieving their stated goal of preventing men getting away with murder, not least by exposing the 'unfaithful wife' narrative as code for 'bereavement separation' from a departing one. For the most part, juries are rejecting tales of woe featuring an 'unfaithful' (read: exiting) woman. But not always. Lingering sympathy can be detected for some non-coping killers, notably some who drew on the all too familiar divorce narrative to plead not guilty murder on the grounds of diminished responsibility due to separation-induced depression. Take for example, the case of a man who killed his wife, Reihana Rezayi, five days after she asked for a divorce. His lawyer likened the offence to 'a crime of passion', somehow overlooking the fact that this was the very crime the reformed law of murder was designed to eliminate. After hearing a psychiatrist testify he would not have committed the offence but for an 'adjustment disorder', the jury cleared him of murder. The judge noted that while 'a human life has been lost', the marriage had been 'happy' and the defendant 'a good, placid and kind husband' who had been greatly distressed by his wife's changed attitude towards him. He imposed a four-year sentence reminiscent of the risibly short sentences that had helped precipitate the reform movement.[62]

Manslaughter convictions for some wife-killers continued to outrage victims' families as keenly as the one handed down to Maddie Humes' husband had her siblings. Pamela Jackson's family was infuriated when her husband was convicted of her manslaughter, a case reported under the headline: 'Manslaughter

Injustice'. Aware that the killer would serve only half of his 18-year term, Pamela's son despaired: 'Nine years for a man that's capable of killing someone and burying them on the moors – there's no justice'.[63] Christine Henderson's family also felt let down by her killer's jury. The prosecution said the stabbing by her former partner was a 'brutal and sustained attack' in revenge for rejecting him. The defence claimed she had taunted him about a previous partner, causing him to lose control. Family members were reported to have rushed distraught from the court when the jury foreman announced a unanimous verdict of not guilty to murder. An incredulous family friend, 'disgusted' at the outcome, despaired saying, 'I'm just wondering, what is murder?'[64]

She might be interested to learn that the cases reveal that juries and some judges are now recognising that her right to leave trumps his right to a conviction for manslaughter. While exculpatory judgments about placid, kind husbands who just 'snap' can still occur, the impassioned, easily defended wife-killer who strutted the courts throughout the second half of the twentieth century is being transformed into a dangerous offender, a pathetic, needy one at that. His credibility is finally starting to falter in the face of the feminist challenge to law's long-standing truth that killing 'your' woman is a lesser form of homicide than murder. As for the lawyer who likened a departure case to a 'crime of passion', it needs emphasising that this was only one of very few diminished responsibility pleas accepted by a jury over the five-year period of the study. Furthermore, as far as can be ascertained from the media reports of hundreds of post-reform cases, this was the only bid to resuscitate 'passion' as a defence. It seems as if defence lawyers and juries alike have heeded the new legal status quo captured in that 2003 newspaper headline, '"Crime of passion" is no defence', that had heralded the planned shake up of the law of murder.

Impassioned homicide today

In her ground-breaking book, *Trauma: Explorations in Memory*, Cathy Caruth said this:

> The difficulty of listening and responding to traumatic stories in a way that does not lose their impact, that does not reduce them to clichés or turn them into versions of the same story, is a problem that remains central to the task of therapists, literary critics, neurobiologists and others who work with trauma survivors.[65]

To that list add the feminist criminologist writing a book about impassioned homicide. A career spent researching 'provocation by infidelity' cases does not inure you to men's violence against women. Familiarity only breeds more anguish. Retrieving historic cases from the archives or contemporary cases from media reports, coming face to face with the sheer number of victims, trying to do justice to as many as is feasibly possible, is deeply traumatic work.

It is all very well to busy oneself dismantling defence narratives featuring she-asked-for-it character assassination clichés. But how to give voice to the victims without falling into the trap Caruth warns against – that of turning their traumatic stories into versions of the same story? The trouble is it *is* largely the same story – the tired cliché-ridden tale of a departing woman provoking a man into a 'red mist' rage. Looking ahead, there's more of the same, though blessedly, less victim-blaming than in the past. Can we even bear to hear any more? I think we must. Victims of intimate partner femicide from the post-reform era, like their predecessors, insist on being heard against the din of self-entitled offender discourse that has pervaded the case law for centuries. Surely we have an ethical obligation to appease 'their groaning shadows that are gone'.[66]

The last case in my study of post-reform cases was that of Nicola Woodman, stabbed 20 times by her partner on Christmas Day, 2016. Her repeated denials of infidelity had enraged him. 'People just snap, you know what I mean', he told the police. But with this historically mandated snapping defence now banned as a trigger for loss of control, he pleaded guilty to murder and was sentenced to life imprisonment with a 23-year minimum. The police hoped this gave the family some satisfaction that justice has been done.[67] Certainly, it provides a sharp contrast to sentences handed down in the pre-reform era.

What has happened since then? An examination of cases decided since 2017 reveals that for the most part, the law reforms are still working as intended. They are stopping femicidal men from getting away with murder. For example, Melanie Clark's husband claimed he had lost control when he killed her in December 2017 because she had belittled the size of his genitals, informed him of a lesbian affair and made other cruel remarks.[68] In 2018 that tale did not wash with the jury as it surely would have in the pre-reform days. Convicted of murder he was sentenced to life with a 15-year minimum. That was a notable increase over the seven-year sentence for manslaughter handed down on appeal in the pre-reform era penis-shaming case of Rowland discussed earlier in this chapter. Such sharply different outcomes in these two 'penis taunting' cases encapsulate how impactful the feminist-led law reforms to defences to murder have been.[69]

With the reformed partial defences restricting the tales that can be told about wayward wives, most femicidal men are pleading guilty to murder. Chrissie Kendall's husband said he 'saw red' when she left him. So he killed her. According to his lawyer, he was 'gripped by an inability to accept the breakdown of his family unit, the loss of the woman he loved and still loves and the loss of his home'. But 'seeing red' and asserting proprietary rights over a wife could no longer found a defence.[70] Susan Gyde's husband killed her and then sent her lover a text with a slight variation on the received script: 'If I can't have her, you can't either. She's dead'.[71] That script no longer exonerated femicidal men. After killing Poppy Devey-Waterhouse in a jealous rage, her former partner claimed he had acted in self-defence. He changed his plea to admit murder on learning that failing to come to terms with a separation no longer excuses murder.[72]

Another measure of the impact of the reforms tightening defences to murder on the disposal of impassioned homicide cases can be seen in the case of Barbara Davidson's partner. He pleaded guilty to her murder in 2018 and was sentenced to life with a minimum of 23 years. That was a very different outcome to the three-year sentence for manslaughter he received in his 1995 trial for strangling his former partner, Jacqueline Aspery. That sentence, according to the prosecutor at the second trial, was 'profoundly merciful by today's standards'. Jacqueline Aspery's daughter put it more strongly: the first trial was a farce that had robbed her mother of justice.[73] She was not the only one to feel like that. Tracy Kearns' partner was cleared of her murder at his 2017 trial. After lying to police about disposing of her body, he claimed she had compared him unfavourably to her new lover and that he 'simply lost it'. He was convicted of manslaughter on the basis of loss of control and given a 13-year sentence. Tracy's family was devastated by the verdict, her mother declaring she would 'never understand how this can be seen as justice'. Nothing less than a life sentence would be justice for what he did to her daughter.[74]

More usually, loss of control defences are failing as they did for the man who killed Sheila Thomas, his wife of 50 years. She had left him for a former lover who allegedly told him that two of the children were not his. Loss of control also failed for Amy Parsons' fiancée who beat her to death after she decided to leave him and for Linda Treeby's partner who 'lost it' when she told him her family hated him.[75] Ann Marie Pomfret's husband hit her with a crow bar more than 30 times. He tried a loss of control defence after initially denying any knowledge of her death. He said he lost his cool after Ann Marie had taunted at him, including calling him 'limp' in reference to his problems with erectile dysfunction. His barrister called him a 'man of impeccable character' who for many years, had been 'a model of self-control, patience and restraint'. He was a 'quiet man who finally snapped', having suffered verbal and physical abuse at her hands. It was to no avail. Convicted of murder, he was sentenced to life with a 20-year minimum.[76]

Occasionally, a 'red mist' can still be counted on to do its traditional excusatory work. In 2019, 77-year-old Mavis Long's husband was sentenced to less than four years for her manslaughter. She had knocked off his glasses, causing him to snap and strangle her. Ordinarily, the appropriate sentence would have been one of eight or nine years but the judge felt it should be reduced given his guilty plea, his previous good character, his remorse and age. Also, he'd had 'a very great deal to cope with', Mavis having suffered from dementia. In the killer's own words, he had snapped because 'the red mist came down', this clouding event still having a purchase in the post-reform era.[77] Contrast the fate of Melissa Belshaw's former partner who stabbed her to death in Wigan in 2020 two months after his discharge from prison. He said he lost control when he became 'overwhelmed' by 'strong suspicions' about her. The judge told him his character assassination of Melissa 'went beyond anything that was justified'. Apparently, a killer's justification for femicide is still a consideration at sentencing, just not in this case. Verdict: murder. Sentence: life with a 32-year minimum.[78]

Concurrently, a victim's 'innocence' or lack thereof, central to the traditional provocation defence, appears to be losing its currency with the growing recognition of a woman's right to leave a relationship notwithstanding the stress it might cause a man. That diminished responsibility defences also rarely succeed today is another indication that defendants once characterised as impassioned killers deserving of sympathy now tend to be condemned as irrationally jealous murderers. Twenty-three-year-old Molly McLaren's killer is a case in point. The jury rejected his diminished responsibility defence at his 2017 trial. According to the judge, he had been 'determined to punish her for ending the relationship' and was clearly 'seeking revenge'. Sentence: life with a 26-year minimum.[79] The same year, 25-year-old Tyler Denton was killed by a man obsessed with her. He found it too hard 'to love someone and not have them love you back'. The jury was unconvinced by psychiatric testimony that he was paranoid and suspicious; that he felt people were plotting against him and had displayed seven of the 14 possible symptoms of a schizotypal disorder. He was convicted of murder and sentenced to life with a minimum of 30 years. That was not enough for her family who said Tyler 'didn't get the justice she deserved'.[80]

Saeeda Hussain's husband's diminished responsibility plea was based on a submission that he suffered from Othello Syndrome when he attacked her in 2018 with a machete and hammer, delivering 46 separate injuries. Like Othello, he had wrongly suspected his wife of having an affair. So he installed CCTV to monitor her movements in his search for 'ocular proof'. His lawyer felt it might sway the jury to submit that there was no evidence to suggest that 'the first 50% of the marriage' was 'anything other than satisfactory and amicable'. For the jury, it was the homicide, not the first half of the marriage that was crucial. Verdict: murder. Sentence: life with a 20-year minimum.[81] Another lawyer's bid to medicalise an offender, or as the judge put it, to 'manipulate the jury' by seeking to 'medicalise' his 'bad behaviour', also failed. He was convicted of the murder of his partner, Maria Gibson. Sentence: life with a 25-year minimum.[82] Juries also rejected the defence offered in the case of Simonne Kerr's former partner. He claimed his depression had impaired his mental function when he 'exploded' in anger and stabbed her more than 70 times. But as the judge told him: 'You killed Simonne Kerr because you are a man of violent disposition prone to outbursts of violent temper'.[83] Another jury rejected the defence presented for Linda Maggs' husband at Cardiff Crown Court in February 2022. He claimed his moderate depression had 'impaired' his ability when he stabbed her to death after a 28-year relationship. He had 'snapped' during their acrimonious divorce. The judge and jury read it otherwise: he resented Linda for 'having the courage to stick up for herself' and following her lawyer's advice not to leave but to remain to protect her interest in the marital home'. Sentence: life with a 20-year minimum.[84]

There have been more cases of men killing their partners and then committing suicide, the familiar *Othello* scenario. These killings were rarely prompted by suspicions of adultery. Once again, the main driving force was rage at a woman's departure. Amy Barnes had asked for a divorce. Reagan Terry was killed by her ex-partner within 24 hours of her confirming on Facebook that she was in a new relationship. Jayde Hall, was also killed by her former partner days after she ended their relationship. All three were stabbed to death. Debbie Zurick was shot by her former husband who was angry that she too had begun a new relationship.[85] Another man was devastated when his 'first ever girlfriend', Jay Edmunds, left for another man. So he killed them both, shouting 'no one else can have you', the standard refrain, before killing himself. Elsie Smith's husband was said to be struggling to cope under the 2020 coronavirus lockdown and so stabbed her to death before killing himself.[86]

Wife-killers who survived Covid-inflected depression and any related suicidal ideation have had mixed success in the courts. Maryan Ismail's husband claimed she had threatened to throw him out for having contracted the disease. Convicted of her murder, he was given life and a 22-year minimum sentence. His self-defence tale was unconvincing, not least because he showed no signs of Covid. As the judge put it: he was 'in the middle of an intense rage' and 'for whatever reason' was intent on killing his wife. Such rage no longer mitigated murder.[87] Compare the case of the man who killed his wife, Ruth Williams. He offered a defence of diminished responsibility on the basis that he had struggled mentally with the 2020 coronavirus restrictions. He had found lockdown 'really hard', becoming depressed just five days after the restrictions were imposed. So he attacked Ruth when she told him to 'get over it'. While one psychiatrist testified that the killer had no history of depression and knew what he was doing, another said his anxiety and depressive illness had been 'heightened' by tough coronavirus measures that had impaired his ability to exercise self-control. Also, he had not coped well since his retirement. Unanimously cleared of murder, he was given a five-year sentence for manslaughter. Protesting against the sentence, domestic violence campaigners demanded that a precedent not be set that allows domestic homicide to be seen as 'an inevitable result' of lockdown restrictions. Femicides often followed years of coercive and controlling abuse and it was essential that this was 'understood by all in our justice system'. While there had been 'an explosion of domestic abuse during the pandemic', the justice system 'must ensure that it takes all action necessary to hold perpetrators to account'.[88]

Such was the outcry over the case that in 2021 there was an attempt to do just that – hold Ruth Williams' killer to account. An appeal was launched against his five-year sentence on the ground of undue leniency. The appeal was dismissed, the court holding that the case was not 'properly classified as a case of domestic abuse'. There had been no controlling behaviour or previous violence against Ruth. In fact, they had a 'long and loving marriage'. This decision surprised Harriet Harman, the Labour MP who led the law reform movement aimed at stopping men getting away with murder. The fact that the appellant judges found that this wife-killing was wholly explained by mental illness showed that the courts were 'simply still too ready to accept excuses'. Domestic abuse does not 'have to be continuous, although it usually is.' It can be 'a one-off homicide'. Moreover, 'to say it's not domestic abuse when a man kills his wife is fatuous. This is the ultimate, most extreme form of domestic abuse'.[89] Harman, who had campaigned so hard to hold femicidal men to account, found it deplorable that English courts are still, a decade after the reforms were implemented, accepting men's excuses for intimate partner femicide.

TikTok murder – impassioned femicide circa 2022

So have the reforms been a failure? Are men still getting away with impassioned femicide? Certainly, there are cases that cause concern. A wife-killer can still win a seven-year sentence for manslaughter as Maddie Humes' killer did. Take the case of the man who said he 'just snapped' when he killed his wife, Jill Sadler, in 2018. He claimed his 'nasty' wife had hastened the death of their daughter from cancer by being rude to her. The judge ruled there was insufficient evidence for a loss of control defence. But the jury unanimously cleared him of murder, believing he did not intend to kill her, he having drunk more than ten pints of lager. That several jurors smiled and waved to him as they left Liverpool Crown Court is vivid testimony to the fact that the wife-killer's nagging, if not shagging, she-caused-me-to-snap defence still has a purchase in some quarters.[90]

Nevertheless, dispositions in other cases suggest that the Williams and Sadler cases, while deeply disturbing, are outliers. Compare these three 2021 cases. The jury rejected the defence offered by Ranjit Gill's husband that he had lost control after she allegedly gave him details about her sexual encounters that made him feel 'worthless'. Verdict: murder. Sentence: life with a 22-year minimum.[91] Sarah Keith's partner stabbed her in the heart because he thought she had cheated on him. With infidelity barred as an excuse for femicide by Harman's reforms, he had no option but to plead guilty to murder. Sentence: life with 25-year minimum.[92] Finally, Beatrice Cenusa's ex-husband pleaded guilty to her murder and in February 2022 was sentenced to life with an 18-year minimum. Posting a TikTok video of herself blowing a kiss to her lover had enraged him: 'you can't be with someone else, you're my wife'. But as it turns out, you can today, most juries deciding that a woman does have a right to be with someone else without being killed. In the eyes of this jury at least, posting a TikTok video of your new partner does not constitute a warrant for your murder.[93]

The English reformers' prediction that they were implementing an important reform that would end the culture of excuses and the injustice of blaming women for their own deaths have largely been fulfilled. Certainly, residual jury sympathy for some enraged killers and occasional risibly short sentences remain causes for concern. But overall, the reforms appear to be working to curtail a woman's 'unfaithfulness', read: departure, as excuse for murder. So many guilty pleas and convictions for murder are testimony to that. As for the reformers' bold claim that 'the days of sexual jealousy as a defence are over', those days still have some way to go.[94] Nevertheless, the chances of a man avoiding a murder conviction for killing an unfaithful or otherwise wayward partner have receded markedly. Astonishingly, adultery finally appears to be losing its status as the highest invasion of property.

In conclusion: the historically mandated provocation by infidelity script has now been exposed as code for a man's murderous rage at being abandoned by a woman who, as criminal courts are increasingly recognising, is entitled to leave a relationship without fatal consequence. As a result, the notion of a mitigating crime of passion is certainly well on track to losing its purchase. Not that it has disappeared altogether. It might be refused in particular cases. For example, in 2019 a judge at Woolwich Crown Court told Sarah Wellgreen's former partner that his killing her was 'no crime of passion or momentary outburst of violence'. It was murder.[95] By implication though, some killings did meet the lower threshold of an impassioned homicide, at least in that judge's view. But tellingly, impassioned homicide is no longer automatically labelled 'hot-blooded' in English courts. Helen Almay's former husband stabbed her and her new partner to death in January 2020 in what a pathologist described as a 'blood bath and the most violent attack' he had encountered in his career. But here the traditional hot-versus-cold blood distinction broke down. Stabbing her 66 times and her new partner 37 times on learning of their relationship was no mitigating 'crime of passion'. It was a 'cold-blooded' attack. That left this angry, cold-blooded killer no alternative than to plead guilty to two counts of murder.[96]

.....

Today, law's traditional wife-killer, reproduced over the centuries as an impassioned man provoked beyond endurance to kill an unfaithful wife in a spur-of-the-moment 'red mist' frenzy, is a shadow of his former self. That legendary *criminel passionnel* emerges from the post-reform cases as a man incapable of coping with relationship breakdown who kills 'his' woman in a frequently planned, far from spontaneous attack, only to find that alleging loss of control in the face of such adversity no longer has much excusatory force. Today he is being reconfigured in the courts as nothing more than a self-entitled 'murderous coxcomb' as Emilia described Othello – 'O murderous coxcomb, what should such a fool/Do with so good a wife?'[97] As for the traditional depiction of his victim as having provoked her own demise, that too is losing its currency in twenty-first-century Britain.

In short, the evidence is overwhelming that the reforms are having their intended effect. Men, at least most of them, are no longer 'getting away' with murdering 'their' women. Accordingly, the reformers, latter-day Emilias, are to be credited with a hard-fought victory. Owning impassioned femicide as the English version of honour killing, refusing to lay it at the door of supposedly emotionally incontinent foreigners, they held the English law of murder to account in the face of near-hysterical opposition from a legal fraternity bent on defending the status quo. What an achievement, exposing English law's hallowed provocation defence, for so long proclaimed as a noble concession to 'human frailty', as nothing more than the fetishising, property-obsessed excuse for murdering women that Shakespeare dismantled and dissected so brilliantly in *Othello* 400 years ago.

Epilogue

The early twenty-first century reform to the English law of murder that banned the age-old 'heat of passion' defence constituted a legal and cultural revolution which up-ended the whole idea of a mitigating 'crime of passion'. That revolution is far from over. Witness residual jury sympathy for some killers cursed with unfaithful or otherwise unsatisfactory wives. Witness judges still able to factor in the victim's 'provocation' when sentencing her killer. For all the success prosecutors have had in securing murder convictions for these killers in the post-reform era, the notion that impassioned men who kill over lost love are deserving of compassion has proved remarkably resilient. This would have surprised Marc Ancel, a French judge who in 1956 delivered a lecture at the University of Cambridge on the subject of '*le crime passionnel*'. He told the audience it was on the wane. With the *criminel passionnel* 'losing his glamour in the public regard', Ancel predicted that it would be possible in the second half of the twentieth century to 'repress' the concept of *crime passionnel* with 'greater effectiveness' than heretofore.[1]

As we have seen, that did not turn out not to be the case in England and Wales. But Ancel's account of the seeming demise of the French *criminel passionnel* is telling in other ways.

He was well aware of how sympathy for the victim is 'counteracted' by pity for the man who kills 'in a fit of passion'. And his example *par excellence* of the killer who, 'swept along by an irresistible force', plays the role of 'a hero hounded by fate'? It is none other than Othello. Despite Desdemona's innocence and virtue, 'everyone is moved by the grandeur and grief of Othello, the classic type of *criminel par passion*'.[2] At least, they were in the nineteenth century. By 1956 not everyone was. Criminologists had come to 'seriously' contest the supposedly 'noble' nature of 'passionate' crimes. They saw them instead as premeditated, motivated by a 'curious mixture of cupidity, egoism and a warped sense of justice' and caused by pathological states such as 'amorous jealousy'. Of course, the 'man in the street' might find himself disposed to excuse impassioned homicide. And not just him. Criminal codes, 'especially' those of the

Latin countries' had for too long held it to be mitigation or even 'an absolutory excuse' if a husband, finding his wife *in flagrante delicto,* kills her or her lover. Nineteenth and early twentieth-century French juries had 'allowed themselves to be carried away by the romantic depiction of the impassioned killer who is 'suddenly flouted by the object of is love, betrayed by her to whom he would have given his all'. Falling under the sway of defence lawyers, they had become 'excessively indulgent towards the "passionate" offender'.[3]

As Ancel tells the story, acquittals and lenient sentences for impassioned homicides declined in France after 1945, the admission of women to juries being a key factor. He was surprised though to discover that women were 'more severe than men' and often 'less disposed to look upon the *criminel passionnel* as a hero' deserving of pity. But recalling that impassioned killings were more often committed by men than by women in France, he speculated that perhaps 'the woman juror feels an instinctive need to defend her own sex against attacks of uncontrolled passion'. Speculation aside, Ancel condemned all such attacks as inspired 'almost entirely by violent jealousy and by a desire for vengeance' or by motives that mingled 'a sort of avarice' with what 'might properly be called passion'. His central point however, was that the tendency to treat passionate murder leniently had been halted by mid-century. Scholars, legislators and ultimately public opinion had started to revolt against the 'too facile solution' of according these crimes 'special and mitigated treatment' when really, they were not 'radically different from ordinary crime'.[4] Crimes of passion – or so he thought – were on their way out.

How wrong that prediction turned out to be and how ironic that he made it in England just a year or two before the Homicide Act 1957 opened up the floodgates to impassioned provocation pleas there. The irony does not stop there. Here was a French judge condemning, at an English university, law's indulgence of 'passion' offenders that 50 years later would be championed by English law lords. Recall Lord Neill railing against law reforms that he felt would deprive stiff upper-lipped Englishmen of the right to kill their wives in the heat of passion. Recall too that Lord Neill laid the notion of a mitigating impassioned homicide at the door of the French, forgetting that Englishmen had been committing 'French style *crime passionnel*', as he called it, for centuries. Herewith, once again, the English propensity to racialise femicidal killers that Shakespeare dramatised in *Othello* in the figures of the out-of-control black Moor and the crafty Italian. This insidious othering practice continuing to this day, is it any wonder the law reformers' arresting claim that provocation by infidelity is 'our own version of honour killings' was such a shock to thought? What, in *our* house?

Shakespeare scholar Mark Breitenberg throws some illuminating light on what feminist critics are up against in contesting the age-old conceit that wife-killing is not murder. Writing in the 1990s, he pinpointed the main problem as 'our' tradition of 'fetishising chastity'. By 'no means', he said, can we claim to have 'freed ourselves' from it, so many men still experiencing sexual jealousy 'as a residual, even old-fashioned response to female sexuality'.[5] The English reformers did their best to challenge that tradition by banning infidelity as an excuse for the old-fashioned, though still prevalent, practice of murdering women. They did well. Today, for the most part, juries in England and Wales are returning murder convictions for femicidal men once deemed worthy of law's compassion.

So what's next for someone who has long advocated abolishing the provocation defence on the ground that it operates as a profoundly sexed excuse for killing women? Write a book explaining exactly what is at stake when men accuse women of provoking them to kill them. Write it from the victims' perspective. Write a play, a Theatre in Education piece, putting Othello, Shakespeare's ludicrous chastity-obsessed fetishiser, on trial for murder.[6] Write it for young people before they succumb to the idea that killing a woman while 'in a red mist' is not murder. Explain that Othello was a white man, a white Englishman's idea of an impassioned killer projected onto a foreign other. Invite them to deliver the verdict. Murder or Manslaughter? So far, the response has been encouraging. Overwhelmingly, young audiences agree with Lord Simon. Even if Iago's insinuations against Desdemona had been true, Othello's crime was murder and nothing else.

.....

This book is dedicated to the memory of Hannah Abbott, the London charwoman who, in 1828, survived her husband's murderous knife attack and lived to tell her story. I like to think she would regard Othello's conviction for murder as just.

Notes

Introduction

1. Reddy 2001 p x.
2. Cited in Verkaik 2008.
3. Cited in Hinsliff 2008; my emphasis.
4. July 7, 2009, House of Lords Debates, Hansard, col 576.
5. October 26, 2009 Ibid, col 1061.
6. Escolme 2013 pp xix–xx.
7. Wortham 2015.
8. Horder 1992.
9. Carol Neely quoted in Loomba 1994 p 24.
10. Ibid.
11. Loomba 1999 pp 187–188.
12. See, for example, Howe 2005.
13. As I argue in Howe 2004 pp 55–57. On my proposed social injury strategy, see Howe 1987.
14. On the use of 'subaltern', see Dayton 2004 p 842.
15. Dixon 2003 pp 1–25.
16. Fernie 2002.
17. Cullen 2019 p 132.
18. Belenky 2008 pp 9–91.
19. Conley 2009 p 153. Compare Peter Stearns' discussion of jealousy's 'gender factor': 1989 pp 36–39.
20. Reddy registers that feeling is 'a domain' to be retrieved from public texts such as court cases. He specifies a 'male world of feeling': 1997 pp 3–5.
21. Early papers include Howe 1994a and 1997.
22. See, for example, Howe 2012a, 2012b, 2014a, 2014b, 2013a and 2013b, 2019a, 2019b and 2022.
23. Smart's *Feminism and the Power of Law* is honoured as a foundational postmodern feminist text in Howe and Alaattinoğlu 2019. This methodology is discussed further in Howe 2019.
24. Howard and O'Connor 1987 p 13.
25. Howard 1987 p 173.
26. See Howe and D. Alaattinoğlu 2019.
27. Greenawalt 1984.
28. Wiener 2004.
29. Cavarero 2000 pp 28 and 38; her emphasis.
30. Pembroke in *King John* 4.2.30–31 in Greenblatt et al 2008.

Chapter 1

1. Citations follow lineation and typesetting in Waith 2008. An earlier version of sections of this chapter was published as Howe 2013b.
2. The 1611 translation is in *The Holy Bible: New International Version* London: Hodder and Stroughton (revised 2011); my emphasis.
3. TS Elliot quoted in Hamilton 1963 p 201. Hamilton was one of the first to challenge the traditional view of the play's 'apparent failure': p 202. The play may have been co-authored with George Peel: Bate 2009 p 359.
4. They are also called the 'cuckoldry plays': Alfar 2017.
5. I am indebted to Eric Heinze for introducing me to this Shakespeare, one who raises a host of socio-legal questions about political and legal orders. See especially his illuminating reading of *The Comedy of Errors* as showing how dominance in law and society flourishes through fictions that erupt in an orchestration of 'errors': Heinze 2009a. See also Heinze 2009b, 2009c and 2009d. For more conventional approaches to legal questions in the plays, see Jordan and Cunningham 2008 and Raffield 2010.
6. Smith 2019 pp 1and 6; Bate 2019 p 19.
7. Bevington 2016 p 42.
8. Garber 2008 pp xxv–xxvi.
9. Howard 1987 p 176. Jean Howard was one of the first Shakespeare scholars to take this Foucauldian approach.
10. Rackin 2016 pp 9–11. As the feminist Shakespeare scholarship is vast, mine is necessarily a selective reading.
11. Bate 2009 p 116.
12. Bate 1994 p 109.
13. Bate 2009 pp 70 and 335.
14. Belsey 2007 p 8. She notes that some enlistments are 'more appalling than others', Nazi ones, for example: p 5.
15. Horder 1992 pp 111 and 138–139; his emphasis.
16. Horder 1992 pp 186 and 197. For the intrinsically normative evaluations made in determinations of criminal responsibility, see Stannard 2002 and Watkins 2006.
17. Horder 1992 pp 7–20.
18. Horder 1992 pp 21–22.
19. Horder 1992 p 24 note 8. He explains that as wives were men's property and not 'capable of rational moral decision-making', they were not to be fully blamed for having been seduced: p 24 note 8.
20. Horder 1992 p 29; his emphasis.
21. *Maddy's Case* (1671) 1 Vent 158. It is sometimes cited as *Manning's Case (1671) 1 Vent 158*. It is also cited as Anonymous (1670) T Raym 212. Horder states incorrectly that it was decided in 1617.
22. Horder 1992 p 39.
23. *R v Mawgridge* (1707) Kel 119.
24. *Mawgridge* at 126–128.
25. *Mawgridge* at 137–138.
26. Horder 1992 40–44.
27. Horder 1992 pp 45–49.
28. Horder 1992 pp 50–51; his emphasis.
29. Horder 1992 pp 52–56; his emphasis.
30. Horder, 1992 pp 72–73.
31. Horder 1992 pp 77 and 85–86.
32. Horder 1992 pp 86–87.
33. *Buckner's Case* (1655) Style 467 at 469. See also Horder 1992 pp 11–15.
34. *Oneby* 92 ER 465 (1727) at 466–468.

35. *Oneby* at 469–471.
36. *Oneby* at 472. Compare Holt's view. Tracking what counted as murder as far back as the Saxons and Normans and laws relating to the killing of Danish and later French invaders, he maintained that it was not murder if an invader killed an Englishman. But it was if an Englishman killed a Frenchman even if it was 'by misfortune'. This was because the conquerors knew the English 'hated' them and so had good reason to enact stricter laws to protect themselves: *Mawgridge* at 121–125.
37. *Oneby* at 472.
38. Horder 1992 pp 74–75; his emphasis.
39. *Mawgridge* at 471. As a jurist writing in 1771 put it: the reasoning faculties of men varied 'as much as their faces' such that it was impossible for the law 'to fix any time in which the passions shall be supposed to become cool': quoted in Horder 1992 p 69.
40. Clark Hulse 1979.
41. Horder cites this widely published statistic with reference to 103 men convicted of killing their partner and former partners in 1989 in Horder 1992 p 186.
42. Kolin 1995 p 21 and James 1995 p 286. See James 1997 and more generally, Kolin's 1995 collection of critical essays. Highlighting the play's use of Ovid against Virgil to parody the epic idiom, James argues that Ovid provides Shakespeare with a precedent for parodying Virgil's *Aeneid,* the epic tale of empire-building, order and piety which the Andronici 'virtually claim as family history':1995 p 287. As Helga Duncan summarises James' reading, the play invokes and then displaces Virgil's authority, turning away from 'the imperial epic of Virgil to the counter-epic of Ovid' as 'part of Shakespeare's critique of Roman imperial ideology as a model for his culture's notion of empire': Duncan 2009 p 434. Bate describes James' argument (first published in 1991) as 'ingenious' and cohering with his 'sense' that Shakespeare uses Ovid to 'destabilise a Virgilian, imperial idiom': Bate 1994 p 103, n 33. He suggests that in questioning 'the commonplace' that Rome stood for civilisation and the Goths for barbarism, the play's final act 'proposes that a Goth invasion led by Lucius will save ancient Rome from decadence. Might that also mean, he asks, that the German religious Reformation 'would save Albion from the decadent influence of modern Rome?': Bate 2019 p 110. He also suggests that the play is about 'the troubled question of succession to the childless Elizabeth': p 132. He points out too that Ovid's *Heroides*, his narrative poems written in the voices of 'lamenting heroines dumped by their lovers', was a key source for Shakespeare's 'animating of "the woman's part"'. This gives 'subjectivity to the female voice, albeit as a victim, yet as a victim who is given the opportunity to state her case at length in the court of audience opinion': Bate 2019 pp 195–196. He addresses the question of how Shakespeare related to the received 'heroic' tradition in Chapter 8.
43. Bate 1994 pp 108–110.
44. Kahn 1997 pp 46–47.
45. Choy 2011 p 46.
46. Rosyter 2000 p 450.
47. Royster 2000 pp 434–435.
48. Little 2021 pp 276–277. Citing Royster's piece as exemplary, Arthur L Little answers his own question as to whether it is possible to 'read Shakespeare through critical white studies' in the affirmative, suggesting that they work to 'disrupt the seeming intractability and permanence of whiteness as a uniquely privileged, adjudicative cultural force': 2021 p 268.
49. Royster 2000 pp 439–444. We return to Shakespeare's glosses on humoural theory in Chapter Two.
50. Loomba 2002 pp 82–83.

51. Lines 1.1.130–131 and 1.1.378.
52. Lines 4.2.71, 4.2. 99 and 4.2.117.
53. White 1997 p 343. See also Bartels 1990.
54. Lines 1.1.23 and 1.1.64–65.
55. Willis 2002 p 23 and Crosbie 2007 pp 147–173. See also Hamilton 1963 and Kyle 2010.
56. Cetin 2010 p 357.
57. Lines 1.1.281, 1.1.292, 4.3.50 and 4.3.24.
58. Heinze 2013.
59. While Virgil's *Aeneid* is featured, it is Ovid's tale in *Metamorphoses* of Procne's revenge on her husband for raping her sister, Philomel, that provides the play's 'main structural model': Bate 1994 p 102.
60. St Hilaire 2009 p 316. See also Starry West 1982 and Miola 1995. For an earlier account of the play's classical origins, see Law 1943 pp 145–153. For its Roman history sources, see Liebler 1994.
61. Aebischer 2004 pp 56–57 citing line 5.3.38.
62. Lines 5.3.42–43; Kendall 1989 p 313. Kahn notes that what she calls 'the murder' of Lavinia confronts us with 'the last of the several textual precedents' with which she has been represented. Earlier in the play, she was compared to several of her classical predecessors: Cornelia, Hebuca, Philomel and Lucrece. Finally she becomes the slaughtered Lavinia whereas she preferred Philomel's fate: Kahn 1997 p 70.
63. James 1995 p 297.
64. Fawcett 1983 pp 269; her emphasis and p 75.
65. Bate 1995 p 267, n 43 citing Line 3.1.106. I note the further irony of Titus deferring to Saturninus on such a grave ethical question given the emperor's brutality and despotism throughout the play. Bate suggests several senses of 'warrant' are relevant here: that of 'authoritative witness, conclusive proof, one whose command justifies an action, sanction, token of authorisation, document or writ licensing execution'.
66. Bate 1995 p 28.
67. Raffield 2010 pp 21 and 28–29. Raffield sees the constitutional significance of the play as lying in the historical context of Elizabeth's last decade when common law adherents were opposing the increasing autocracy of the government. He argues that 'the triumph of unwritten law is symbolised' in the Emperor's death and the succession of Lucius who has 'respect for ceremony, precedent and ritual': p 49. Alternatively, Lorna Hutson argues that the play exemplifies how Elizabethan revenge tragedy distinguished the emergent participatory and open jury trial from the inquisitorial system that preceded it: Huston 2007 pp 66–68.
68. Crosbie 2007 pp 148, 158–159 and 163–164. Crosbie sees Titus' murderous acts as an example of Aristotle's theory of 'justice in exchange'. He suggests that 'it might seem radical to see his revenge as structured by the rational principles of Aristotelian exchange theory': 169–170.
69. Raffield 2010 p 48.
70. Grace Starry West was one of the first to query the warrant to kill Lavinia: 1982 p 71.
71. Dickson 2008 pp 6 and 15. See also Willis 2002. One critic suggests that the fly scene, where Titus protests Marcus' killing of a fly, is a parody of 'the humanist appeal to sympathetic understanding'. Yet such sentimental understanding of subjectivity 'as *interior* experience is precisely not the project that the play stages for its audience': Rowe 1994 p 301 her emphasis.
72. Lines 1.1.23 and 1.1.64–65. James 1995 p 298.
73. Anderson 2003 p 311–313. Such is the play's obsession with precedent texts that, as one critic puts it, even the play's own precedent text, Ovid's *Metamorphosis* – 'the

grandfather of rape stories' – is 'literally brought on to the stage': Detmer-Goebel 2001 p 76.

74. Line 5.3.46; my emphasis. Aebischer 2004 pp 58–59. As Asp succinctly puts it, she must die to 'assuage his woe': Asp 1995 p 341,
75. Ines 5.3.49–51.
76. Line 3.2.79; Starry West 1982 p 74. See also Cutts 1968. To be sure, this is not the idea of anger as justifiable outrage that Horder attributed to Aristotle. It is more akin to rashness, as Titus acknowledges. Deborah Willis argues that Titus performs his 'own self-critique'. He 'knows his killing of Lavinia is horrible': Willis 2002 p 50.
77. Hunt 1988 pp 210–213.
78. Line 3.2.39.
79. Raffield 2010 p 39.
80. Packard 2010 pp 282, 287-288 and 294–295. For the 'explosion of scholarly interest' in the play in North American literary studies that focuses on Lavinia as author see Solga 2006 pp 63–64. In Ovid's tale, Philomel's sister, Procne, is turned into a nightingale and Philomel to a swallow after getting her revenge on her rapist.
81. Detmer-Goebel 2001 pp 83 and 88.
82. Line 4.1.50.
83. Frederick 2008 p 211.
84. Line 4.1.50; Bate 1994 p 117.
85. Lines 2.1.65 and 3.1.63–64; my emphasis. Oakley-Brown 2005 pp 331-332.
86. Rutkoski 2006 pp 211–212.
87. Zamir 2008 pp 294–296. The piece of wood is the 'faggot' in line 3.1.68.
88. Willis 2002 pp 49–50.
89. Aebischer 2004 p 57.
90. Cunningham 1990 p 153. For a Lacanian gloss on Lavinia's silence, see Asp 1995 pp 338–339.
91. Horder 1992 pp 194–197.
92. Spelman 1989 pp 263–264.

Chapter 2

1. Citations are from Honigmann 1997. References will also be made to other editions, notably Neill 2008 and Hall 2007. Lines cited from other Shakespeare plays are from Greenblatt et al 2008. An earlier version of sections of this chapter was published as Howe 2012b.
2. Riley 2005 p 13.
3. Lines 4.2.117–121.
4. Lines 1.1.66, 1.188, 1.1.111, 1.125, 1.1.135, 1.2.69 and 2.3.200.
5. Line 3.3.363.
6. Lines 4.3.59 and 68–70.
7. Neill 1998 p 361 note 2.
8. Howard 2016 p 112 and Rackin 2016 p 13. Barbara Hodgson suggests that the OJ Simpson trial 'made *Othello* perhaps the timeliest' of his plays for late twentieth-century America: 1998 p 72.
9. An annotated bibliography of Shakespeare and Feminist Criticism was already available by the early 1990s: Kolin 1991. Foundational texts include Wayne 1991, Traub 1992 and Hendricks and Parker 1994.
10. My reading of *Othello* clearly falls within 'presentism', an interpretative framework that reads the Shakespeare text in relation to current affairs, arguing for 'the crucial importance of Shakespeare *now*': Fernie 2005 p 169; his emphasis.

11. See Heinze 2013 pp 153–155. See Prawer 2012 for a fascinating account of Marx's engagement with Shakespeare.
12. Capitalist angst is surely on display in the opening scene of *The Merchant of Venice* with Antonio expressing inexplicable sadness. Is he worried about the potential loss of his 'merchandise'? Antonio's sadness is famously cryptic and may stem from the loss of his homoerotic companion Bassanio or from mixed emotions. After all, Antonio denies that he is worried about his investments. But inasmuch as his cronies declare they would be worried in the same circumstances, capitalist angst is surely on display. See Heinze 2013 pp.110 and 130–131.
13. Warren 1998 p 19.
14. FH Mares quoted in Warren 1998 p 19.
15. See Marjorie Garber's intriguing critique – in the context of her reading of *The Merchant of Venice* – of the persistent critical interest in recapturing the elusive matter of intention: Garber 2008 pp 124–153.
16. See Heinze 2009d p 73.
17. Howard 2008 p 2971.
18. *Cymbeline* Line 5.1.2–5.
19. Honigmann 1997 pp 43–44.
20. Lines 2.1.295–300.
21. Lines 3.3.167–169, 3.4.152–157, 4.3.63 and 4.1.193.
22. Singh 1994 p 46. Line 4.1.197.
23. Honigmann 1997 p 61.
24. Lines 3.3.324–326 and 5.2. 344–345; Matheson 2004 p 181.
25. Michael Nagle 1978 pp 104–109. The murder/manslaughter crux in the play is also discussed in Strier and McAdams 2016.
26. Hawley 1998 pp 12–15; my emphases. In North American reform jurisdictions that have adopted the Model Penal Code, male jealousy in relation to 'unfaithful' women has been enshrined as mitigating excuse for murder under the rubric of 'extreme mental or emotional disturbance'.
27. Leader-Elliot 1997, pp 162–165; his emphasis.
28. Neely 1987 pp 108–110. Philippa Berry, amongst other feminist critics, adopts a similar interpretive stance, reading *Othello* as having unsettled the authority of the 'masculine subject position' by dislocating the 'masculine eye of its heroic protagonists: Berry 1999: 72. Marjorie Garber notes that 'in Shakespearean comedy there is *always* a tragedy embedded, somewhere': Garber 2008 p 146; her emphasis.
29. Lines 2.3.253–255. Horns as odious as they are necessary appear in *As You Like It*: Line 3.3.49.
30. Neely 1987 pp 118–119 citing line 1.3.270.
31. Fernie 2002 pp 136–137.
32. Lines 1.3.374–376.
33. Fernie 2002 p 143.
34. Fernie 2002 pp 160 citing Line 5.2.282; my emphasis.
35. Line 2.3.21–22.
36. Fernie 2002 pp 170–172.
37. Headlam Wells 2000 pp 111–113.
38. Lines 3.4.104–107; Neely 1987 pp 133–134.
39. Breitenberg 1993 pp 383–384.
40. Snow 1980 pp 384–412.
41. Snow 1980 pp 384–386.
42. Line 5.2.143.
43. Snow 1980 pp 386–389.
44. Lines 5.2.3; Snow 1980 pp 390–393.

45. Snow 1980 p 400.
46. Snow 1980 pp 401–402 and 410–411. See also Breitenberg 1996.
47. Parker 1996 pp 251–252 citing Line 3.3.430. The husband's 'judicial proceeding' against this female 'chose' or 'thing' cannot be named to stars that are figured as 'the virginal coldness of a closed perfection'.
48. Parker 1992 p 208.
49. Rutter 2001 pp 165–167.
50. Burke 1951 pp 166–167.
51. Neely p 119.
52. Bruster 1992 pp 42–44.
53. Bruster 1992 00 45–54 citing lines 3.3.362 and 3.3.251–252 and drawing on Bourdieu's famous concept symbolic capitalism.
54. Lines 3.3.368 and 3.3. 251–252; Bruster 2002 pp 50–54. Bruster explains that, according to the myth, the cuckoo finding a man at work 'testifies symbolically to that man's inadequacy' while the source of cuckoldry's association with labour is 'the historical gendering of patient production as feminine'.
55. Bruster 1992 pp 65–68.
56. There has been much discussion of the handkerchief's significance. See especially Bose's 1975 brilliant discussion of its strawberry patterning and Dympna Callaghan's 2001 equally engaging Marxist reading, one that nevertheless finds it 'inappropriate' to apply the concept of commodity fetishism to the handkerchief's production.
57. Yachnin 1996 p 203.
58. Lines 4.1.13–14.
59. Yachnin 1996 p 203 referencing lines 4.1.13–14 and 3.3.278.
60. Yachnin 1996 p 204.
61. Yachnin 1996 p 205. See my exploration of Marxist and Freudian theories of fetishism in the context of intimate partner femicide: Howe 2017.
62. Korda 2002 pp 11–12. She argues that women's control over household property was *de facto* and *de jure* more extensive than accounts of the common law doctrine of coverture imply: pp 39–40.
63. Korda 2002 pp 113–116.
64. Korda 2002 p 146.
65. Ross 2010 pp 91–92 citing lines 1.2.62–63.
66. Hall 2007 p 328.
67. See Hall 2007 pp 315–340. Informed by Aristotelian ethics and Stoicism, the central humoural idea was that the human body was constituted of four humours; phlegm, yellow bile, black bile and blood, each having an effect on moods. Suggesting a continuum between passion and cognition, physiology, psychology and environment, humoural theory's recognition of the interdependence of mind and body has, it has been argued, 'an explanatory power' that has 'never gone away': Arikha 2007 p xix. See Kern Paster 2004.
68. Lines 3.4.26–28.
69. Floyd-Wilson 2003 pp.1–12 and 135–140.
70. Floyd-Wilson 2003 pp 132–140. Neill notes the 'notorious indeterminacy of the term *Moor* itself': Neill 1998 p 364.
71. Leo Africanus 1600 p 233.
72. Floyd-Wilson 2003 pp 133–147.
73. *Othello* thus aims to 'validate the northern complexion while forgetting its origins in a tripartite geohumoral system'. It displays that system being challenged by an emergent theory that suggests that blackness, whether it is 'the black poison of suspicion or the blackness of melancholy, necessarily destroys the inherent virtues of a white complexion': 2003 pp 150–157.

74. Korda 2002 pp 136–138.
75. Varchi 1615 pp 18–19 and Korda 2002 p 138. Tofte also claims that more extreme forms of jealousy are found in women. Korda points out the 'clear contradiction' between reserving jealousy as a male privilege associated with property ownership and his bid to locate it in humoral theory according to which women should be more jealous: 2002 p 243 note 86 citing Varchi 1615 p 25.
76. Varchi 1615 pp 21–23.
77. Varchi makes it explicit he is speaking of the 'Masculine Gender'. Tofte is not so sure, tripping himself up in contradictions as he tries to claim women are more jealous: Varchi 1615 pp 33–34.
78. Varchi 1615 pp 57–59.
79. Line 1.2.68.
80. Burton 1932 pp 264–265 and 283–284. See Breitenberg's 1996 discussion of Burton's text.
81. Brown 2004 p 151.
82. Hall 1996 pp 267–268. Hall was one of the first Shakespeare scholars to insist that a sustained critique of whiteness is essential to stop the derisory practice of only regarding people of colour as racial subjects. See also Hendricks and Parker 1996 and Barbara Hodgson's suggestion that *Othello* 'represents a site through which the problem of the black body in the white imaginary becomes visible, gets worked through': 1998 p 43. On Othello's whiteness, see the discussion in Howe 2022. It was Dympna Callaghan who famously declared that 'Othello was a white man': 1996. Compare the suggestion that he is 'a mixture of black and tawny, of negroid and Arab; he is almost any colour one pleases, so long as it permits his easier isolation and destruction by his enemies and himself': Everett 2000 p 72. See also Newman 1987.
83. Lines 2.3.29, 1.1.88–89 and 1.2.70–71.
84. Bristol 1990 pp 3–21, p 18; his emphasis.
85. Bristol 1990 pp 10–15. Or as Ruth Vanita puts it, the play ultimately presents Othello's jealousy as 'not at all different from any white husband': 1994 p 342. See Vaughan 1994 for an extended discussion of Othello's jealousy.
86. Bristol 1990 pp 16–18.
87. Howard 2016 p112.
88. Neill 1989 pp 383–412, pp 385 and 404–408.
89. Neill 1989 p 406.
90. The statistics she cites indicate that husbands murdered wives two to three times more often than wives murdered husbands, with one study revealing women to be the victims in almost 75 per cent of marital killings. Only after 1650 did literary attention shift from the murderous wife to the murderous husband: Dolan 1994 pp 25 and 89.
91. Dolan 1994 pp 112–118.
92. Neill 2008 pp 21–22.
93. Line 4.1.232.
94. Volpp 1994 pp 57–101, p 67; her emphasis. I draw on Volpp' work in my critique of the deployment of cultural defences in the Australian context in Howe 2009.
95. Lines 5.2.290–292 and 5.2.340–346. For extreme mental or emotional disturbance defences deployed in provocation by infidelity femicides in Model Penal Code states, see Lee 2003 pp 33–45. One critic has argued that Othello's 'judicial language' suggests that 'he speaks as if he were already in a court of law': Headlam Wells 2000 p108.
96. Line 3.3.394.
97. Lines 4.1.166, 4.1.175 and 4.1.178–180.
98. Line 4.1.197–207.
99. Lines 4.1.263–266.

100. 'My lord has fallen into an epilepsy/This is his second fit, he had one yesterday': Lines 4.1.50–51.
101. Lines 5.2.6 and 3.3.351.
102. See further Korda 2002 pp 112–114 and Neill 2008 Appendix F (iii) on the Indian/Judean crux in Othello's final speech.
103. Lines 5.2. 351 and 353.
104. Lines 3.3.363–364.
105. Tamora is unfaithful to her husband Saturninus in *Titus Andronicus*, but that is the least of her offences and does not bring about her demise.
106. For Carol Rutter, the play's domestic narrative 'speaks through the entirely colloquial, even banal discourse of misogynist gender stereotyping, mobilising (male) cultural fantasies that work to regulate women's bodies by regulating their speech': Rutter 2001 pp 145–146. See Lynne Magnusson's 2004 Bourdieu-inflected reading of 'voice potential' in the play, focusing on Othello's voice.
107. Lines 5.2.190–194.
108. Lines 5.2.231–232.

Chapter 3

1. Wiener 2004 pp 160–162.
2. Wiener 2004 p 227, note 74.
3. Cavararo 2000 p 28.
4. Wiener 2004 p 6. See Howe and Alaattinoğlu 2019 for an appreciation of Carol Smart's work focusing on law as a site of contestation over gendered questions.
5. My main sources are court records, Home Office papers and newspaper reports of the trials. There is, as Shani D'Cruze points out, a complex interrelationship between the stories told in official written accounts, in verbal courtroom exchanges and in witness testimony. Press representations were shaped through these different kinds of reported speech and were 'coloured by the addition of investigative journalism': D'Cruze 2007 p 709.
6. *Times* 16 April, 1791 p 3. In her victim-orientated study of 38 wife murder cases in London from 1690 to 1750, Jennine Hurl-Eamon found that 70 per cent of the killers were convicted of murder: 2008 p 227.
7. *Bath Chronicle and Weekly Gazette*, 1 September 791, p 2; *Times* 17 September, 1791, p 3.
8. Lines 5.2.16–19.
9. *Old Bailey Proceedings Online* [hereafter OBP] (www.oldbaileyonline.org), October 1819, John Holmesby.
10. Wiener 2004 p 212.
11. *Times* 30 October 1819 p 3; Wiener 2004 p 212.
12. *Times* 17 March 1826 p 4.
13. *Times* 25 July 1828 p 3.
14. Wiener 1999a 481 note 44. The 'exertions' made day and night on behalf of the condemned man were said to be 'beyond all precedent': *Times 9 December* 1828 p 3. Not everyone was sympathetic. Some thought the evidence showed it was 'a deliberate attempt to commit murder': *Times* 9 December 1828 p 3.
15. Gatrell 1994 pp 413–416. Compare Lizzie Seal's reading of twentieth-century petitions for mercy: 2014 pp 101–104.
16. *Times 3* October p 3 and 6 October 1828 p 3.
17. OBP: October 1828, James Abbott.
18. *Morning Advertiser* 6 December 1828 p 3. See also *Times* 6 December 1828 p 3. Sarah Burrell, the nurse at the birth of Hannah's last child, deposed that Abbott wandered

around the birthing room 'like a mad man' and that when he looked at the child, he 'appeared very much agitated and said it was not his': HO17/82/80 (Abbott).

19. HO17/82/80.
20. *Times* 29 October 1828 p 3. The woman with whom she lodged at this last address said she could no longer maintain her there. Hannah is difficult to trace thereafter. On her release from hospital, she had requested that she not be sent to a workhouse outside London as she had better prospects of work there. Did she stay in London? Or is she the charwoman listed in a Nottinghamshire census as a mother-in-law living in her daughter Ann's household? If so, she altered her place of birth and was still living there in 1871. Or is she the Hannah Abbott, a widower and pauper, living in Hampshire in 1861? Probably not. Again, the listed birthplace is not hers. Another Hannah Abbott, aged 70, was admitted to a London workhouse in 1874. Is it her? She would have been 77 then, so maybe not. I shall keep searching for her.
21. *Times* 27 March 1868 p 12; HO144/30/75392 (Quigley). Wiener 2004 p 228. A drunkard, yes, but does Wiener overstate his case against Dinah? The trial report in the *Times* does not mention adultery.
22. *Sheffield Independent* 27 March p 3.
23. *Pearson's Case* (1832) 2 Lewin 216; *Times* 14 March 1835 p 6.
24. *R v Kirkham* (1837) 173 ER 422 at 425.
25. *Kirkham* at 423.
26. *Kirkham* at 425.
27. *R v Welsh* (1869) 11 Cox CC 336 at 338.
28. *R v Fisher* (1837) 173 ER 452; pp 453–454.
29. *Times* 24 October 1839. p 7; Wiener 2004 p 213.
30. Wiener 2004 p 205.
31. Wiener 2004 p 180; *Times* 10 April 1843 p 6; HO12/102/24. He hanged.
32. *R v Mark Sherwood* (1844) 174 ER 936 at 937; *Evening Mail* 5 August 1844 p 6; Wiener 2004 pp 180–181; HO18/146/2 (Sherwood).
33. *R v Matthias Kelly* (1848) 175 ER 342 at 342–343.
34. *Times* 10 August 1844 p 8.
35. HO18/376/21 (Mobbs); *Times* 27 August 1853, p 9 and *Times* 28 October 1853, p 10. See Wiener 2004 p 229 note 78 where even he finds the claims against Caroline Mobbs unconvincing. See Hammerton 1992 pp 22–26 for an account of London demonstrations against General Haynau.
36. *Times* 8 March 1856 p 11; Wiener 2004 p 214.
37. *Times* 31 July 1858 p 11.
38. *Times* 8 August 1859 p 11; Wiener 2004 p 178. D'Cruze notes that newspapers often remarked on the large number of women attending murder trials. They were especially interested in domestic or courtship homicides. She suggests this reflects women's investment and interest in a growing middle-class interwar domestic culture: 2007 pp 716–717. Perhaps they also had an investment in the fate of the victims.
39. *Times* 15 December 1856 p 9.
40. *Times* 31 March 1862; my emphasis, p 11; *Liverpool Mercury* 31 March 1862 p 11; Wiener 2004 p 221.
41. Wiener 2004 p 204.
42. Wiener 2004 p 226.
43. *Times* 4 March 1864 p 11; Wiener p 215.
44. *Times* 19 December 1864 p 11; Wiener 2004 pp 213–214.
45. *Times* 28 March 1867 p 11.
46. *Times* 25 November 1869 p 9; Wiener 2004 p 207.
47. HO12/189/89255 (Hinson).
48. *Daily News* 10 July 1846.

49. *R v Rothwell* (1871) 12 Cox CC.
50. *Rothwell* at 146-7; *Huddersfield Chronicle*, 14 October 1871 p 3.
51. *Morning Post* July 24 1872 p 7; *Times* 24 July 1872 p 11. On the same page, *The Times* reported another murder trial of a man who alleged his wife had been unfaithful. He was acquitted, the jury accepting his defence that she had committed suicide.
52. *Times* 14 March 1872 p 11; *Tavistock Gazette* 22 March 1872 p 6.
53. *Times* 19 December 1872 p 9; *Yorkshire Post* 19 December 1872 p 4.
54. Wiener 2004 p 227; HO45/9374/39497 (Poplett); *Times* 23 November 1874 p 11; 26 November p 4; 28 November 1874 p 12 and 15 December 1874 p 10.
55. Wiener 2004 p 183; *Times* 9 July 1878 p 4; *London Evening Standard* 9 July 1878 p 4.
56. *Times* 17 January 1879 p 11; Wiener pp 217–218.
57. OBP: Charles Taylor, November 1882.
58. *Times* 28 October 1880 p 8.
59. Wiener 2004 p 220; *Times* 7 February 1881 p 10.
60. It was granted. HO144/135/35383 (Smith); *Times* 29 April 1884 p 10; *Sunderland Daily Echo* 29 April 1884 p 4. Wiener p 223.
61. *Times* 17 September 1885 p 12.
62. *Times* 15 February 1887 p.8.
63. *Leicester Chronicle* 5 February 1887 p 8.
64. OBP: March 1892, John Noble; *Times* 28 March 1892 p 10.
65. OBP: July 1894, John Goldie Round; *Reynold's Newspaper* 24 June 1894 p 3.
66. HO144/549/A57211 (Harris); *Times* 15 November 1895 p 10.
67. OBP: June 1896, James Robert Allison.
68. Cited in Wiener 2004 pp 230–231, note 82.
69. *Times* 27 June 1898 p 3. Wiener 2004 p 218.
70. Wiener 2004 pp 2-6, 11–12, 25–30.
71. Wiener 2004 pp 165–166.
72. Wiener 2004 pp 147, 175 and 201–202.
73. Wiener 2004 pp 235–239 citing *Lloyd's Weekly* 30 November 1884 pp 6–7.
74. Wiener 2004 p 31. Caroline Conley (2007) charts the pernicious othering practice as it occurred within the British Isles with Irish, Scottish, English and Welsh accusing each other of being more homicidally inclined and more violent towards their wives.
75. Wiener 2004 pp 31–34. See further Wiener 2008.
76. Wiener 2004 p 238.
77. Wiener 2004 pp 158, 187–188 and 225–226.
78. *Times* 10 March 1864 p 7 and 7 March 1864 p 11.
79. Wiener 1999b p 176, note 11 and 177.
80. Wiener 2004 pp 290–291.
81. Relatedly, see my book-length Foucauldian feminist critique of penal regimes: Howe 1994b.
82. *Times* 9 May 1887 p 7; Wiener 2004 pp 202 and 216.
83. Wiener 2004 pp 203–204.
84. *Times* 10 August 1840 p 7; Wiener 2004 p 203.
85. *R v Townley* (1863) 176 ER 384 388.
86. *Times* 10 March 1864 p 11.
87. *Times* December 14 1863 p 8.
88. Ibid. Wiener notes that given the great legitimacy given to medical evidence, defence lawyers opted for insanity defences in the face of the 'continuing delegitimisation' of provocation and drunkenness defences: 2004 p 282.

Chapter 4

1. Corbett Roberts, a Jamaican immigrant hanged in a Birmingham prison in August 1955 was the last wife-killer hanged in England. He lost his self-control in a dispute with her over a bus fare: *British Executions*. John Christie, executed in 1953, was the last English born wife-killer to be hanged for murdering his wife. He also killed several other women: *British Executions*.
2. Of the four women executed for murdering their husbands in twentieth-century Britain, his infidelity was raised as a motive in just one case. Ethel Major, hanged in 1934 for poisoning her husband, was said to be jealous of a woman neighbour: *Times* 30 October 1934. The court noted that Mr Major was 'addicted to drink, had a violent temper and uttered many threats': *Times* 4 December 1934. Ruth Ellis, hanged in 1955 for killing an unfaithful male partner, is well-known as the last woman executed in England, but who can name the two men hanged in the same year for murdering women partners? Answer: Winston Shaw, hanged at Leeds prison in 1955 for murdering his former partner and Corbett Roberts (see note 1).
3. In some years over half the men hanged had killed wives, rising as high as 8 of the 12 executed in 1900, 7 of the 8 in 1906, 8 of the 10 in 1912 and 7 of the 9 in 1915: http://www.capitalpunishmentuk.org/
4. Of the six men hanged in Scotland in that decade, three had killed women partners.
5. OBP: October 1902, Henry Williams.
6. *Dundee Courier* 28 January 1905 p 5; OBP: 6 February 1905, Edward Harrison.
7. *Nottingham Evening Post* 6 March 1905 p 4.
8. *Liverpool Mercury* 9 November 1900 p 9; *Times* 28 December 1900 p 4.
9. OBP: June 1900, Alfred Highfield.
10. *Derby Daily Telegraph*, 13 September 1906 p 4.
11. *Manchester Courier* 6 February 1906 p 10; *Derby Daily Telegraph*, 6 February 1906 p 3; HO 144/809/135941 (Reynolds).
12. *Dundee Evening Telegraph* 18 November 1908 p 2; *Driffield Times* 28 November 1908 p 4; *North Devon Gazette* 8 December 1908 p 3.
13. *Evening Telegraph* 14 February 1908 p 3.
14. *Sheffield Daily Telegraph* 7 July 1903 p 8.
15. *Nottingham Evening Post* 5 December 1906 pp 5–6.
16. His appeal against his conviction was dismissed, and he too hanged: *Dundee Courier* 15 April 1909 p 4.
17. *Faversham Times* 28 November 1908; *Canterbury Journal* 28 November 1908 p 7.
18. *Northampton Mercury* 25 July 1902 p 2
19. *Derby Daily Telegraph*, 25 June 1907 p 3; *Nottingham Evening Post* 26 June 1907 p 4.
20. *Manchester Courier* 28 July 1900 p 3.
21. *Wrexham Weekly Advertiser* 14 July 1900 p 8; *Shields Daily News* 21 August 1900 p 3.
22. OBP: March 1903: Timothy Donovan.
23. *Aberdeen Press and Journal* 12 July 1902 p 6.
24. He asked for, and received, the death sentence. *Edinburgh Evening News*, 8 July 1904 p 2; HO 144/765/120419 (Breeze).
25. *Dundee Courier* 13 December 1902 p 5; HO 144/682/102522 (Callaghan).
26. *Essex Newsman* 20 June 1903 p 1. He hanged when no trace of a mental disorder could be found.
27. *Times* 30 November 1903 p 7.
28. *Times* 24 June 1904 p 7.
29. *Sheffield Daily Telegraph* 17 August 1904 p 8.
30. HO 144/580/A63488 (Churcher); *Isle of Wight Times* 24 July 1902 p 5.
31. *Belfast News Letter* 4 May 1909 p 7.
32. *Manchester Courier* 11 April 1902 p 6; *Dundee Courier* 3 May 1902 p 5.

33. *Globe* 29 October 1903 p 3. Asked why he had not said it was an accident before he came to trial, he said he had been warned, presumably by his court-appointed lawyer, that whatever he said would be used as evidence against him. A no-comment interview was a strategy lawyers would hone in future wife-killing cases.
34. *Shipley Times and Express* 12 February 1909 p 10; *Leeds Mercury* 11 February 1909 p 3.
35. *Nottingham Evening Post* 7 August 1906 p 3.
36. *Bicester Herald* 1 January 1909 p 3.
37. *Dundee Evening Telegraph* 30 December 1908 p 5.
38. OBP: September 1901, Alfred Palmer.
39. OBP*:* October 1901, John Price; *Sheffield Daily Telegraph* 28 October 1901 p 9; *Manchester Courier* 4 November 1901 p 7.
40. *Boston Guardian* 30 March 1901 p 3; *Portsmouth Evening News*19 July 1901 p 4.
41. That's what Churchill told parliament during the 1948 debate about capital punishment. See Chapter 5.
42. *Times* 17 November 1902 p 7*: Sheffield Evening Telegraph* 14 November 1902 p 8.
43. *Worcestershire Chronicle* 8 November 1902 p 1 and 15 November 1902 p 4.
44. *Exmouth Journal* 23 March 1907 p 7.
45. *Times* 13 September 1900 p 10.
46. *Times* 24 July 1901 p 13.
47. *Times* 16 January 1902 p 14.
48. *Times* 16 January 1902 p 14.
49. *Times* 23 October 1902 13.
50. *Othello* lines 4.1.50–51.
51. OBP: October 1902, William Barnaby; *Times* 23 October 1902 p 13; *Globe* 23 October 1902 p 9.
52. OBP: July 1903, Thomas Washington Gibbs; *Tamworth Herald* 11 July 1903 p 2; *Sheffield Daily Telegraph* 7 August 1903 p 8.
53. *Times* 29 June 1905 p 4; OBP: June 1905, James Henry Cornfield; *Daily Telegraph 29 June 9 5.* OBP: June 1905, Henry Capon.
54. *Times* 14 March 1907 p 12; *Huddersfield Daily Examiner* 13 March 1907 p 1.
55. OBP: April 1907, James Albert Jones; *Leicester Daily Post* 2 May 1907 p 5.
56. OBP: November 1908, George Leaning.
57. *Manchester Courier* 12 August 1909; *Times* 1 November 1909 p 3.
58. Elizabeth Rapaport refers to the resistance to treating domestic homicide as 'of the first rank of seriousness' as the 'domestic discount': 1994 p 227. For the application of the domestic discount in the Australian context see Strange 2003.
59. *South London Mail* 20 September 1902 p 4.
60. *Nottingham Evening* Post 15 September 1902; *Hull Daily Mail* 15 September 1902 p 3; *Sheffield Evening Telegraph* 15 September 1902 p 3; *Aberdeen Journal*, 16 September 1902 p 5.
61. *Edinburgh Evening News* 15 September 1902 p 3.
62. *Edinburgh Evening News* 15 September 1902 p 3; 'Two Sentences', *Times* 30 September 1902 p 6 and 7 October 1902 p 10. The killer in the 1895 case was Frank Miles.
63. *Times* 5 April 1907 p 7. The killer was Horace Rayner.
64. *Derby Daily Telegraph* 3 July 1903. In her study of eighteenth-century wife murder cases, Hurl-Eamon suggests that saying these words was a 'form of empowerment' for battered wives, their deaths giving them an opportunity to publicise their husbands' violence: 2008 p 229.
65. *Manchester Courier* 28 July 1900 p 3.
66. *Nottingham Evening Post* 5 December 1906 pp 5–6.

67. *Hull Daily Mail* 14 July 1908, p 5; HO 144/884/167791 (Siddle).
68. *Lloyds Weekly Newspaper* 2 September 1900 p 8; *Times* 1 September 1900 p 4; *Dundee Courier* 3 October 1900 p 7.
69. *Derby Daily Telegraph* 30 August 1900 p 2; *Times* 15 September 1900 p 3; *Sheffield Daily Telegraph* 15 September 1900 p 8.
70. *Illustrated Police News* 8 September 1900, p 3.
71. *Brecon County Times* 21 September 1900 p 7.
72. *Shields Daily Gazette* 26 November 1900 p 3; *Carlisle Journal*, 27 November, 1900, p 3.
73. *Bromyard News* 14 March 1900 p 2.
74. All three were hanged. *Tamworth Herald* 13 July 1901 p 6; *Gloucester Citizen* 5 December 1901 p 4.
75. *Northampton Mercury* 12 July 1901 p 6. Not that all women celebrated the fate handed down to Louisa Claydon's killer. One, signing herself 'Autres Temps, Autres Moeurs', condemned the 'needless' postponement of his execution caused by the declaration of a holiday for a royal visit to Northampton. This only extended his suffering. She preferred the ancient Roman practice of pardoning condemned criminals if they 'accidently met a Vestal Virgin': *Times* 13 December 1901 p 13.
76. *Times* 2 August 1901 p 11; *Aberdeen Press and Journal* 1 August 1901 p 4; *Nuneaton Observer* 2 August 1901 p 8; *Lloyd's Weekly Newspaper* 4 August 1901 p 22. What the densely crowded courtroom thought of the verdict, described by the judge as 'merciful', and the 20-year sentence for manslaughter is not recorded. Might there have been a different outcome had the court proceeded with a charge of murdering his daughter?
77. HO 144/576/A63141 (Wigley); *Lakes Chronicle and Reporter* 4 December 1901, p 7; *Iris News and Belfast Morning News* 2 December 1901 p 8.
78. *Times* 23 October 1902 p 13.
79. *Times* 24 October 1902 p 5. Evidence was submitted at the trial that she had been seeing a married man to support the killer's claim that Emily was a 'false cat'. That was not enough to save him from the gallows.
80. *Western Times* 8 December 1903 p 12.
81. He hanged despite a strong recommendation to mercy and petitions for a reprieve: HO ASSI 6/40/1 (Yarnold).
82. Lines 5.2.122–123.
83. *Leominster News* 21 November 1902, p 6.
84. *Dundee Evening Post* 15 November 1902 p 4.
85. Characterising the case as one on 'the verge of murder', the judge sentenced him to ten years' imprisonment: *Manchester Times* 16 November 1900 p 2; *Times* 16 November 1900 p 10.
86. Nor was the Home Office always inclined to reprieve men who killed women in circumstances far removed from the classic adultery scenario. Over the first two decades of the twentieth century, 130 (or 53%) of the men hanged had killed their wives or women partners, a percentage peaking in 1920 when 13 (or 62%) of the 21 hanged were in this category and dropping to 69 (or 32%) of the total hanged over the next two decades. They increased again to 10 of the 23 hanged in 1952 before tapering off after 1955 to close to zero as the movement to abolish capital punishment gathered pace: http://www.capitalpunishmentuk.org/
87. *Dundee Courier* 27 May 1912 p 5; *Dundee Evening Telegraph* 13 July p 1, 20 July p 1 and 23 July 1912 p 1; *Lancashire Evening Post* 17 July 1912 p 2.
88. OBP: July 1912, John Henry Kay; *Derby Daily Telegraph* 6 July 1912 p 3.
89. *R v Philpot* (1912) 7 Cr App R 140 at 141-2. A petition with 11,000 signatures attached helped secure his reprieve: *Illustrated Police News* 24 February 1912 p 14.

90. OBP: May 1912, George Fitzgibbons; *R v Fitzgibbons* (1912) 7 Cr App R 264 at 265.
91. *Dundee Evening Telegraph* 6 December 1912 p 2; *R v Mason* (1913) 8 Cr App R 121 at 124; *Daily Citizen (Manchester)* 17 December 2012 p 5.
92. *R v Palmer* (1913) 8 Cr App 207 at 210. There was no mercy recommendation.
93. *R v Birchall* (1914) 9 Cr App 91 at 93. This killer was reprieved.
94. *R v Frank Greening* [1913] 3 KB 846 at 847-850. He hanged. The press reported that Elizabeth, known as 'Birmingham Lizzie', had been visiting a friend, not a house of ill repute, and that he had served prison sentences for assaults on other women: *Dundee Evening Telegraph* 15 August 1913 p 1.
95. *R v Ellor* (1921) 15 Cr App R 41 at 41-46; citing *Palmer, Birchall* and *Greening*; *Daily Herald* 29 March 1920 p 5; *Lincolnshire Echo* 27 July 1920 p 2.
96. *Dundee Evening Telegraph* 12 July 1943 p 4; *Belfast News-Letter* 13 July 4 1943 p 4.
97. HO 144/21864 (Gauthier).
98. *R v Gauthier* (1944) 29 Cr App R 113 at 119; *Aberdeen Evening Express* 24 September 1943 p 2.
99. HO 144/21864 (Gauthier).
100. *Holmes v Director of Public Prosecutions* [1946] AC 588.
101. *Nottingham Journal* 1 March 1946 p 4.
102. *Holmes* at 594.
103. *Holmes* at 596.
104. *Holmes* at 598.
105. *Leicester Evening Mail* 5 April 1946 p 5.
106. *Dundee Evening Herald* 4 July 1946 p 3; *Halifax Evening* Courier 4 July 1946 p 4; Hartlepool *Northern Daily Mail* 4 July 1946 p 5; *Nottingham Journal* 5 July 1946 p 1; *Leicester Evening Mail* 4 July 1946 p 5; *Daily Mirror* 5 July 1946. *The Times*, which reported the case at length, included clues from *Othello* in its crossword puzzles later that month: 23 July and 26 July 1946 p 6. Londoners had a choice of three *Othello* productions in the weeks before the trial started and notification of the release of a filmic version a few weeks after Holmes was executed: *Daily News* 16 February 1946 p 2; *Kinematograph Weekly* 27 June 1946 p 21.
107. *Holmes* at 599; my emphasis.
108. Eighteen other men were executed in 1946, seven of whom had killed wives or partners. One had only known his victim for a week, not long enough to found a defence around the provocative woman narrative. He thought 23-year-old Joyce Jacques had 'jilted' him. He admitted murdering her in a court hearing lasting two minutes: *Times* 17 July 1946 p 8.
109. *Hartlepool Northern Daily Mail* 11 December 1946 p 12.
110. *Birmingham Daily Gazette* 12 December 1946 p 3; *Daily Mirror* 12 December 1946 p 4. For an analysis of this much debated line see Law (1935) who suggests that 'in' is a typo for 'as', Iago implying Cassio was 'effeminate'. See also Neill 2008 p 197 note 20.

Chapter 5

1. These sections of the Act were in force from March 1957 to 9 November 1965 when the Murder Act (Abolition of the Death Penalty) came into force. See Bailey 2019 p 342; see also Block 1997.
2. Glanville Williams cited in Bailey 2019: 372–373 and Bailey 2000 p 348. Compare Bailey's inaccurate suggestion that the inclusion of murder by shooting meant that most *crimes passionnel* would *ipso facto* be capital murder: Bailey 2019 p 368. Very few wife-killers shot their victims, knives being the weapon of choice. See also Seal 2014.
3. See Bailey 2019 pp 351 and 368; Brown 2007 p 683.
4. Edwards 1957 pp 54–55; Preverer 1957 p 645.

5. Hughes 1957 pp 526–528. He notes that lead abolitionist Silverman wanted the diminished responsibility defence's qualification out, suggesting that the 'probable aim was to exclude those whose only manifestation of disease of the mind is their anti-social behaviour'.
6. Preverer 1957 pp 642–643; Hughes 1957 pp 528–529. See also Blom-Cooper 1989.
7. Langhamer 2012 pp 437–438. This study cites a woman who said she once threw a knife at her husband and who, on that account, supported the provocation defence. See also Bailey 2019 p 368.
8. Langhamer 2012 p 429 citing Francis 2002 p 358.
9. Francis 2002: pp 358 and 380. That is not all that is problematic about this account. Consider Francis' claim that only now was British reserve 'deliberately counterpoised to the unregulated emotional cultures of various others'. From the mid-1950s 'the boundary between emotional control and expression was to be constructed along racial, rather than ethnic or national lines. Only now, were people of colour 'increasingly identified as the undisciplined other against which a British national identity rooted in restraint was given meaning'. Only now were Africans and West Indians seen as 'lacking restraint', the 'very reverse of English reserve and self-control' with the black male typecast as 'closer to nature, more intuitive, emotional and sexual than the detached and passionless white man'. Francis 2002 pp 363–366. As we saw in Chapter 2, this process was well under way by Shakespeare's time.
10. 15 July 1948, Hansard vol 453, 15 July 1948 col 1443. However, he lost touch with reality when he added that there was 'a reciprocal set of cases which can arise on the part of the weaker sex'. It comes as no surprise that his example of a reprieved murderer who said he preferred a death sentence to life imprisonment was yet another wife-killer: col 1439.
11. *R v Duffy* (1949) 1 All ER 932.
12. *Duffy* at 933. She was reprieved.
13. *James Frank Rivett v R* (1950) 34 Cr App R 87 at 92–93 and 95.
14. *Weekly Dispatch (London)* 26 February 1950 p 3.
15. *Daily Herald* 11 December 1951 p 1; *Formby Times* 15 December 1951 p 2. He received a life sentence with a 14-year minimum.
16. Harris: *Liverpool Echo* 4 February 1952 p 6; Cull: *Times* September 13 1952, p 3; Simon: *Shields Daily Mail* 23 October 1952 p 3; Norcliffe: *Nottingham Evening Post* 21 November 1953 p 10. Simon's lawyer attributed the killing to 'a typical history of a psychopathic personality'. The court of appeal found no evidence of insanity. Six other men were executed in 1952 for killing their common law wives. The Home Office rejected the application of Jean Cull's killer for a reprieve on the same day as they rejected one for the man who killed celebrated wartime secret agent Christine Granville: *Portsmouth Evening News* 27 September 1952 p 1.
17. *Times* 20 December 1955 p 10; *Belfast Telegraph* 31 December 1955 p 7.
18. *Times* 17 January 1956 p 6; *Aberdeen Evening Express* 19 September 1955 p 7. Dissenting, one judge would have sentenced him to be permanently detained as 'a menace to society' on the ground that he was 'so obviously near the border of insanity'. In the event, the appellant withdrew his appeal, apparently believing it would fail.
19. *Times* 5 May 1959 p 13.
20. *Times* 16 August 1961 p 12. Her killer was known as the last man hanged at Wandsworth Prison. Less well-known is that he was also the last man hanged for intimate partner homicide.
21. *Daily Mirror* 14 January 1961 p 5; *Birmingham Daily Post* 17 January 1961 p 4.
22. *Aberdeen Evening Express* 30 November 1961 p 5.
23. *Liverpool Echo* 5 March 1962 p 14; *Times* 7 March 1962 p 9. He got a five-year sentence. Not that every femicidal man got away with murder. The man who killed his

wife, Florence Regan, mother of his four children, in their Slough home and hid her body for three months in their bedroom was convicted of her murder in September 1962. But Florence was not his first victim. He was acquitted of killing a man at a trial in 1950 and given a ten-year sentence for the manslaughter of a woman the following year. Florence sat through his trials and waited for him to serve his various prison sentences: *Newcastle Journal* 20 September 1962 p 7.

24. *Times* 22 March 1963 p 7; *Times* 27 March 1963 p 16; *Times* 29 March 1963 p 7.
25. *Times* 29 March 1963 p 9; *Times* 30 March 1963 p 6.
26. *Times* 30 March 1963 p 6; *Sunday Mirror* 31 March 1963 p 2. He received the standard three-year sentence.
27. *Daily Mail* 7 July 2006. The reference to 'damaged goods' recalled evidence given in court that the killer's mother had sex with him as a child, thereby allowing another woman to share the blame for Christine's death.
28. *Times* 18 June 1963 p 17; *Daily Mirror* 18 June 1963 p 4. The defence could backfire though. In 1961, the Court of Appeal refused to interfere with a life sentence for a man convicted of the manslaughter of his wife, the same sentence he would have got for murder. He had strangled his 'girl wife', 17-year-old Violet Faulkner after what one newspaper called 'a tiff over tea'. He claimed she also said she wished she had not married him. The jury accepted his diminished responsibility defence after hearing a medical expert say he had a psychopathic personality and the 'emotional control of a child'. But in the court's view, there were some defendants whose mental condition required that they be kept in custody for the rest of their lives. He was one of them. He 'could not be trusted not to strangle people when annoyed with them': *Daily Mirror* 12 February p 2; 24 February p 7 and 10 March 1961 p 7; *Times* 18 August 1961 p 12.
29. The judge had no time for this vindictive and 'sulky' man and handed down an indeterminate sentence: *Times* 10 February 1965 p 15; *Birmingham Daily Post* 12 February 1965 p 9.
30. *Daily Mirror* 21 July 1964 p 12. He won his appeal on the ground that the judge should not have withheld the defence of provocation, the court overturning his murder conviction and substituting a three-year sentence for manslaughter.
31. *Times* 20 July 1965 p 13.
32. *Daily Mirror* 28 July 1965 p 3.
33. *Times* 26 November 1965 p 5. He got a three-year sentence. Of course, had he known she had lied about her marital status that might also have provoked him to kill her.
34. *Daily Mirror* 24 February 1966 p 24. He received a two-year sentence for manslaughter.
35. *Times* 30 March 1966 p 13.
36. *Times* 12 May 1967 p 2; *Daily Mail* 12 May 1967 p 20.
37. *Liverpool Echo* 20 July p 20; 21 July p 7; 26 July 1966 p 5. He was sentenced to seven years.
38. *Times* 15 April 1967 p 2; *Reading Evening Post* 15 April 1967 p 3.
39. Koessler 1960 p 138.
40. *R v Reid* [1973] QB 299 at 302–303; *Reading Evening Post* 30 August 1968 p 7; *Birmingham Daily Post* 17 June 1972 p 14.
41. *R v Turner* (1974) 60 Cr App R 80 at 83.
42. *R v Vinagre* (1979) 69 Cr App.R 104 at 105; *Daily Mirror* 25 July 1978 p 13.
43. *Vinagre* at 106–107. There was an additional difficulty. What if he had a recurrence of Othello Syndrome? That would make him a danger to the public (read: women). The court decided that as he was no longer suffering from 'the kind of mental imbalance' that would justify a life sentence, 'justice' demanded that his sentence be reduced to seven years' imprisonment: at 107.

44. He was however, given a life sentence. *Times* 20 June p 3; 26 June 1984 p 3; 29 June 1984 p 3; 30 June 1984 p 3; *Aberdeen Press and Journal* 30 June 1984 p 4.
45. *Times* 9 October 1984 p 4; *Aberdeen Press and Journal* 9 October 1984 p 2; *Daily Mirror* 9 October 1984 p 7.
46. *Times 1 December* 1984 p 3; *Daily Mail* 1 December 1984 p 7; *Daily Mirror* 6 December 1984 p 9.
47. *R v Mellentin* (1985) 7 Cr App R (S) 9 at 10.
48. *Liverpool Echo* 6 March 1985 p 17; *Times* 9 March 1985 p 1. He received an extra 12 months for making a false statement and obstructing an inquest by disposing of her body.
49. *Daily Mail* 23 April 1985 p 7; *Reading Evening Post* 23 April 1969 p 15.
50. *Times* 31 October 1985 p 5.
51. *Times* 9 October p 5 and 10 October 1985 p 3. He received six years for manslaughter and two for disposing of the body, to run concurrently.
52. *R v Doughty* (1986) 83 Cr App R 319.
53. *Doughty* at 325–326; *Newcastle Journal* 24 May 1986 p 2 where the claim that he was 'provoked' by the baby's cries is placed in inverted commas. It is not in the *Times* 24 May 1986 p 3.
54. *R v Townsend* (1979) 1 Cr App R (S) 333.
55. *R v Green* (1986) 8 Cr App R (S) 284 at 287 discussing *Townsend*; *R v Haines* (1983) 5 Cr App R (S) 58 and *R v Donnelly* (1983) 5 Cr App R (S) 70.
56. *Newcastle Journal* 30 January 1988 p 7; *R v Drinkald* (1988) 10 Cr App R (S) 380 at 381–382.
57. *R v Dearn* (1990–1991) 12 Cr App R (S) 527 at 528. The trial judge found it 'very hard to think of a worse case of attempted murder than this.... Its consequences have been utterly disastrous, some would say as bad if not worse' than if he had killed her: Ibid.
58. *R v Casseeram* (1992) 13 Cr Ap R (S) 384 at 387–388.
59. *R v Bedford* (1993) 14 Cr App R (S) 336 at 338. But it suggested that the level of sentencing in this type of case – setting wives alight – might need to be reviewed.
60. *R v Jason Clement* [1995] 16 Cr Ap R (S) 811 at 815.
61. *R v Giboin* (1980) 2 Cr App R (S) 99; my emphasis. Nevertheless, the court reduced this appellant's sentence from six to five years. For a comparison of sentencing in attempted murder and manslaughter cases at this time, see Horder 1989 pp 547–548. See also Burton 2003 pp 282–286.
62. Radford 1982. Radford's critique of marriage as a 'licence to kill' in the context of the 1981 Jane Asher case was quoted in the press.
63. *Times* March 2 1990 p 3; *Dundee Courier* 2 March 1900 p 9.
64. *Times* 21 April 1990 p 6.
65. *Times* 1 August 1991 p 2; *Sandwell Evening Mail* 1 August 1991 p 6; *Dundee Courier* 14 August 1991 p 15 and 19 August 1991 p 3; *Lichfield Mercury* 1 November 1991 p 27; Edwards 2004 p 182.
66. *Times* 4 December 1993 p 9.
67. *Times* 2 February 1994 p 5; *Aberdeen Press and Journal* 22 February 1994 p 14.
68. *Times* 29 October 1994 p 3; *Daily Mail* 29 October 1994 p 17.
69. *Times*13 September 1995 p 3 and 27 September 1995 p 2. At the same time, the release of Sarah Thornton spurred on Justice for Women to press for reforms to address the fact that nearly 40 per cent of women who killed their partners were convicted of murder compared to 25 per cent of men: *Times* 29 July 1995 p 2.
70. *Times* 10 December 1996 p 2.
71. *Times* 15 December 1998 p 5.

72. Edwards 1987. There were in fact two strings to the critique. On the one hand, the defence was seen as too restrictive for women who killed violent male partners. They usually did so in circumstances that do not found a provocation defence – he was asleep; there was no obvious provocative act aside from his nearly lethal violent assaults and threats to kill over many years. On the other hand, the defence was too expansive for male defendants. Men kill women partners for the slightest reason – she laughed at him, taunted him about his sexual inadequacies, she left him. The literature on the operation of provocation defences in intimate partner femicide cases is vast. Excellent critiques from other Anglophone jurisdictions include Coker 1992, Tarrant 1990, Boyle 1994. In the United States, for example, critics commentating on the criminal law's 'receding sympathy for the rage of the cuckold', noted that 'what was once settled law – that marital infidelity can provoke a reasonable man to homicidal rage' – was being contested in some criminal courts. The cuckold's rage was no longer assumed to be reasonable when raised as a provocation defence: Kahan & Nussbaum, 1996, pp 274 and 347.
73. Allen 1988, pp 423 and 427–429. These critiques were instrumental in convincing Horder that the provocation defence should be abolished. One critic noted that by 2000, the collapse of the objective standard in provocation cases resulted in us 'going backwards', rather than 'advancing towards' a higher measure of self-control, such as Lord Simon had called for in *Holmes*: Allen 2000 p 240.
74. Bandalli 1995 p 399.
75. Wells 2000 pp 86 and 104 and at p 95 citing my 1997 paper on homosexual advance defences.

Chapter 6

1. *R v Suratan, R v Humes and R v Wilkinson* (Attorney General's Reference No 74 of 2002, No. 95 of 2002 and No 118 of 2002 [2002] EWCA Crim 2982.
2. *BBC News Online* 28 October 2002.
3. Quoted in Wainwright, 2002.
4. Quoted in Hinsliff 2003. This alliance of families with reform-minded politicians provides yet another instance of a Foucauldian 'insurrection of subjugated knowledges' that I have documented elsewhere. Such an insurrection takes place when different forms of subjugated knowledge, here that of a feminist-informed senior legal officer, unites with the local knowledge of victims' immediate family to challenge received or dominant knowledges in this case, the notion that a woman asks for it when she annoys a man. For other examples, see Howe 2005 and 2008, Chapter 3.
5. Quoted in Kite 2002 p 10.
6. Attorney General's Reference No. 74 of 2002 at 277-282 and 285 citing *Taylor* (1987) 9 Cr App R (S) 175, *Gilbey* (1990) 12 Cr App R (S) 49 and *Light* (1995) 16 Cr App R (S) 824 at 827. The third appellant, Suratan, denied killing his partner. His manslaughter conviction was overturned in April 2005: *Manchester Evening News* 9 April 2005.
7. Nicky's mother vowed not to dwell on her anger, determining instead to accept a place on the board of the women's refuge where Nicole had once fled: quoted in Watson 2002. Maddie Humes' sister, Paula Watt, continued to advocate for law reform, urging the Scottish parliament to follow the proposed changes to the English law of provocation. Maddie, she said, would have been 'immensely proud that her name' would be associated with the reform proposals: quoted in *Aberdeen Press and Journal* 3 November 2003.
8. Hinsliff 2003. By now, a movement to reform or, better still, abolish the defence was well under way in Australia and Canada. See, for example, Howe 1994a, 1997,

1998, 1999, 2002, 2004; Morgan 1997 and Tyson 2013 on Australian cases. For the superlative Canadian case made for abolishing provocation, see Côté, A *et al* 2000. As Horder observed, the provocation defence has been the subject of more decisions of the House of Lords, the Privy Council and the Court of Appeal since the 1940s than perhaps any other area of the substantive criminal law: Horder 2005 pp 131–132. Gough's observation in 1999 that provocation has 'long been a puzzle' which scholarly debates have 'often seemed to deepen' remains relevant in those jurisdictions that have retained the defence: Gough 1999 p 492. The defence has also been the subject of thousands of scholarly articles. A search of law-based e-resources I conducted in 2013 reveals over 16,000 law journal articles and commentaries on the law of provocation. See Quick and Wells 2006 pp 524–525 on the importance of the 'gender context' and the 'general denial of gender as relevant factor' in domestic provocation cases.

9. Law Commission 2004 para 3.59. See Brown 2007 pp 695 and 872.
10. Law Commission 2004 para 3.143 citing *Smith (Morgan)* [2001] 1 AC 146 at 169.
11. Para 3.145 citing *Holmes* [1946] AC 588 at 598.
12. Paras 3.52-54 citing Nourse 1997 p 1338.
13. Nourse 1997 pp 1370, 1332–1336 and 1345. Interestingly, one of the abolitionists Nourse cites is Jeremy Horder who came to revise his abolitionist position in the light of her argument.
14. Horder 1992 p 112.
15. Horder 1992 pp 186 and 197. See also Stannard 2002. On the intrinsically normative evaluations made in determinations of criminal responsibility, see Watkins 2006. It is always important when citing homicide statistics to observe that women usually kill men after a history of violence and rarely over 'infidelity'.
16. Law Commission 2006 paras 5. 11 and 5.74–77 Horder's shift from an abolitionist to a reformist position is discernible as early as 1999 when he criticised *Holmes* for 'wrongly' turning the strong excuse theory into 'a theory that disregards *all* individual characteristics': Horder 1999 p 145; his emphasis. By 2004 he was considering modifying rather than abolishing the provocation defence: pp 97–98.
17. This is not to say that battered women cases were not of concern, only that they were not the cases that precipitated the law reform movement.
18. It is perhaps worth noting that the Commissioners were all men. Without wishing to essentialise gendered differences, I might just note Mark Breitenberg's comment about a critique mounted by a male subject position. He says it potentially realises what Gayatri Spivak called a 'political or historical and indeed ideological differential that irreducibly separates the male from the female critics of phallogocenterism': quoted in Breitenberg 1993 p 395.
19. Payne 2002.
20. *R v Rowland* [2003] EWCA Crim 3636. See further Howe 2004.
21. *R v Rush* [2008] Cr App R(S) 45 at para 26.
22. *R v Birks* [2011] 1 Cr App R (S) 48.
23. Sections 54–56 of the Act. For commentaries, see Edwards 2010 pp 230–232 and Miles 2009.
24. Quoted in Verkaik 2008.
25. Horder, Memorandum to Public Bill Committee, January 2009.
26. Testimony to Public Bill Committee, February 4, 2009, Hansard, col 28.
27. Spencer 2009.
28. Quoted in Verkaik 2008.
29. Quoted in Hinsliff 2008; my emphasis.
30. *Macbeth* Lines 2.3.84–85.
31. July 7 2009, House of Lords Debates, Hansard, col 576–578.

32. Ibid col 581.
33. Ibid col 589–590 referring to *R v Mawgridge* (1706) Kel 119 at 135.
34. Ibid col 1061–1062.
35. House of Commons Debates, Hansard, 9 November 2009 cols 85–95.
36. Hansard November 11 2009, col 839.
37. McDonagh 2008.
38. Attorney General's Reference (No.80 of 2009) [2010] EWCA Crim. 470 at para 19.
39. *R v Thompson* Attorney General's Reference (No. 1 of 2010) [2010] EWCA Crim 748 at para 21–22.
40. *R v Edwards* Attorney General's Reference No. 008 of 2011 [2011] EWCA Crim 1461 at para 15; *BBC News* 16 June 2011.
41. *R v Williams (Sanchez)* Attorney General's Reference No 23 of 2011 [2001] EWCA Crim 1496 at paras 32 and 33; *Daily Mail* 19 October 2011.
42. *Telegraph* 17 January 2012.
43. *R v Clinton, Parker and Evans* [2012] 1 Cr App R 26 at [77]
44. *R v Clinton* at [37].
45. A more detailed account of the facts can be found at [50]–[75].
46. Baker and Zhao 2012 pp 255, 259–260 and 268.
47. Baker and Zhao 2012 pp 273–275; their emphasis.
48. The literature critiquing the gender-biased operation of provocation defences in Anglophone jurisdictions is too vast to cite here but see, for example, the list of references in Howe 2002 and Howe 2004. Key foundational feminist critiques include Taylor (1986), Allen (1988), Coker (1992), Lees 1994 and Bandalli (1995).
49. *R v Clinton* at [2].
50. *R v Clinton* at [16].
51. *R v Mawgridge* (1706) Kel 119 at 137.
52. As we have seen, exiting a relationship is a hazardous operation for women, her desire to depart frequently trigging his murderous fury. The feminist literature is vast but see, for example, Mahoney 1991, Dick 2011, Nourse 1997.
53. *R v Oakes* [2012] EWCA Crim 2435 [33] pp 34–37 and 41.
54. *Oakes* pp 44–45.
55. Horder cites this widely published statistic to support his argument to abolish provocation in 1992 p 186 and again in Horder 2005, p 124. See Ingala Smith's 'Counting Dead Women' lists for 2012–2022.
56. Ingala Smith is co-founder of the Femicide Census which monitors femicide cases in the UK.
57. My study's findings are fully reported in my chapters in Howe and Allatinoğlu 2019. See further for discussions of femicides and law reforms in other jurisdictions.
58. Silverman 2013. I have come across only two English cases where 'Othello Syndrome' was raised for a wife-killer – the 1979 case of *Vinagre* discussed in Chapter 5 and a 2018 case discussed later in this chapter. Nevertheless, it is notable that *Othello* thus continues to 'fiction truth' in wife-killing cases, as Foucault might have said had he given any critical attention to femicide. Instead, he adopted the standard pro-offender viewpoint. See my critique in Howe 2008, Chapter 3 and Howe 2014.
59. Lines 5.2.209–210; BBC 2015.
60. The new diminished responsibility plea, introduced by Section 52 of the Coroners and Justice Act, provided that a person not be convicted of murder if suffering from an abnormality of mental functioning that arises from a recognised medical condition and that substantially reduced their responsibility for their actions. For assessments of the new plea see Reed and Bohlander 2011.
61. Most were given hospital orders, some indefinite, under the Mental Health Act. One man was found not guilty by reason of insanity. Two were unfit to plead.

62. Anonymous 2013.
63. Rush 2013.
64. Passant 2015.
65. Caruth 1995 p vii.
66. As Titus Andronicus referred to his sons killed by the Goths: *Titus Andronicus* 1.1.126.
67. BBC 2017.
68. BBC 2018a. Such 'provocation' can still, however, be taken into account at sentencing in order to reduce the minimum term.
69. For more on the prominence of penis anxiety in these cases, see Howe 2010.
70. Osuh 2017.
71. Vernalls 2019.
72. BBC 2019a.
73. Jones 2019.
74. Hemming 2017. The justice question is raised only very occasionally in the judgments and then only in relation to offenders, justice for victims not entering the equation. See Howe 2022.
75. See Ingala Smith's lists for 2018–2019.
76. BBC 2019b.
77. Williams 2019.
78. BBC 2020. He was sentenced to life with a 32-year minimum.
79. Siddique 2018.
80. Roberts 2018.
81. Quoted in Rodger 2019.
82. Quoted BBC 2018b.
83. Quoted in Christian 2019.
84. BBC 2022. For a more pessimistic assessment of post-reform era sentencing practices, see Horder and Fitz-Gibbon 2015.
85. See Ingala Smith's 'Counting Dead Women' lists for 2017–2020 for these cases. They included 71-year-old Christina Arnold who was suffocated by her husband of 50 years before he killed himself, and 29-year-old Chenise Gregory who was lured to her death by her suicidal former partner.
86. See Ingala Smith's 2020 list for these cases.
87. BBC 2021a.
88. Gayle 2021.
89. Cited in Topping 2021.
90. Boyle 2018.
91. BBC 2021b.
92. BBC 2021b.
93. Evans 2022.
94. Quoted in McDonagh 2008.
95. Gregory 2019. He was sentenced to life with a 27-year minimum
96. Hitchenor and Thomson 2020. He was jailed for life with a 31-year minimum.
97. Lines 5. 2.231–232.

Epilogue

1. Ancel 1957 p 47.
2. Ancel 1957 p 37 note 3. Everyone, he continues, momentarily forgetting the gendered pattern of impassioned homicide, is 'ready to attribute the real responsibility for such a crime to that Iago which every man bears within himself'.
3. Ancel 1957 pp 37–39 and 44–45.

4. Ancel 1957 p 47. Thirty-two of the 33 cases in which heavy sentences were imposed between 1946 and 1953 for crimes that could be regarded as '*passionnel*' were committed by men.
5. Breitenberg 1993 p 378.
6. *Othello on Trial – or the Tragedy of Desdemona, the Wife* has been performed in London and Melbourne, Australia. This project's aims as well as its trials and tribulations are discussed in Howe 2014, 2015, 2016 and 2021.

Bibliography

Archival Resources

British Executions: List of Hangings in England British Executions http://www.britishexecutions.co.uk/

The British Newspaper Archive https://www.britishnewspaperarchive.co.uk/

Capital Punishment UK http://www.capitalpunishmentuk.org/

Ingala Smith, K *Counting Dead Women* https://kareningalasmith.com/counting-dead-women/

The National Archives, Home Office (HO)

Old Bailey Proceedings Online (OBP) www.oldbaileyonline.org

The Times Digital Archive https://www.thetimes.co.uk

Newspapers 2002–2022

Anonymous 2013 'Leicester Man Jailed for Killing Wife' *Leicester Mercury* https://ssristories.org/leicester-mercury

BBC 2015 'Dawlish Killer James McDonald "Laughed at Abduction Question"' www.bbc.com/news/uk-england-devon

BBC 2017 'Pregnant Woman's Christmas Day Murderer James Hutchinson Jailed' www.bbc.com/news/uk-england-leeds

BBC 2018a 'David Clark Jailed for Killing Wife Over Penis Taunts' https://www.bbc.com/news/uk-england-hereford-worcester

BBC 2018b '"Savage" Baseball Bat Murderer Shane Murphy Jailed' https://www.bbc.com/news/uk-england-lincolnshire

BBC 2019a 'Poppy Devey Waterhouse Murder: Ex-Partner Jailed for Life' https://www.bbc.com/news/uk-england-leeds

BBC 2019b 'Ann Marie Pomphret Trial: Husband Killed Wife after "Useless" Taunt' https://www.bbc.com/news/uk-england-manchester

BBC 2020 'Former Cage Fight Jailed for 32 Years for Murder of Ex-Girlfriend' https://www.bbc.com/news/uk-england-manchester

BBC 2021a 'Hussein Egal: Bus Driver Jailed for Wife's "Covid-19 Row" Murder' https://www.bbc.com/news/uk-england-london

BBC 2021b 'Milton Keynes Murder: Anil Gill Jailed for Stabbing Ranjit Gill' https://www.bbc.com/news/uk-england-beds-bucks-herts

BBC 2021c 'Sarah Keith Murder: Jealous Boyfriend Stabbed and Strangled Partner' https://www.bbc.com/news/uk-england-leeds

BBC 2022 'Pontypool Murder: Husband Found Guilty after Stabbing Wife' https://www.bbc.com/news/uk-wales-60196520

Boyle, D 2018 'Jury Waives at Grandfather' *Daily Mail* https://www.dailymail.co.uk/news/article

Christian, B 2019 'Simonne Kerr Murder Trial' https://www.standard.co.uk/news/crime/simonne-kerr

Evans, H 2022 'Jealous Ex-husband Stabbed Mum to Death in Rage as She Made Dying Call to Boyfriend with Knife in her Chest' https://www.mylondon.news/news/south-london-news/

Gayle, D 2021 'Man Who Killed Wife "In Act of Great Violence" Jailed for Five Years' *Guardian* https://www.theguardian.com/uk-news/2021/feb/18

Gregory, A 2019 'Taxi Driver Ben Lacomba Jailed for Life for Murdering Mother of Five' *Independent* https://www.independent.co.uk/news/uk/crime/sarah-wellgreen-murder

Hemming, J 2017 'What Tracy Kearns' Mum Had to Say about Anthony Bird Being Cleared of her Daughter's Murder' *Daily Post* https://www.dailypost.co.uk/news/north-wales

HInsliff, G 2003 '"Crime of Passion" is No Defence' https://www.theguardian.com/politics/2003/jan/19/ukcrime.prisonsandprobation

Hinsliff, G 2008 'Harman and Law Lord Clash Over Wife Killers' *Guardian* https://www.theguardian.com/politics

Hitchenor, T and Thomson, G 2020 '"Sadistic" Former Headteacher Stabbed Wife and Her New Lover 103 Times in Savage Bloodbath' https://www.dailyrecord.co.uk/news/crime/

Jones, S 2019 'Chilling Echoes from the Past' *Teesidelive* https://www.gazettelive.co.uk/news/teesside-news/

Kite, M 2002 'Jail Sentences for Domestic Killings are "Too Lenient"' *Times* 4 December https://www.thetimes.co.uk/article/jail-sentences-for-domestic-killings-are-too- lenient-

McDonagh, M 2008 'An Unjust, Feminist View of Murder' *The Times* https://www.thetimes.co.uk/article/an-unjust-feminist-view-of-murder

Osuh, C 2017 'Much-loved Nursery Manager Chrissy Kendall Strangled to Death' *Manchester Evening News* https://www.manchestereveningnews.co.uk/news/greater-manchester-news

Passant, A 2015 'Friend's Disgust at Christine Henderson Murder Trial Verdict' *GazetteLive* www.gazettelive.co.uk/news/local-news/

Payne, S 2002 'Six Years for Teacher Who Beat to Death His Unfaithful Wife' *Telegraph* https://www.telegraph.co.uk/news/uknews/

Roberts, E 2018 'Redvers. Bickley Blames his Evil Alter Ego "James" for Killing Tyler Denton' *Daily Post* https://www.dailypost.co.uk/news/north-wales-news/redvers-bickley-blames-evil-alter-14445055

Rodger, J 2019 'Jealous Husband Jailed Over Murdering Wife with Hammer after Believing She Was Having Affair' *Birmingham Mail* https://www.birminghammail.co.uk/news/midlands-news/jealous-husband-jailed-over-murdering-16469195\

Rush, R 2013 '"Nine Years for a Man that's Capable of Killing Someone"' *Daily Mail* www.dailymail.co.uk/news/article-2439304/Adrian-Muir-Pamela-Jacksons-sons-anger-unjust-sentence-given-manslaughter.html

Siddique, H 2018 'Joshua Simpson Gets Life Sentence or Former Girlfriend's Murder' *Guardian* https://www.theguardian.com/uk-news/

Silverman, R 2013 'Diamond Thief Who Killed Himself and Wife Had "Othello Syndrome"' *Telegraph* www.telegraph.co.uk/news/uknews/law-and-order

Topping, A 2021 'Welsh Man Who Killed Wife Will Not Have Five-Year Sentence Increased' *Guardian* https://www.theguardian.com/uk-news/2021/apr/30/wales

Verkaik, R 2008 'Judge Backs Infidelity Defence for Killers' *The Independent* https://www.independent.co.uk/news/uk/crime/judge-backs-infidelity-defence-for-killers

Vernalls, R. 2019. 'If I Can't Have Her, You Can't Either. She's Dead' *Daily Record* https://www.dailyrecord.co.uk/news/crime

Wainwright, M 2002 'Family Protests at Manslaughter Verdict for Stabbing of Wife' https://www.theguardian.com/uk/2002/jul/25

Watson, J 2002 'Judges Refuse to Increase Killer's Four-Year Jail Term' https://www.thefreelibrary.com

Williams, T 2019 'Husband Jailed for Three Years for Manslaughter' *Daily Mail* https://www.dailymail.co.uk/news/article

References

Aebischer, P 2004 *Shakespeare's Violated Bodies* Cambridge: CUP

Alfar, CL 2017 *Women and Shakespeare's Cuckoldry Plays: Shifting Narratives of Marital Betrayal* London and New York: Routledge

Allen, H 1988 'One Law for All Reasonable Persons?' 16 *International Journal of the Sociology of Law* 419

Allen, MJ 2000 'Provocation's Reasonable Man: A Plea for Provocation's Self Control' 64 *Journal of Criminal Law* 216

Anderson, TP 2003 'What is Written Shall be Executed: Nude Contracts and Lively Warrants in *Titus Andronicus*' 45 *Criticism* 301

Arikha, N 2007 *Passions and Tempers: A History of the Humours* New York: Harper Collins

Asp, C 1995 '"Upon her Wit Doth Earthly Honour Wait": Female Agency in *Titus Andronicus*' in PC Kolin (ed) *Titus Andronicus: Critical Essays* London: Routledge

Baker, D and Zhao, L 2012 'Contributory Qualifying and Non-Qualifying Triggers in the Loss of Control Defence: A Wrong Turn on Sexual Infidelity' 76(3) *Journal of Criminal Law* 254

Bailey, V 2000 *The Shadow of the Gallows: The Death Penalty and the British Labour Government, 1945–1951* Cambridge: CUP

Bailey, V 2019 *The Rise and Fall of the Rehabilitative Ideal* London: Routledge

Bandalli, S 1995 'Provocation – A Cautionary Note' 22 *Journal of Law and Society* 398

Bartels, E 1990 'Making More of the Moor' 41(4) *Shakespeare Quarterly* 444

Bate, J 1994 *Shakespeare and Ovid* Oxford: Clarendon Press

Bate, J (ed) 1995 *Titus Andronicus* London: Arden Shakespeare

Bate, J 2009 *The Soul of the Age: A Biography of the Mind of William Shakespeare* London: Penguin Books

Bate, J 2019 *How the Classics Made Shakespeare* Princeton: Princeton University Press

Belenky, M 2008 *The Anxiety of Dispossession: Jealousy in Nineteenth-Century French Culture* Lewisburg PA: Bucknell University Press

Belsey, C 2007 *Why Shakespeare?* London: Palgrave Macmillan

Berry, P 1999 *Shakespeare's Feminine Endings: Disfiguring Death in Tragedies* New York: Routledge

Bevington, D 2016 'The Classroom' in D Callaghan and S Gossett (eds) *Shakespeare in Our Time* London: Bloomington

Block, BP and Hostettler, J 1997 *Hanging in the Balance: A History of the Abolition of Capital Punishment in Britain* Winchester: Waterside Press

Blom-Cooper, L 1989 'Criminal Justice and Social Change: The Morality of the Homicide Act 1957' 20 *Cambrian Law Review* 83

Bose, LE 1975 'Othello's Handkerchief: The Recognisance and Pledge of Love' 5 *English Literary Renaissance* 360

Boyle, C 1994 'The Role of Equality in the Criminal Law' 58 *Saskatchewan Law Review* 203

Breitenberg, M 1993 'Anxious Masculinity: Sexual Jealousy in Early Modern England' 19(2) *Feminist Studies* 377

Breitenberg, M 1996 *Anxious Masculinity: Sexual Jealousy in Early Modern England* Cambridge: CUP

Bristol, EM 1990 'Charivari and the Comedy of Abjection in "*Othello*"' 21 *Renaissance Drama* 3

Brown, DJ 2007 'Disentangling Concessions to Human Frailty' 39 *International Law and Politics* 675

Brown, PA 2004 '*Othello* Italicised: Xenophobia and the Erosion of Tragedy' in M Marrapodi (ed) *Shakespeare, Italy and Intertextuality* Manchester: Manchester University Press

Bruster, D 1992 *Drama and the Market in the Age of Shakespeare* Cambridge: CUP

Burke, K 1951 '*Othello*: An Essay to Illustrate a Method' 4 *Hudson Review* 165

Burton, M 2003 'Case Note: Sentencing Domestic Homicide upon Provocation: Still "Getting Away with Murder"' 11 *Feminist Legal Studies* 279

Burton, R 1932 *The Anatomy of Melancholy* Vol 3 H Jackson (ed) New York: JM Dent & Sons

Callaghan D 1996 '"Othello was a White Man": Properties of Race on Shakespeare's Stage' in T Hawkes (ed) *Alternative Shakespeares 2* London: Routledge

Callaghan, D 2001 'Looking Well to Linens: Women and Cultural Production in *Othello* and Shakespeare's England' in JE Howard and SC Shershow (eds) *Marxist Shakespeares* London: Routledge

Caruth, C 1995 *Trauma: Explorations in Memory* Baltimore: John Hopkins University Press

Cavarero, A 2000 *Relating Narratives: Storytelling and Selfhood* London: Routledge

Cetin, I 2010 '*Titus Andronicus* A Comedy of Blood' 28 *Shakespeare Bulletin* 356

Choy, HYF 2011 'Toward a Poetic Minimalism of Violence: On Tang Shu-wing's *Titus Andronicus*' 1 *Asian Theatre Journal* 44

Clark Hulse, S 1979 'Wresting the Alphabet: Oratory and Action in *Titus Andronicus*' 21 *Criticism* 106

Coker, DK 1992 'Heat of Passion and Wife Killing: Men Who Batter/Men Who Kill' 2 *Southern California Review of Law and Women's Studies* 71

Conley, C 2009 *Certain Other Countries: Homicide, Gender and National Identity in Late Nineteenth Century England, Ireland, Scotland and Wales* Ohio: Ohio State University Press

Côté, A et al 2000 *Stop Excusing Violence Against Women: NAWL's Position Paper on the Defence of Provocation* Ottowa: National Association of Women and the Law

Crosbie, C 2007 'Fixing Moderation: *Titus Andronicus* and the Aristotelian Determination of Value' 58 *Shakespeare Quarterly* 147

Cullen, N 2019 *Love, Honour and Jealousy: An Intimate History of the Italian Economic Miracle* Oxford: OUP

Cunningham, K 1990 '"Scars Can Witness": Trials by Ordeal and Lavinia's Body in *Titus Andronicus*' in KA Ackley (ed) *Women and Violence in Literature* New York: Routledge

Cutts, JP 1968 'Shadow and Substance: Structural Unity in *Titus Andronicus*' 2 *Comparative Drama* 161

Dayton, CH 2004 'Rethinking Agency, Recovering Voices' 109(3) *American Historical Review* 827

D'Cruze, S 2007 'Intimacy, Professionalism and Domestic Homicide in Interwar Britain: The Case of Buck Ruxton' 16(5) *Women's History Review* 701

Detmer-Goebel, E 2001 'The Need for Lavinia's Voice: Titus Andronicus and the Telling of Rape' 29 *Shakespeare Studies* 75

Dick, C 2011 'A Tale of Two Cultures: Intimate Femicide, Cultural Defences and the Law of Provocation' 23 *Canadian Journal of Women and the Law* 519

Dickson, L 2008 '"High and "Low" Blows: *Titus Andronicus* and the Critical Language of Pain' 26 *Shakespeare Bulletin* 1

Dixon, T 2003 *From Passions to Emotions: The Creation of a Secular Category* Cambridge: CUP

Dolan, F 1994 *Dangerous Familiars: Representations of Domestic Crime in England, 1550–1700* Ithaca: Cornell University Press

Duncan, HL 2009 '"Sumptuously Re-edified": The Reformation of Sacred Space in *Titus Andronicus*' 43(4) *Comparative Drama* 425

Edwards, J 1957 'The Homicide Act, 1957 — A Critique' 8(1) *British Journal of Delinquency* 49

Edwards, S 1987 '"Provoking Her Own Demise": From Common Assault to Homicide' in J Hanmer and M Maynard (eds) Women, Violence and Social Control London: Routledge

Edwards, S 2004 'Abolishing Provocation and Reframing Self-Defence — The Law Commission's Options for Reform' March *Criminal Law Review* 181

Edwards, S 2010 'Anger and Fear as Justifiable Preludes for Loss of Self-control' 74 *Journal of Criminal Law* 223

Escolme B 2013 *Emotional Excess on the Shakespearean Stage: Passion's Slaves* London: Bloomsbury

Everett, B 2000 '"Spanish" Othello: The Making of Shakespeare's Moor' in CMS Alexander and S Wells (eds) *Shakespeare and Race* Cambridge: CUP

Fawcett, ML 1983 'Arms/Words/Tears: Language and the Body in *Titus Andronicus*' 50(2) *English Literary History* 261

Fernie, E 2002 *Shame in Shakespeare* London Routledge

Fernie, E 2005 'Shakespeare and the Prospect of Presentism' 58 *Shakespeare Survey* 169

Floyd-Wilson, M 2003 *English Ethnicity and Race in Early Modern Drama* Cambridge: CUP

Francis, M 2002 'Tears, Tantrums and Bared Teeth: The Emotional Economy of Three Conservative Prime Ministers, 1951–63' 41(3) *Journal of British Studies* 354

Frederick, D 2008 'Titus Androgynous: Foul Mouths and Troubled Masculinity' 41(1) *Arethusa* 205

Garber, M 2008 *Shakespeare and Modern Culture* New York: Pantheon Books

Greenawalt, K 1984 'The Perplexing Borders of Justification and Excuse' 84(8) *Columbia Law Review* 1897

Greenblatt, S et al 2008 *The Norton Shakespeare* New York: WW Norton & Company

Gatrell, VAC 1994 *The Hanging Tree: Executions and the English People, 1770–1868* Oxford: OUP

Gough, S 1999 'Taking the Heat out of Provocation' 19 *Oxford Journal of Legal Studies* 481

Hall, KF 1996 *Things of Darkness: Economies of Race and Gender in Early Modern England* Ithaca and London: Cornell University Press

Hall, KF (ed) 2007 *William Shakespeare: Othello, the Moor of Venice* Boston: Bedford/St Martin's

Hammerton, AK 1992 *Cruelty and Companionship: Conflict in Nineteenth-Century Married Life* London: Routledge

Hamilton, AC 1963 'Titus Andronicus: The Form of Shakespearean Tragedy' 14(3) *Shakespeare Quarterly* 201

Hawley, W 1998 *Shakespearean Tragedy and the Common Law* New York: Peter Lang

Headlam Wells, R 2000 *Shakespeare on Masculinity* Cambridge: CUP

Heinze, E 2009a '"Were it not Against our Laws": Oppression and Resistance in Shakespeare's *Comedy of Errors*' 29 *Legal Studies* 230

Heinze, E 2009b 'Power Politics and the Rule of Law: Shakespeare's First Historical Tetralogy and Law's "Foundations"' 29(1) *Oxford Journal of Legal Studies* 139

Heinze, E 2009c 'Heir, Celebrity, Martyr, Monster: Legal and Political Legitimacy in Shakespeare and Beyond' 20(1) *Law and Critique* 79

Heinze, E 2009d 'Imperialism and Nationalism in Early Modernity: The "Cosmopolitan" and the "Provincial" in Shakespeare's *Cymbeline*' 18 *Social & Legal Studies* 373

Heinze, E 2013 *The Concept of Injustice* Abingdon, Oxon: Routledge

Hendricks, M and Parker, P (eds) 1994 *Women, 'Race' and Writing in the Early Modern Period* London: Routledge

Hodgson, B 1998 *The Shakespeare Trade: Performances and Appropriations* Philadelphia: University of Pennsylvania Press

Honigmann, E (ed) 1997 *Othello* London: Arden 3rd series Cengage Learning

Horder, J 1992 *Punishment and Responsibility* Oxford: Clarendon Press

Horder, J 1999 'Between Provocation and Diminished Responsibility' 10 *King's College Law Journal* 143

Horder, J 2004 *Excusing Crime* Oxford: Oxford University Press

Horder, J 2005 'Reshaping the Subjective Element in the Provocation Defence' 25 *Oxford Journal of Legal Studies* 123

Horder, J and Fitz-Gibbon, K 2015 'When Sexual Infidelity Triggers Murder: Examining the Impact of Homicide Law Reform on Judicial Attitudes in Sentencing' 74(2) *Cambridge Law Journal* 307

Howard, JE 1987 'Renaissance Antitheatricality and the Politics of Gender and Rank in *Much Ado About Nothing*' in JE Howard and MF O'Connor (eds) *Shakespeare Reproduced: The Text in History and Ideology* London: Routledge

Howard, JE and O'Connor, MF (eds) *Shakespeare Reproduced: The Text in History and Ideology* London: Routledge

Howard, JE 2008 'Cymbeline' in S Greenblatt et al (eds) *The Norton Shakespeare* New York: WW Norton & Company

Howard, JE 2016 'Is Black so Base a Hue?' in D Callaghan and S Gossett (eds) *Shakespeare in Our Time* London: Bloomsbury

Howe, A 1987 'Social Injury Revisited; Towards a Feminist Theory of Social Justice' 15 *International Law Journal* 428

Howe, A 1994a 'Provoking Comment: The Question of Gender Bias in the Provocation Defence – A Victorian Case Study' in N Grieve and A Burns (eds) *Australian Women: New Feminist Perspectives* Oxford: Oxford University Press

Howe, A 1994b *Punish and Critique: Towards a Feminist Analysis of Penality* London: Routledge

Howe, A 1997 'More Folk Provoke Their Own Demise (Revisiting the Provocation Defence Debate Courtesy of the Homosexual Advance Defence)' 19 *Sydney Law Review* 366

Howe, A 1998 'The Provocation Defence: Finally Provoking its Own Demise?' 22 *Melbourne University Law Review* 466

Howe, A 1999 'Reforming Provocation (More or Less)' 12 *Australian Feminist Law Journal* 127

Howe, A 2002 'Provoking Polemic: Provoked Killings and the Ethical Paradoxes of the Postmodern Feminist Condition' 10 *Feminist Legal Studies* 39

Howe, A 2004 'Provocation in Crisis—Law's Passion at the Crossroads? New Directions for Feminist Strategists' 21 *Australian Feminist Law Journal* 55

Howe, A 2005 *Lindy Chamberlain Revisited: A 25th Anniversary Retrospective* Sydney: Lhr Press

Howe, A 2008 *Sex, Violence and Crime: Foucault and the 'Man' Question* Abingdon, Oxon: Routledge

Howe, A 2009 '*R v Wunungmurra*: "Culture" as Usual in the Courts' 30 *Australian Feminist Law Journal* 163

Howe, A 2010 'Every Time You Said "Penis" (Men's) Violence, Victim Advocacy and Impermissible Speech' 25(64) *Australian Feminist Studies* 209

Howe, A 2012a 'A Right to Passions? Compassion's Sexed Asymmetry and a Minor *Comedy of Errors*' 23(2) *Law and Critique* 83

Howe, A 2012b 'Enduring Fictions of Possession – Sexual Infidelity and Homicidal Rage in Shakespeare and Late Modernity (glossing *Othello*)' 21 *Griffith Law Review* 772

Howe, A 2013a "Mastering Emotions or Still Losing Control? – Seeking Public Engagement with Sexual Infidelity Homicide' 21(2) *Feminist Legal Studies* 141

Howe, A 2013b '"Red Mist" Homicide—Sexual Infidelity and the English Law of Murder (Glossing *Titus Andronicus*)' 33(3) *Legal Studies* 407

Howe, A 2014 'Dramatising Intimate Femicide—Petitions, Plays, Public Engagement (with a Shakespearean Gloss)' 26 *Canadian Journal of Women and the Law* 276

Howe, A 2015 '*Othello on Trial*: Engaging with the "Extra-Academic Outside World' 2(1) *Queen Mary Human Rights Law Review* 133

Howe, A 2016 '*Othello on Trial*: The Politics of Performance' 42(4) *Australian Feminist Law Journal* 197

Howe, A 2017 '(Dis) Affectionate Fetishism—Dispossessed Love in *Othello* and Late Modernity' in M Gratzke and A Malinowska (eds) *The Materiality of Love: Essays on Affection and Cultural Practice* New York: Routledge

Howe, A 2019 '"Endlessly Valuable" Discursive Work—Intimate Partner Femicide, an English Case Study' 8(4) *Laws* 1

Howe, A 2020 'Speaking Out Against Violence—For an Embodied Feminist Law Agenda?' 20 *Australian Feminist Law Journal* 1

Howe, A 2021 'White Angst Meets *Othello* – Casting Conundrums' 15(1) *Journal of Artistic and Creative Education* 1

Howe, A 2022 'Sensing Injustice? Defences to Murder' in K Atkinson et al (eds) *Feminist Responses to Injustices of the State and its Institutions: Politics, Intervention, Resistance* Bristol: Bristol University Press

Howe, A and Alaattinoğlu, D (eds) 2019 *Contesting Femicide: Feminism and the Power of Law Revisited* Abingdon, Oxon: Routledge

Hughes, G 1959 'The English Homicide Act of 1957: The Capital Punishment Issue and Various Reforms in the Law of Murder and Manslaughter' 49(6) *Journal of Criminal Law and Criminology* 521

Hunt, M 1988 'Compelling Art in *Titus Andronicus*' 28(2) *Studies in English Literature* 197

Hurl-Eamon, J 2008 '"I Will Forgive You if the World Will": Wife Murder and Limits on Patriarchal Violence in London, 1690–1750' in JP Ward (ed) *Violence, Politics and Gender in Early Modern England* London: Palgrave Macmillan

Hutson L 2007 *The Invention of Suspicion: Law and Mimesis in Shakespeare and Renaissance Drama* Oxford: Oxford University Press

James, H 1995 'Cultural Disintegration in *Titus Andronicus*: Mutilating Titus, Vergil and Rome' in PC Kolin (ed) *Titus Andronicus: Critical Essays* London: Routledge

James, H 1997 *Shakespeare's Troy: Drama, Politics and the Translation of Empire* Cambridge: CUP

Jordan, C and Cunningham, K (eds) 2007 *The Law in Shakespeare* London: Palgrave Macmillan

Kahn, C 1997 *Roman Shakespeare: Warriors, Wounds and Women* New York: Routledge

Kahan, D and Nussbaum, M 1996 'Two Conceptions of Emotion in Criminal Law' 96 *Columbia Law Review* 269

Kendall, GM 1989 '"Lend Me Thy Hand": Metaphor and Mayhem in *Titus Andronicus*' 40 *Shakespeare Quarterly* 299

Kern Paster, G 2004 *Humouring the Body: Emotions and the Shakespearean Stage* Chicago: University of Chicago Press

Koessler, M 1960 'Comparative Aspects of the English Homicide Act of 1957' 25(2) *Missouri Law Review* 107

Kolin, PC 1991 *Shakespeare and Feminist Criticism: An Annotated Bibliography and Commentary* New York: Garland Publishing

Kolin, PC (ed) 1995 *Titus Andronicus: Critical Essays* London: Routledge.

Korda, N 2002 *Shakespeare's Domestic Economies: Gender and Property in Early Modern England* Philadelphia: University of Pennsylvania Press

Kyle, CK 2010 'The Wilde Side of Justice in Early Modern England and *Titus Andronicus*' in C Jordan and K Cunningham (eds) *The Law in Shakespeare* London: Palgrave Macmillan

Langhamer, C 2012 '"The Live Dynamic Whole of Feeling and Behaviour": Capital Punishment and the Politics of Emotion, 1945–1957' 51(2) *Journal of British Studies* 416

Law, RA 1935 '"Almost Damn'd in a Fair Wife"' 15 *Studies in English* 19

Law, RA 1943 'The Roman Background of *Titus Andronicus*' 40 *Studies in Philology* 145

Law Commission 2004 *Partial Defences to Murder* No 290

Law Commission 2006 *Murder, Manslaughter and Infanticide* No 304

Leader-Elliot, I 1997 'Passion and Insurrection in the Law of Sexual Provocation' in N Naffine and R Owens (eds) *Sexing the Subject of Law* North Ryde, NSW: LBC Information Services

Lee, C 2003 *Murder and the Reasonable Man: Passion and Fear in the Criminal Court* New York: New York University Press

Lees, S 1994 'Lawyer's Work as Constitutive of Gender Relations' in ME Cain and CB Harrington (eds) *Lawyers in a Postmodern World: Translation and Transgression* New York: New York University Press

Leo Africanus, J 1600 *A Geographical History of Africa* Trans. John Pory. London
Liebler, NC 1994 'Getting it All Right: *Titus Andronicus* and Roman History' 45 *Shakespeare Quarterly* 263
Little, AL 2021 'Is it Possible to Read Shakespeare through Critical White Studies? in A Thompson (ed) *The Cambridge Companion to Shakespeare and Race* Cambridge: Cambridge University Press
Loomba, A 1994 'The Colour of Patriarchy: Critical Difference, Cultural Difference and Renaissance Drama' in M Hendricks and P Parker (eds) *Women, 'Race' and Writing in the Early Modern Period* London: Routledge
Loomba, A 1999 'Overworlding the "Third-World"' 13(1) *Oxford Literary Review* 164
Loomba, A 2002 *Shakespeare, Race and Colonialism* Oxford: OUP
Magnusson, L 2004 '"Voice Potential": Language and Symbolic Capital in *Othello*' in CMS Alexander (ed) *Shakespeare and Language* Cambridge: Cambridge University Press
McCandless, D 2002 'A Tale of Two Tituses: Julie Taymor's Vision in Stage and Screen' 53 *Shakespeare Quarterly* 487
Mahoney, MR 1991 'Legal Images of Battered Women: Redefining the Issue of Separation' 90 *Michigan Law Review* 1
Matheson, M 2004 'Venetian Culture and the Politics of Othello' in C Alexander (ed) *Shakespeare and Politics* Cambridge: CUP
Michael Nagle, P 1978 '*Commonwealth v Othello*' 7 *The Maryland Law Forum* 104
Miles, J 2009 'The Coroners and Justice Act 2009: A "Dog's Breakfast" of Homicide Reform' 10 *Archibold News* 6
Miola, RS 1995 '*Titus Andronicus* Rome and the Family' in PC Kolin (ed) *Titus Andronicus: Critical Essays* New York: Garland
Morgan, J 1997 'Provocation Law and Facts' 21 *Melbourne University Law Review* 237
Neely, C 1987 *Broken Nuptials in Shakespeare's Plays* New Haven: Yale University Press
Neill, M 1989 'Unproper Beds: Race, Adultery and the Hideous in *Othello*' 40(4) *Shakespeare Quarterly* 382
Neill, M 1998 '"Mulatttos and Indian Moors' 49(4) *Shakespeare Quarterly* 361
Neill, M (ed) 2008 *William Shakespeare: Othello on the Moor of Venice* Oxford: Oxford University Press
Newman, K 1987 '"And wash the Ethiop White": Femininity and the Monstrous in *Othello*' in JE Howard and MF O'Conner (eds) *Shakespeare Reproduced: The Text in History and Ideology* London: Routledge
Nourse, V 1997 'Passion's Progress: Modern Law Reform and the Provocation Defence' 106 *Yale Law Journal* 1331
Oakley-Brown, L 2005 'Titus Andronicus and the Cultural Politics of Translation in Early Modern England' 19(3) *Renaissance Studies* 325
Parker, P 1992 'Preposterous Events' 43(2) *Shakespeare Quarterly* 186
Parker, P 1996 *Shakespeare from the Margins: Language, Culture, Context* Chicago: University of Chicago Press
Packard, B 2010 'Lavinia as Co-author of Shakespeare's *Titus Andronicus*' 2 *Studies in English Literature* 281
Prawer, SS 2012 *Karl Marx and World Literature* London: Verso
Preverer, S 1957 'The English Homicide Act: A New Attempt to Revise the Law of Murder' 57(5) *Columbia Law Review* 624
Quick, OL and Wells, C 2006 'Getting Tough with Defences' 38 *Criminal Law Review* 514

Rackin, P 2016 'Why Feminism Still Matters' in D Callaghan and S Gossett (eds) *Shakespeare in Our Time* London: Bloomsbury

Radford, J 1982 'Marriage Licence or Licence to Kill? Womanslaughter in the Criminal Law' 11 *Feminist Review* 88

Raffield, P and Watt, G (eds) 2008 *Shakespeare and the Law* Oxford: Hart Publishing

Raffield, P 2010 *Shakespeare's Imaginary Constitution: Late Elizabethan Politics and the Theatre of Law* Oxford: Hart Publishing

Rapaport, E 1994 'The Death Penalty and the Domestic Discount' in MA Fineman (ed) *The Public Nature of Private Violence* New York: Routledge

Reddy, WM 1997 *The Invisible Code Honour and Sentiment in Postrevolutionary France, 1814–1848* Berkeley: University of California Press

Reddy, WM 2001 *The Navigation of Feeling: A Framework for the History of Emotions* Cambridge: CUP

Reed, A and Bohlander, M (eds) 2011 *Loss of Control and Diminished Responsibility* Farnham, Surrey: Ashgate

Riley, D 2005 *Impersonal Passion: Language and Affect* Durham: Duke University Press

Ross, C 2010 'Avoiding the Issue of Fraud' in C Jordan and K Cunningham (eds) *The Law in Shakespeare* London: Palgrave Macmillan

Rowe, KA 1994 'Dismembering and Forgetting in *Titus Andronicus*' 45 *Shakespeare Quarterly* 279

Royster, FT 2000 'White-Limed Walls: Whiteness and Gothic Extremism in Shakespeare's *Titus Andronicus*' 51(4) *Shakespeare Quarterly* 432

Rutkoski, M 2006 '"Arm the Minds of Infants": Interpreting Childhood in Titus Andronicus' 48(2) *Criticism* 203

Rutter, C 2001 *Enter the Body: Women and Representation on Shakespeare's Stage* London: Routledge

Seal, L 2014 *Capital Punishment in Twentieth-Century Britain* London: Routledge

Singh, J 1994 'Othello's Identity, Postcolonial Theory and Contemporary African Rewritings of *Othello*' in M Hendricks and P Parker (eds) *Women, 'Race' and Writing in the Early Modern Period* New York: Routledge

Smart, C 1989 *Feminism and the Power of Law* London: Routledge

Smith, E 2019 *This is Shakespeare* London: Penguin

Solga, K 2006 'Rape's Metaphorical Return: Rehearsing Sexual Violence Among the Early Moderns' 58 *Theatre Journal* 53

Snow, EA 1980 'Sexual Anxiety and the Male Order of Things in *Othello*' 10(3) *English Literary Renaissance* 384

Spelman, E 1989 'Anger and Insubordination' in A Garry and M Pearsall (eds) *Women, Knowledge and Reality: Explorations in Feminist Philosophy* Boston: Unwin Hyman

Spencer, JR 2009 'Response to Ministry of Justice Consultation Paper Murder, Manslaughter and Infanticide: Proposals for Reform' www.docstoc.com/docs

Stannard, JE 2002 'Towards a Normative Defence of Provocation in England and Ireland' 66 *Journal of Criminal Law* 528

Starry West, G 1982 'Going by the Book: Classical Allusions in Shakespeare's *Titus Andronicus*' 79 *Studies in Philology* 62

Stearns, P 1989 *Jealousy: The Evolution of an Emotion in American History* New York: New York University Press

Sterling Brown, D 2018 '"Is Black So Base a Hue?" Black Life Matter's in Shakespeare's *Titus Andronicus*' in CLJ Smith et al (eds) *Early Modern Black Diaspora Studies* London: Palgrave Macmillan

St Hilaire, DA 2009 'Allusion and Sacrifice in *Titus Andronicus*' 49(2) *Studies in English Literature* 311

Strange, C 2003 'Masculinities, Intimate Femicide and the Death Penalty in Australia, 1890–1920' 43 *British Journal of Criminology* 310

Strier, R and McAdams, RH 2016 'Cold-Blooded and High-Minded Murder' in AL LaCroix et al (eds) *Fatal Fictions: Crime and Investigation in Law and Literature* Oxford: OUP

Tarrant, S 1996 'Something is Pushing Them to the Side of Their Own Lives: A Feminist Critique of Law and Laws' 26 *Western Australian Law Review* 190

Taylor, L 1986 'Provoked Reason in Men and Women: Heat-of-Passion Manslaughter and Imperfect Self-Defence' 33 *UCLA Law Review* 1679

Traub, V 1992 *Desire and Anxiety: Circulations of Sexuality in Shakespearean Drama* New York: Routledge

Tyson, D 2013 *Sex, Culpability and the Defence of Provocation* London: Routledge

Watkins, J 2006 'Responsibility in Context' 26 *Oxford Journal of Legal Studies* 593

White, JS 1997 '"Is Black so Base a Hue": Shakespeare's Aaron and the Politics and Poetics of Race' 40(3) *CLA Journal* 336

Willis, D 2002 '"The Gnawing Vulture": Revenge, Trauma Theory and *Titus Andronicus*' 53 *Shakespeare Quarterly* 21

Vanita, R 1994 'Proper Men and Fallen Women' 34(2) *Studies in English Literature* 341

Varchi, B 1615 *The Blazon of Jealousy* Trans. Robert Tofte. London

Vaughan, VM 1994 *Othello: A Contextual History* Cambridge: Cambridge University Press.

Volpp, L 1994 'Mis)identifying Culture; Asian Women and the "Culture Defence"' 17 *Harvard Women's Law Journal* 57

Waith, EM (ed) 2008 *William Shakespeare: Titus Andronicus* Oxford: OUP

Warren, R (ed) 1998 *Shakespeare's Cymbeline* Oxford: Oxford University Press

Wayne, V 1991 *The Matter of Difference: Materialist Feminist Criticism of Shakespeare* New York: Harvester Wheatsheaf

Wells, C 2000 'Provocation: The Case for Abolition' in A Ashworth and B Mitchell (eds) *Rethinking English Homicide Law* Oxford: OUP

White, JS 1997 '"Is Black so Base a Hue?" Shakespeare's Aaron and the Politics and Poetics of Race' 40(3) *College Language Association Journal* 336

Wiener, MJ 1999a 'Judges *v* Jurors: Courtroom Tensions in Murder Trials and the Law of Criminal Responsibility in Nineteenth-Century England' 17(3) *Law and History Review* 467

Wiener, MJ 1999b 'The Sad Story of George Hall: Adultery, Murder and the Politics of Mercy in Mid-Victorian England' 24(2) *Social History* 174

Wiener, MJ 2004 *Men of Blood: Manliness and Criminal Justice in Victorian England* Cambridge: CUP

Wiener, MJ 2008 *Empire on Trial: Race, Murder and Justice Under British Rule* Cambridge: CUP

Wortham, C 2015 'Displacement: Maps and Emotions in *Othello*' in RS White et al (eds) *Shakespeare and Emotions: Inheritances, Enactments, Legacies* London: Palgrave Macmillan

Yachnin, P 1996 'Magical Properties: Vision, Possession and Wonder in *Othello*' 48(2) *Theatre Journal* 197

Zamir, T 2008 'Wooden Subjects' 39(2) *New Literary History* 277

Index